T&p BOOKS

THAI
VOCABULARY

ENGLISH-
THAI

The most useful words
To expand your lexicon and sharpen
your language skills

7000 words

Thai vocabulary for English speakers - 7000 words

By Andrey Taranov

T&P Books vocabularies are intended for helping you learn, memorize and review foreign words. The dictionary is divided into themes, covering all major spheres of everyday activities, business, science, culture, etc.

The process of learning words using T&P Books' theme-based dictionaries gives you the following advantages:

- Correctly grouped source information predetermines success at subsequent stages of word memorization
- Availability of words derived from the same root allowing memorization of word units (rather than separate words)
- Small units of words facilitate the process of establishing associative links needed for consolidation of vocabulary
- Level of language knowledge can be estimated by the number of learned words

T&P Books Publishing
www.tpbooks.com

ISBN: 978-1-78767-233-8

This book is also available in E-book formats.
Please visit www.tpbooks.com or the major online bookstores.

THAI VOCABULARY
for English speakers

T&P Books vocabularies are intended to help you learn, memorize, and review foreign words. The vocabulary contains over 7000 commonly used words arranged thematically.

- Vocabulary contains the most commonly used words
- Recommended as an addition to any language course
- Meets the needs of beginners and advanced learners of foreign languages
- Convenient for daily use, revision sessions, and self-testing activities
- Allows you to assess your vocabulary

Special features of the vocabulary

- Words are organized according to their meaning, not alphabetically
- Words are presented in three columns to facilitate the reviewing and self-testing processes
- Words in groups are divided into small blocks to facilitate the learning process
- The vocabulary offers a convenient and simple transcription of each foreign word

The vocabulary has 198 topics including:

Basic Concepts, Numbers, Colors, Months, Seasons, Units of Measurement, Clothing & Accessories, Food & Nutrition, Restaurant, Family Members, Relatives, Character, Feelings, Emotions, Diseases, City, Town, Sightseeing, Shopping, Money, House, Home, Office, Working in the Office, Import & Export, Marketing, Job Search, Sports, Education, Computer, Internet, Tools, Nature, Countries, Nationalities and more ...

TABLE OF CONTENTS

PRONUNCIATION GUIDE

T&P phonetic alphabet	Thai example	English example

Vowels

[a]	ห้า [hâ:] – hâa	shorter than in ask
[e]	เป็นลม [pen lom] – bpen lom	elm, medal
[i]	วินัย [wiʔ naj] – wí–nai	shorter than in feet
[o]	โกน [ko:n] – gohn	pod, John
[u]	ขุ่นเคือง [kʰùn kʰɯːaŋ] – khùn kheuang	book
[aa]	ราคา [ra: kʰa:] – raa–khaa	calf, palm
[oo]	ภูมิใจ [pʰuːm tɕaj] – phoom jai	pool, room
[ee]	บัญชี [ban tɕʰiː] – ban–chee	feet, meter
[eu]	เดือน [dɯːan] – deuan	similar to a longue schwa sound
[er]	เงิน [ŋɤn] – ngern	e in "the"
[ae]	แปล [plɛ:] – bplae	longer than bed, fell
[ay]	เลข [lê:k] – lâyk	longer than in bell
[ai]	ไปป์ [paj] – bpai	time, white
[oi]	โพย [pʰoːj] – phoi	oil, boy, point
[ya]	สัญญา [sǎn ja:] – sǎn–yaa	Kenya, piano
[oie]	อบเชย [ʔòp tɕʰɤːj] – òp–choie	Combination [ə:i]
[ieo]	หน้าเชียว [nâ: si:aw] – nâa sieow	year, here

Initial consonant sounds

[b]	บาง [ba:ŋ] – baang	baby, book
[d]	สีแดง [sǐ: dɛ:ŋ] – sěe daeng	day, doctor
[f]	มันฝรั่ง [man fà ràŋ] – man fà–ràng	face, food
[h]	เฮลซิงกิ [he:n siŋ kiʔ] – hayn–sing–gì	home, have
[y]	ยี่สิบ [jîː sìp] – yêe sìp	yes, New York
[g]	กรง [kroŋ] – grorng	game, gold
[kh]	เลขา [le: kʰǎ:] – lay–khǎa	work hard
[l]	เล็ก [lék] – lék	lace, people
[m]	เมลอน [me: lɔ:n] – may–lorn	magic, milk
[n]	หนัง [nǎŋ] – nǎng	name, normal
[ng]	เงือก [ŋɯːak] – ngêuak	English, ring
[bp]	เป็น [pen] – bpen	pencil, private
[ph]	เผ่า [pʰàw] – phào	top hat

T&P phonetic alphabet	Thai example	English example
[r]	เบอรรี่ [bɤː ríː] – ber–rêe	rice, radio
[s]	ซอน [sôn] – sôm	city, boss
[dt]	ดนตรี [don triː] – don–dtree	tourist, trip
[j]	ปั้นจั้น [pân tɕàn] – bpân jàn	cheer
[ch]	วิชา [wíʔ tɕʰaː] – wí–chaa	hitchhiker
[th]	แถว [tʰɛːw] – thǎe	don't have
[w]	เคียว [kʰiːaw] – khieow	vase, winter

Final consonant sounds

[k]	แม่เหล็ก [mɛː lèk] – mâe lèk	clock, kiss
[m]	เพิ่ม [pʰɤːm] – phêrm	magic, milk
[n]	เนียน [niːan] – nian	name, normal
[ng]	เป็นห่วง [pen hùːaŋ] – bpen hùang	English, ring
[p]	ไม่ขยับ [mâj kʰà ja p] – mâi khà–yàp	pencil, private
[t]	ลูกเป็ด [lûːk pèt] – lôok bpèt	tourist, trip

Comments

Mid tone - [ā] การคูณ [gaan khon]
Low tone - [à] แจกจ่าย [jàek jàai]
Falling tone - [â] แต้ม [dtâem]
High tone - [á] แซ็กโซโฟน [sáek-soh-fohn]
Rising tone - [ǎ] เน้นเขา [nern khǎo]

ABBREVIATIONS
used in the vocabulary

English abbreviations

ab.	-	about
adj	-	adjective
adv	-	adverb
anim.	-	animate
as adj	-	attributive noun used as adjective
e.g.	-	for example
etc.	-	et cetera
fam.	-	familiar
fem.	-	feminine
form.	-	formal
inanim.	-	inanimate
masc.	-	masculine
math	-	mathematics
mil.	-	military
n	-	noun
pl	-	plural
pron.	-	pronoun
sb	-	somebody
sing.	-	singular
sth	-	something
v aux	-	auxiliary verb
vi	-	intransitive verb
vi, vt	-	intransitive, transitive verb
vt	-	transitive verb

BASIC CONCEPTS

Basic concepts. Part 1

1. Pronouns

you	คุณ	khun
he	เขา	khăo
she	เธอ	ther
it	มัน	man
we	เรา	rao
you (to a group)	คุณทั้งหลาย	khun tháng lăai
you (polite, sing.)	คุณ	khun
you (polite, pl)	คุณทั้งหลาย	khun tháng lăai
they (masc.)	เขา	khăo
they (fem.)	เธอ	ther

2. Greetings. Salutations. Farewells

Hello! (fam.)	สวัสดี!	sà-wàt-dee
Hello! (form.)	สวัสดี ครับ/ค่ะ!	sà-wàt-dee khráp/khâ
Good morning!	อรุณสวัสดิ์!	a-run sà-wàt
Good afternoon!	สวัสดีตอนบ่าย	sà-wàt-dee dtorn-bàai
Good evening!	สวัสดีตอนค่ำ	sà-wàt-dee dtorn-khâm
to say hello	ทักทาย	thák thaai
Hi! (hello)	สวัสดี!	sà-wàt-dee
greeting (n)	คำทักทาย	kham thák thaai
to greet (vt)	ทักทาย	thák thaai
How are you? (form.)	คุณสบายดีไหม?	khun sà-baai dee măi
How are you? (fam.)	สบายดีไหม?	sà-baai dee măi
What's new?	มีอะไรไหม?	mee à-rai mài
Goodbye!	ลาก่อน!	laa gòrn
Bye!	บาย!	baai
See you soon!	พบกันใหม่	phóp gan mài
Farewell! (to a friend)	ลาก่อน!	laa gòrn
Farewell! (form.)	สวัสดี!	sà-wàt-dee
to say goodbye	บอกลา	bòrk laa
So long!	ลาก่อน!	laa gòrn
Thank you!	ขอบคุณ!	khòrp khun

Thank you very much!	ขอบคุณมาก!	khòrp khun mâak
You're welcome	ยินดีช่วย	yin dee chûay
Don't mention it!	ไม่เป็นไร	mâi bpen rai
It was nothing	ไม่เป็นไร	mâi bpen rai
Excuse me! (fam.)	ขอโทษที!	khŏr thôht thee
Excuse me! (form.)	ขอโทษ ครับ/ค่ะ!	khŏr thôht khráp / khâ
to excuse (forgive)	ให้อภัย	hâi a-phai
to apologize (vi)	ขอโทษ	khŏr thôht
My apologies	ขอโทษ	khŏr thôht
I'm sorry!	ขอโทษ!	khŏr thôht
to forgive (vt)	อภัย	a-phai
It's okay! (that's all right)	ไม่เป็นไร!	mâi bpen rai
please (adv)	โปรด	bpròht
Don't forget!	อย่าลืม!	yàa leum
Certainly!	แน่นอน!	nâe norn
Of course not!	ไม่ใช่แน่!	mâi châi nâe
Okay! (I agree)	โอเค!	oh-khay
That's enough!	พอแล้ว	phor láew

3. Cardinal numbers. Part 1

0 zero	ศูนย์	sŏon
1 one	หนึ่ง	nèung
2 two	สอง	sŏrng
3 three	สาม	săam
4 four	สี่	sèe
5 five	ห้า	hâa
6 six	หก	hòk
7 seven	เจ็ด	jèt
8 eight	แปด	bpàet
9 nine	เก้า	gâo
10 ten	สิบ	sìp
11 eleven	สิบเอ็ด	sìp èt
12 twelve	สิบสอง	sìp sŏrng
13 thirteen	สิบสาม	sìp săam
14 fourteen	สิบสี่	sìp sèe
15 fifteen	สิบห้า	sìp hâa
16 sixteen	สิบหก	sìp hòk
17 seventeen	สิบเจ็ด	sìp jèt
18 eighteen	สิบแปด	sìp bpàet
19 nineteen	สิบเก้า	sìp gâo
20 twenty	ยี่สิบ	yêe sìp
21 twenty-one	ยี่สิบเอ็ด	yêe sìp èt

| 22 twenty-two | ยี่สิบสอง | yêe sìp sŏrng |
| 23 twenty-three | ยี่สิบสาม | yêe sìp sǎam |

30 thirty	สามสิบ	sǎam sìp
31 thirty-one	สามสิบเอ็ด	sǎam-sìp-èt
32 thirty-two	สามสิบสอง	sǎam-sìp-sŏrng
33 thirty-three	สามสิบสาม	sǎam-sìp-sǎam

40 forty	สี่สิบ	sèe sìp
41 forty-one	สี่สิบเอ็ด	sèe-sìp-èt
42 forty-two	สี่สิบสอง	sèe-sìp-sŏrng
43 forty-three	สี่สิบสาม	sèe-sìp-sǎam

50 fifty	ห้าสิบ	hâa sìp
51 fifty-one	ห้าสิบเอ็ด	hâa-sìp-èt
52 fifty-two	ห้าสิบสอง	hâa-sìp-sŏrng
53 fifty-three	หาสิบสาม	hâa-sìp-sǎam

60 sixty	หกสิบ	hòk sìp
61 sixty-one	หกสิบเอ็ด	hòk-sìp-èt
62 sixty-two	หกสิบสอง	hòk-sìp-sŏrng
63 sixty-three	หกสิบสาม	hòk-sìp-sǎam

70 seventy	เจ็ดสิบ	jèt sìp
71 seventy-one	เจ็ดสิบเอ็ด	jèt-sìp-èt
72 seventy-two	เจ็ดสิบสอง	jèt-sìp-sŏrng
73 seventy-three	เจ็ดสิบสาม	jèt-sìp-sǎam

80 eighty	แปดสิบ	bpàet sìp
81 eighty-one	แปดสิบเอ็ด	bpàet-sìp-èt
82 eighty-two	แปดสิบสอง	bpàet-sìp-sŏrng
83 eighty-three	แปดสิบสาม	bpàet-sìp-sǎam

90 ninety	เก้าสิบ	gâo sìp
91 ninety-one	เก้าสิบเอ็ด	gâo-sìp-èt
92 ninety-two	เก้าสิบสอง	gâo-sìp-sŏrng
93 ninety-three	เกาสิบสาม	gâo-sìp-sǎam

4. Cardinal numbers. Part 2

100 one hundred	หนึ่งร้อย	nèung rói
200 two hundred	สองร้อย	sŏrng rói
300 three hundred	สามร้อย	sǎam rói
400 four hundred	สี่ร้อย	sèe rói
500 five hundred	หารอย	hâa rói

600 six hundred	หกร้อย	hòk rói
700 seven hundred	เจ็ดร้อย	jèt rói
800 eight hundred	แปดร้อย	bpàet rói
900 nine hundred	เการอย	gâo rói

1000 one thousand	หนึ่งพัน	nèung phan
2000 two thousand	สองพัน	sŏrng phan
3000 three thousand	สามพัน	săam phan
10000 ten thousand	หนึ่งหมื่น	nèung mèun
one hundred thousand	หนึ่งแสน	nèung săen
million	ล้าน	láan
billion	พันล้าน	phan láan

5. Numbers. Fractions

fraction	เศษส่วน	sàyt sùan
one half	หนึ่งส่วนสอง	nèung sùan sŏrng
one third	หนึ่งส่วนสาม	nèung sùan săam
one quarter	หนึ่งส่วนสี่	nèung sùan sèe
one eighth	หนึ่งส่วนแปด	nèung sùan bpàet
one tenth	หนึ่งส่วนสิบ	nèung sùan sìp
two thirds	สองส่วนสาม	sŏrng sùan săam
three quarters	สามสวนสี่	săam sùan sèe

6. Numbers. Basic operations

subtraction	การลบ	gaan lóp
to subtract (vi, vt)	ลบ	lóp
division	การหาร	gaan hăan
to divide (vt)	หาร	hăan
addition	การบวก	gaan bùak
to add up (vt)	บวก	bùak
to add (vi, vt)	เพิ่ม	phêrm
multiplication	การคูณ	gaan khon
to multiply (vt)	คูณ	khoon

7. Numbers. Miscellaneous

digit, figure	ตัวเลข	dtua lâyk
number	เลข	lâyk
numeral	ตัวเลข	dtua lâyk
minus sign	เครื่องหมายลบ	khrêuang măai lóp
plus sign	เครื่องหมายบวก	khrêuang măai bùak
formula	สูตร	sòot
calculation	การนับ	gaan náp
to count (vi, vt)	นับ	náp
to count up	นับ	náp
to compare (vt)	เปรียบเทียบ	bprìap thîap

| How much? | เท่าไหร่? | thâo rài |
| How many? | กี่...? | gèe...? |

sum, total	ผลรวม	phŏn ruam
result	ผลลัพธ์	phŏn láp
remainder	ที่เหลือ	thêe lĕua

a few (e.g., ~ years ago)	สองสาม	sŏrng săam
little (I had ~ time)	นิดหนอย	nít nòi
few (I have ~ friends)	นอย	nói
the rest	ที่เหลือ	thêe lĕua
one and a half	หนึ่งครึ่ง	nèung khrêung
dozen	โหล	lŏh

in half (adv)	เป็นสองส่วน	bpen sŏrng sùan
equally (evenly)	เท่าเทียมกัน	thâo thiam gan
half	ครึ่ง	khrêung
time (three ~s)	ครั้ง	khráng

8. The most important verbs. Part 1

to advise (vt)	แนะนำ	náe nam
to agree (say yes)	เห็นดวย	hĕn dûay
to answer (vi, vt)	ตอบ	dtòrp
to apologize (vi)	ขอโทษ	khŏr thôht
to arrive (vi)	มา	maa

to ask (~ oneself)	ถาม	thăam
to ask (~ sb to do sth)	ขอ	khŏr
to be (vi)	เป็น	bpen

to be afraid	กลัว	glua
to be hungry	หิว	hĭw
to be interested in ...	สนใจใน	sŏn jai nai
to be needed	ตองการ	dtôrng gaan
to be surprised	ประหลาดใจ	bprà-làat jai

to be thirsty	กระหายน้ำ	grà-hăai náam
to begin (vt)	เริ่ม	rêrm
to belong to ...	เป็นของของ...	bpen khŏrng khŏrng...
to boast (vi)	โออวด	ôh ùat
to break (split into pieces)	แตก	dtàek

to call (~ for help)	เรียก	rîak
can (v aux)	สามารถ	săa-mâat
to catch (vt)	จับ	jàp
to change (vt)	เปลี่ยน	bplìan
to choose (select)	เลือก	lêuak
to come down (the stairs)	ลง	long
to compare (vt)	เปรียบเทียบ	bprìap thîap

to complain (vi, vt)	บ่น	bòn
to confuse (mix up)	สับสน	sàp sǒn
to continue (vt)	ทำต่อไป	tham dtòr bpai
to control (vt)	ควบคุม	khûap khum
to cook (dinner)	ทำอาหาร	tham aa-hǎan
to cost (vt)	ราคา	raa-khaa
to count (add up)	นับ	náp
to count on …	พึ่งพา	phêung phaa
to create (vt)	สร้าง	sâang
to cry (weep)	ร้องไห้	rórng hâi

9. The most important verbs. Part 2

to deceive (vi, vt)	หลอก	lòrk
to decorate (tree, street)	ประดับ	bprà-dàp
to defend (a country, etc.)	ปกป้อง	bpòk bpôrng
to demand (request firmly)	เรียกร้อง	rîak rórng
to dig (vt)	ขุด	khùt
to discuss (vt)	หารือ	hǎa-reu
to do (vt)	ทำ	tham
to doubt (have doubts)	สงสัย	sǒng-sǎi
to drop (let fall)	ทิ้งให้ตก	thíng hâi dtòk
to enter (room, house, etc.)	เข้า	khâo
to excuse (forgive)	ให้อภัย	hâi a-phai
to exist (vi)	มีอยู่	mee yòo
to expect (foresee)	คาดหวัง	khâat wǎng
to explain (vt)	อธิบาย	à-thí-baai
to fall (vi)	ตก	dtòk
to find (vt)	พบ	phóp
to finish (vt)	จบ	jòp
to fly (vi)	บิน	bin
to follow … (come after)	ไปตาม…	bpai dtaam...
to forget (vi, vt)	ลืม	leum
to forgive (vt)	ให้อภัย	hâi a-phai
to give (vt)	ให้	hâi
to give a hint	บอกใบ้	bòrk bâi
to go (on foot)	ไป	bpai
to go for a swim	ไปว่ายน้ำ	bpai wâai náam
to go out (for dinner, etc.)	ออกไป	òrk bpai
to guess (the answer)	คาดเดา	khâat dao
to have (vt)	มี	mee
to have breakfast	ทานอาหารเช้า	thaan aa-hǎan cháo

to have dinner	ทานอาหารเย็น	thaan aa-hǎan yen
to have lunch	ทานอาหารเที่ยง	thaan aa-hǎan thîang
to hear (vt)	ได้ยิน	dâai yin
to help (vt)	ช่วย	chûay
to hide (vt)	ซ่อน	sôrn
to hope (vi, vt)	หวัง	wǎng
to hunt (vi, vt)	ล่า	lâa
to hurry (vi)	รีบ	rêep

10. The most important verbs. Part 3

to inform (vt)	แจ้ง	jâeng
to insist (vi, vt)	ยืนยัน	yeun yan
to insult (vt)	ดูถูก	doo thòok
to invite (vt)	เชิญ	chern
to joke (vi)	ลอเล่น	lór lên
to keep (vt)	รักษา	rák-sǎa
to keep silent, to hush	นิ่งเงียบ	nîng ngîap
to kill (vt)	ฆ่า	khâa
to know (sb)	รู้จัก	róo jàk
to know (sth)	รู้	róo
to laugh (vi)	หัวเราะ	hǔa rór
to liberate (city, etc.)	ปลดปล่อย	bplòt bplòi
to like (I like …)	ชอบ	chôrp
to look for … (search)	หา	hǎa
to love (sb)	รัก	rák
to make a mistake	ทำผิด	tham phìt
to manage, to run	บริหาร	bor-rí-hǎan
to mean (signify)	หมาย	mǎai
to mention (talk about)	กล่าวถึง	glàao thěung
to miss (school, etc.)	พลาด	phlâat
to notice (see)	สังเกต	sǎng-gàyt
to object (vi, vt)	ค้าน	kháan
to observe (see)	สังเกตการณ์	sǎng-gàyt gaan
to open (vt)	เปิด	bpèrt
to order (meal, etc.)	สั่ง	sàng
to order (mil.)	สั่งการ	sàng gaan
to own (possess)	เป็นเจ้าของ	bpen jâo khǒrng
to participate (vi)	มีส่วนร่วม	mee sùan rûam
to pay (vi, vt)	จ่าย	jàai
to permit (vt)	อนุญาต	a-nú-yâat
to plan (vt)	วางแผน	waang phǎen
to play (children)	เล่น	lên
to pray (vi, vt)	ภาวนา	phaa-wá-naa

to prefer (vt)	ชอบ	chôrp
to promise (vt)	สัญญา	sǎn-yaa
to pronounce (vt)	ออกเสียง	òrk sǐang
to propose (vt)	เสนอ	sà-něr
to punish (vt)	ลงโทษ	long thôht

11. The most important verbs. Part 4

to read (vi, vt)	อ่าน	àan
to recommend (vt)	แนะนำ	náe nam
to refuse (vi, vt)	ปฏิเสธ	bpà-dtì-sàyt
to regret (be sorry)	เสียใจ	sǐa jai
to rent (sth from sb)	เช่า	châo

to repeat (say again)	ซ้ำ	sám
to reserve, to book	จอง	jorng
to run (vi)	วิ่ง	wîng
to save (rescue)	กู้	gôo
to say (~ thank you)	บอก	bòrk

to scold (vt)	ดุด่า	dù dàa
to see (vt)	เห็น	hěn
to sell (vt)	ขาย	khǎai
to send (vt)	ส่ง	sòng
to shoot (vi)	ยิง	ying

to shout (vi)	ตะโกน	dtà-gohn
to show (vt)	แสดง	sà-daeng
to sign (document)	ลงนาม	long naam
to sit down (vi)	นั่ง	nâng

to smile (vi)	ยิ้ม	yím
to speak (vi, vt)	พูด	phôot
to steal (money, etc.)	ขโมย	khà-moi
to stop (for pause, etc.)	หยุด	yùt
to stop (please ~ calling me)	หยุด	yùt

to study (vt)	เรียน	rian
to swim (vi)	ว่ายน้ำ	wâai náam
to take (vt)	เอา	ao
to think (vi, vt)	คิด	khít
to threaten (vt)	ขู่	khòo

to touch (with hands)	แตะต้อง	dtàe dtôrng
to translate (vt)	แปล	bplae
to trust (vt)	เชื่อ	chêua
to try (attempt)	พยายาม	phá-yaa-yaam
to turn (e.g., ~ left)	เลี้ยว	líeow
to underestimate (vt)	ดูถูก	doo thòok

to understand (vt)	เข้าใจ	khâo jai
to unite (vt)	สมาน	sà-mǎan
to wait (vt)	รอ	ror

to want (wish, desire)	ต้องการ	dtôrng gaan
to warn (vt)	เตือน	dteuan
to work (vi)	ทำงาน	tham ngaan
to write (vt)	เขียน	khǐan
to write down	จด	jòt

12. Colors

color	สี	sěe
shade (tint)	สีอ่อน	sěe òrn
hue	สีสัน	sěe sǎn
rainbow	สายรุ้ง	sǎai rúng

white (adj)	สีขาว	sěe khǎao
black (adj)	สีดำ	sěe dam
gray (adj)	สีเทา	sěe thao

green (adj)	สีเขียว	sěe khǐeow
yellow (adj)	สีเหลือง	sěe lěuang
red (adj)	สีแดง	sěe daeng

blue (adj)	สีน้ำเงิน	sěe nám ngern
light blue (adj)	สีฟ้า	sěe fáa
pink (adj)	สีชมพู	sěe chom-poo
orange (adj)	สีส้ม	sěe sôm
violet (adj)	สีม่วง	sěe mûang
brown (adj)	สีน้ำตาล	sěe nám dtaan

| golden (adj) | สีทอง | sěe thorng |
| silvery (adj) | สีเงิน | sěe ngern |

beige (adj)	สีน้ำตาลอ่อน	sěe nám dtaan òrn
cream (adj)	สีครีม	sěe khreem
turquoise (adj)	สีเขียวแกม น้ำเงิน	sěe khǐeow gaem náam ngern
cherry red (adj)	สีแดงเชอร์รี่	sěe daeng cher-rêe
lilac (adj)	สีม่วงอ่อน	sěe mûang-òrn
crimson (adj)	สีแดงเข้ม	sěe daeng khâym

light (adj)	อ่อน	òrn
dark (adj)	แก่	gàe
bright, vivid (adj)	สด	sòt

colored (pencils)	สี	sěe
color (e.g., ~ film)	สี	sěe
black-and-white (adj)	ขาวดำ	khǎao-dam

plain (one-colored)	สีเดียว	sĕe dieow
multicolored (adj)	หลากสี	làak sĕe

13. Questions

Who?	ใคร?	khrai
What?	อะไร?	a-rai
Where? (at, in)	ที่ไหน?	thêe năi
Where (to)?	ที่ไหน?	thêe năi
From where?	จากที่ไหน?	jàak thêe năi
When?	เมื่อไหร?	mêua rài
Why? (What for?)	ทำไม?	tham-mai
Why? (~ are you crying?)	ทำไม?	tham-mai

What for?	เพื่ออะไร?	phêua a-rai
How? (in what way)	อย่างไร?	yàang rai
What? (What kind of ...?)	อะไร?	a-rai
Which?	ไหน?	năi

To whom?	สำหรับใคร?	săm-ràp khrai
About whom?	เกี่ยวกับใคร?	gìeow gàp khrai
About what?	เกี่ยวกับอะไร?	gìeow gàp a-rai
With whom?	กับใคร?	gàp khrai

How many?	กี่...?	gèe...?
How much?	เท่าไหร?	thâo rài
Whose?	ของใคร?	khŏrng khrai

14. Function words. Adverbs. Part 1

Where? (at, in)	ที่ไหน?	thêe năi
here (adv)	ที่นี่	thêe nêe
there (adv)	ที่นั่น	thêe nân

somewhere (to be)	ที่ใดที่หนึ่ง	thêe dai thêe nùung
nowhere (not in any place)	ไม่มีที่ไหน	mâi mee thêe năi

by (near, beside)	ข้าง	khâang
by the window	ข้างหน้าต่าง	khâang nâa dtàang

Where (to)?	ที่ไหน?	thêe năi
here (e.g., come ~!)	ที่นี่	thêe nêe
there (e.g., to go ~)	ที่นั่น	thêe nân
from here (adv)	จากที่นี่	jàak thêe nêe
from there (adv)	จากที่นั่น	jàak thêe nân

close (adv)	ใกล้	glâi
far (adv)	ไกล	glai

near (e.g., ~ Paris)	ใกล้	glâi
nearby (adv)	ใกล้ๆ	glâi glâi
not far (adv)	ไม่ไกล	mâi glai
left (adj)	ซ้าย	sáai
on the left	ทางซ้าย	khâang sáai
to the left	ซ้าย	sáai
right (adj)	ขวา	khwǎa
on the right	ทางขวา	khâang kwǎa
to the right	ขวา	khwǎa
in front (adv)	ข้างหน้า	khâang nâa
front (as adj)	หน้า	nâa
ahead (the kids ran ~)	หน้า	nâa
behind (adv)	ข้างหลัง	khâang lǎng
from behind	จากข้างหลัง	jàak khâang lǎng
back (towards the rear)	หลัง	lǎng
middle	กลาง	glaang
in the middle	ตรงกลาง	dtrorng glaang
at the side	ข้าง	khâang
everywhere (adv)	ทุกที่	thúk thêe
around (in all directions)	รอบ	rôrp
from inside	จากข้างใน	jàak khâang nai
somewhere (to go)	ที่ไหน	thêe nǎi
straight (directly)	ตรงไป	dtrorng bpai
back (e.g., come ~)	กลับ	glàp
from anywhere	จากที่ใด	jàak thêe dai
from somewhere	จากที่ใด	jàak thêe dai
firstly (adv)	ข้อที่หนึ่ง	khôr thêe nèung
secondly (adv)	ข้อที่สอง	khôr thêe sǒrng
thirdly (adv)	ขอที่สาม	khôr thêe sǎam
suddenly (adv)	ในทันที	nai than thee
at first (in the beginning)	ตอนแรก	dtorn-râek
for the first time	เป็นครั้งแรก	bpen khráng râek
long before ...	นานก่อน	naan gòrn
anew (over again)	ใหม	mài
for good (adv)	ให้จบสิ้น	hâi jòp sîn
never (adv)	ไม่เคย	mâi khoie
again (adv)	อีกครั้งหนึ่ง	èek khráng nèung
now (at present)	ตอนนี้	dtorn-née
often (adv)	บอย	bòi
then (adv)	เวลานั้น	way-laa nán
urgently (quickly)	อย่างเรงดวน	yàang râyng dùan

usually (adv)	มักจะ	mák jà
by the way, ...	อนึ่ง	à-nèung
possibly	เป็นไปได้	bpen bpai dâai
probably (adv)	อาจจะ	àat jà
maybe (adv)	อาจจะ	àat jà
besides ...	นอกจากนั้น...	nôrk jàak nán...
that's why ...	นั่นเป็นเหตุผลที่...	nân bpen hàyt phǒn thêe...
in spite of ...	แม้ว่า...	máe wâa...
thanks to ...	เนื่องจาก...	nêuang jàak...
what (pron.)	อะไร	a-rai
that (conj.)	ที่	thêe
something	อะไร	a-rai
anything (something)	อะไรก็ตาม	a-rai gôr dtaam
nothing	ไม่มีอะไร	mâi mee a-rai
who (pron.)	ใคร	khrai
someone	บางคน	baang khon
somebody	บางคน	baang khon
nobody	ไม่มีใคร	mâi mee khrai
nowhere (a voyage to ~)	ไม่ไปไหน	mâi bpai nǎi
nobody's	ไม่เป็นของของใคร	mâi bpen khǒrng khǒrng khrai
somebody's	ของคนหนึ่ง	khǒrng khon nèung
so (I'm ~ glad)	มาก	mâak
also (as well)	ด้วย	dûay
too (as well)	ด้วย	dûay

15. Function words. Adverbs. Part 2

Why?	ทำไม?	tham-mai
for some reason	เพราะเหตุผลอะไร	phrór hàyt phǒn à-rai
because ...	เพราะว่า...	phrór wâa
for some purpose	ด้วยจุดประสงค์อะไร	dûay jùt bprà-sǒng a-rai
and	และ	láe
or	หรือ	rěu
but	แต่	dtàe
for (e.g., ~ me)	สำหรับ	sǎm-ràp
too (~ many people)	เกินไป	gern bpai
only (exclusively)	เท่านั้น	thâo nán
exactly (adv)	ตรง	dtrorng
about (more or less)	ประมาณ	bprà-maan
approximately (adv)	ประมาณ	bprà-maan
approximate (adj)	ประมาณ	bprà-maan
almost (adv)	เกือบ	gèuap

the rest	ที่เหลือ	thêe lĕua
the other (second)	อีก	èek
other (different)	อื่น	èun
each (adj)	ทุก	thúk
any (no matter which)	ใดๆ	dai dai
many (adj)	หลาย	lăai
much (adv)	มาก	mâak
many people	หลายคน	lăai khon
all (everyone)	ทุกๆ	thúk thúk
in return for ...	ที่จะเปลี่ยนเป็น	thêe jà bplìan bpen
in exchange (adv)	แทน	thaen
by hand (made)	ใช้มือ	chái meu
hardly (negative opinion)	แทบจะไม่	thâep jà mâi
probably (adv)	อาจจะ	àat jà
on purpose (intentionally)	โดยเจตนา	doi jàyt-dtà-naa
by accident (adv)	บังเอิญ	bang-ern
very (adv)	มาก	mâak
for example (adv)	ยกตัวอย่าง	yók dtua yàang
between	ระหว่าง	rá-wàang
among	ทามกลาง	tâam-glaang
so much (such a lot)	มากมาย	mâak maai
especially (adv)	โดยเฉพาะ	doi chà-phór

Basic concepts. Part 2

16. Opposites

rich (adj)	รวย	ruay
poor (adj)	จน	jon
ill, sick (adj)	เจ็บป่วย	jèp bpùay
well (not sick)	สบายดี	sà-baai dee
big (adj)	ใหญ่	yài
small (adj)	เล็ก	lék
quickly (adv)	อย่างเร็ว	yàang reo
slowly (adv)	อยางชา	yàang cháa
fast (adj)	เร็ว	reo
slow (adj)	ชา	cháa
glad (adj)	ยินดี	yin dee
sad (adj)	เสียใจ	sĭa jai
together (adv)	ด้วยกัน	dûay gan
separately (adv)	ตางหาก	dtàang hàak
aloud (to read)	ออกเสียง	òrk sĭang
silently (to oneself)	อยางเงียบๆ	yàang ngîap ngîap
tall (adj)	สูง	sŏong
low (adj)	ต่ำ	dtàm
deep (adj)	ลึก	léuk
shallow (adj)	ตื้น	dtêun
yes	ใช่	châi
no	ไม่ใช่	mâi châi
distant (in space)	ไกล	glai
nearby (adj)	ใกล	glâi
far (adv)	ไกล	glai
nearby (adv)	ใกลๆ	glâi glâi
long (adj)	ยาว	yaao
short (adj)	สั้น	sân
good (kindhearted)	ใจดี	jai dee

evil (adj)	เลวร้าย	leo ráai
married (adj)	แต่งงานแล้ว	dtàeng ngaan láew
single (adj)	เป็นโสด	bpen sòht
to forbid (vt)	ห้าม	hâam
to permit (vt)	อนุญาต	a-nú-yâat
end	จบ	jòp
beginning	จุดเริ่มต้น	jùt rêrm-dtôn
left (adj)	ซ้าย	sáai
right (adj)	ขวา	khwǎa
first (adj)	แรก	râek
last (adj)	สุดท้าย	sùt tháai
crime	อาชญากรรม	àat-yaa-gam
punishment	การลงโทษ	gaan long thôht
to order (vt)	สั่ง	sàng
to obey (vi, vt)	เชื่อฟัง	chêua fang
straight (adj)	ตรง	dtrorng
curved (adj)	โค้ง	khóhng
paradise	สวรรค์	sà-wǎn
hell	นรก	ná-rók
to be born	เกิด	gèrt
to die (vi)	ตาย	dtaai
strong (adj)	แข็งแรง	khǎeng raeng
weak (adj)	อ่อนแอ	òrn ae
old (adj)	แก่	gàe
young (adj)	หนุ่ม	nùm
old (adj)	เก่าแก่	gào gàe
new (adj)	ใหม่	mài
hard (adj)	แข็ง	khǎeng
soft (adj)	อ่อน	òrn
warm (tepid)	อุ่น	ùn
cold (adj)	หนาว	nǎao
fat (adj)	อ้วน	ûan
thin (adj)	ผอม	phǒrm
narrow (adj)	แคบ	khâep
wide (adj)	กว้าง	gwâang

good (adj)	ดี	dee
bad (adj)	ไม่ดี	mâi dee
brave (adj)	กล้าหาญ	glâa hǎan
cowardly (adj)	ขี้ขลาด	khêe khlàat

17. Weekdays

Monday	วันจันทร์	wan jan
Tuesday	วันอังคาร	wan ang-khaan
Wednesday	วันพุธ	wan phút
Thursday	วันพฤหัสบดี	wan phá-réu-hàt-sà-bor-dee
Friday	วันศุกร์	wan sùk
Saturday	วันเสาร์	wan sǎo
Sunday	วันอาทิตย์	wan aa-thít
today (adv)	วันนี้	wan née
tomorrow (adv)	พรุ่งนี้	phrûng-née
the day after tomorrow	วันมะรืนนี้	wan má-reun née
yesterday (adv)	เมื่อวานนี้	mêua waan née
the day before yesterday	เมื่อวานซืนนี้	mêua waan-seun née
day	วัน	wan
working day	วันทำงาน	wan tham ngaan
public holiday	วันนักขัตฤกษ์	wan nák-khàt-rêrk
day off	วันหยุด	wan yùt
weekend	วันสุดสัปดาห์	wan sùt sàp-daa
all day long	ทั้งวัน	tháng wan
the next day (adv)	วันรุ่งขึ้น	wan rûng khêun
two days ago	สองวันก่อน	sǒrng wan gòrn
the day before	วันก่อนหน้านี้	wan gòrn nâa née
daily (adj)	รายวัน	raai wan
every day (adv)	ทุกวัน	thúk wan
week	สัปดาห์	sàp-daa
last week (adv)	สัปดาห์ก่อน	sàp-daa gòrn
next week (adv)	สัปดาห์หน้า	sàp-daa nâa
weekly (adj)	รายสัปดาห์	raai sàp-daa
every week (adv)	ทุกสัปดาห์	thúk sàp-daa
twice a week	สัปดาห์ละสองครั้ง	sàp-daa lá sǒrng khráng
every Tuesday	ทุกวันอังคาร	túk wan ang-khaan

18. Hours. Day and night

| morning | เช้า | cháo |
| in the morning | ตอนเช้า | dtorn cháo |

noon, midday	เที่ยงวัน	thîang wan
in the afternoon	ตอนบ่าย	dtorn bàai
evening	เย็น	yen
in the evening	ตอนเย็น	dtorn yen
night	คืน	kheun
at night	กลางคืน	glaang kheun
midnight	เที่ยงคืน	thîang kheun

second	วินาที	wí-naa-thee
minute	นาที	naa-thee
hour	ชั่วโมง	chûa mohng
half an hour	ครึ่งชั่วโมง	khrêung chûa mohng
a quarter-hour	สิบห้านาที	sìp hâa naa-thee
fifteen minutes	สิบห้านาที	sìp hâa naa-thee
24 hours	24 ชั่วโมง	yêe sìp sèe · chûa mohng

sunrise	พระอาทิตย์ขึ้น	phrá aa-thít khêun
dawn	ใกล้รุ่ง	glâi rûng
early morning	เช้า	cháo
sunset	พระอาทิตย์ตก	phrá aa-thít dtòk

early in the morning	ตอนเช้า	dtorn cháo
this morning	เช้านี้	cháo née
tomorrow morning	พรุ่งนี้เช้า	phrûng-née cháo
this afternoon	บ่ายนี้	bàai née
in the afternoon	ตอนบ่าย	dtorn bàai
tomorrow afternoon	พรุ่งนี้บ่าย	phrûng-née bàai
tonight (this evening)	คืนนี้	kheun née
tomorrow night	คืนพรุ่งนี้	kheun phrûng-née

at 3 o'clock sharp	3 โมงตรง	săam mohng dtrorng
about 4 o'clock	ประมาณ 4 โมง	bprà-maan sèe mohng
by 12 o'clock	ภายใน 12 โมง	phaai nai sìp sŏng mohng

in 20 minutes	อีก 20 นาที	èek yêe sìp naa-thee
in an hour	อีกหนึ่งชั่วโมง	èek nèung chûa mohng
on time (adv)	ทันเวลา	than way-laa

a quarter to ...	อีกสิบห้านาที	èek sìp hâa naa-thee
within an hour	ภายในหนึ่งชั่วโมง	phaai nai nèung chûa mohng
every 15 minutes	ทุก 15 นาที	thúk sìp hâa naa-thee
round the clock	ทั้งวัน	tháng wan

19. Months. Seasons

January	มกราคม	mók-gà-raa khom
February	กุมภาพันธ์	gum-phaa phan
March	มีนาคม	mee-naa khom
April	เมษายน	may-săa-yon

| May | พฤษภาคม | phréut-sà-phaa khom |
| June | มิถุนายน | mí-thù-naa-yon |

July	กรกฎาคม	gà-rá-gà-daa-khom
August	สิงหาคม	sǐng hǎa khom
September	กันยายน	gan-yaa-yon
October	ตุลาคม	dtù-laa khom
November	พฤศจิกายน	phréut-sà-jì-gaa-yon
December	ธันวาคม	than-waa khom

spring	ฤดูใบไม้ผลิ	réu-doo bai máai phlì
in spring	ฤดูใบไม้ผลิ	réu-doo bai máai phlì
spring (as adj)	ฤดูใบไมผลิ	réu-doo bai máai phlì

summer	ฤดูร้อน	réu-doo rórn
in summer	ฤดูร้อน	réu-doo rórn
summer (as adj)	ฤดูรอน	réu-doo rórn

fall	ฤดูใบไม้ร่วง	réu-doo bai máai rûang
in fall	ฤดูใบไม้ร่วง	réu-doo bai máai rûang
fall (as adj)	ฤดูใบไมรวง	réu-doo bai máai rûang

winter	ฤดูหนาว	réu-doo nǎao
in winter	ฤดูหนาว	réu-doo nǎao
winter (as adj)	ฤดูหนาว	réu-doo nǎao

month	เดือน	deuan
this month	เดือนนี้	deuan née
next month	เดือนหน้า	deuan nâa
last month	เดือนที่แลว	deuan thêe láew

a month ago	หนึ่งเดือน กอนหนานี้	nèung deuan gòrn nâa née
in a month (a month later)	อีกหนึ่งเดือน	èek nèung deuan
in 2 months (2 months later)	อีกสองเดือน	èek sǒrng deuan
the whole month	ทั้งเดือน	tháng deuan
all month long	ตลอดทั้งเดือน	dtà-lòrt tháng deuan

monthly (~ magazine)	รายเดือน	raai deuan
monthly (adv)	ทุกเดือน	thúk deuan
every month	ทุกเดือน	thúk deuan
twice a month	เดือนละสองครั้ง	deuan lá sǒrng kráng

year	ปี	bpee
this year	ปีนี้	bpee née
next year	ปีหน้า	bpee nâa
last year	ปีที่แลว	bpee thêe láew

a year ago	หนึ่งปีก่อน	nèung bpee gòrn
in a year	อีกหนึ่งปี	èek nèung bpee
in two years	อีกสองปี	èek sǒng bpee

| the whole year | ทั้งปี | tháng bpee |
| all year long | ตลอดทั้งปี | dtà-lòrt tháng bpee |

every year	ทุกปี	thúk bpee
annual (adj)	รายปี	raai bpee
annually (adv)	ทุกปี	thúk bpee
4 times a year	ปีละสี่ครั้ง	bpee lá sèe khráng

date (e.g., today's ~)	วันที่	wan thêe
date (e.g., ~ of birth)	วันเดือนปี	wan deuan bpee
calendar	ปฏิทิน	bpà-dtì-thin

half a year	ครึ่งปี	khrêung bpee
six months	หกเดือน	hòk deuan
season (summer, etc.)	ฤดูกาล	réu-doo gaan
century	ศตวรรษ	sà-dtà-wát

20. Time. Miscellaneous

time	เวลา	way-laa
moment	ครูหนึ่ง	khrôo nèung
instant (n)	ครู่เดียว ๆ	khrôo dieow
instant (adj)	เพียงครู่เดียว	phiang khrôo dieow
lapse (of time)	ช่วงเวลา	chûang way-laa
life	ชีวิต	chee-wít
eternity	ตลอดกาล	dtà-lòrt gaan

epoch	สมัย	sà-măi
era	ยุค	yúk
cycle	วัฏจักร	wát-dtà-jàk
period	ช่วง	chûang
term (short-~)	ระยะเวลา	rá-yá way-laa

the future	อนาคต	a-naa-khót
future (as adj)	อนาคตู	a-naa-khót
next time	ครั้งหน้า	khráng nâa
the past	อดีต	a-dèet
past (recent)	ที่ผ่านมา	thêe phàan maa
last time	ครั้งที่แล้ว	khráng thêe láew

later (adv)	ภายหลัง	phaai lăng
after (prep.)	หลังจาก	lăng jàak
nowadays (adv)	เวลานี้	way-laa née
now (at this moment)	ตอนนี้	dtorn-née
immediately (adv)	ทันที	than thee
soon (adv)	อีกไม่นาน	èek mâi naan
in advance (beforehand)	ล่วงหน้า	lûang nâa

| a long time ago | นานมาแล้ว | naan maa láew |
| recently (adv) | เมื่อเร็ว ๆ นี้ | mêua reo reo née |

destiny	ชะตากรรม	chá-dtaa gam
memories (childhood ~)	ความทรงจำ	khwaam song jam
archives	จดหมายเหตุ	jòt mǎai hàyt

during ...	ระหว่าง...	rá-wàang...
long, a long time (adv)	นาน	naan
not long (adv)	ไม่นาน	mâi naan
early (in the morning)	ลวงหนา	lûang nâa
late (not early)	ชา	cháa

forever (for good)	ตลอดกาล	dtà-lòrt gaan
to start (begin)	เริ่ม	rêrm
to postpone (vt)	เลื่อน	lêuan

at the same time	ในเวลาเดียวกัน	nai way-laa dieow gan
permanently (adv)	อย่างถาวร	yàang thǎa-won
constant (noise, pain)	ต่อเนื่อง	dtòr nêuang
temporary (adj)	ชั่วคราว	chûa khraao

sometimes (adv)	บางครั้ง	baang khráng
rarely (adv)	ไม่บ่อย	mâi bòi
often (adv)	บ่อย	bòi

21. Lines and shapes

square	สี่เหลี่ยมจัตุรัส	sèe lìam jàt-dtù-ràt
square (as adj)	สี่เหลี่ยมจัตุรัส	sèe lìam jàt-dtù-ràt
circle	วงกลม	wong glom
round (adj)	กลม	glom
triangle	รูปสามเหลี่ยม	rôop sǎam lìam
triangular (adj)	สามเหลี่ยม	sǎam lìam

oval	รูปกลมรี	rôop glom ree
oval (as adj)	กลมรี	glom ree
rectangle	สี่เหลี่ยมมุมฉาก	sèe lìam mum chàak
rectangular (adj)	สี่เหลี่ยมมุมฉาก	sèe lìam mum chàak

pyramid	พีระมิด	phee-rá-mít
rhombus	รูปสี่เหลี่ยม ขนมเปียกปูน	rôop sèe lìam khà-nǒm bpìak bpoon
trapezoid	รูปสี่เหลี่ยมคางหมู	rôop sèe lìam khaang mǒo
cube	ลูกบาศก์	lôok bàat
prism	ปริซึม	bprì seum

circumference	เส้นรอบวง	sên rôrp wong
sphere	ทรงกลม	song glom
ball (solid sphere)	ลูกกลม	lôok glom
diameter	เส้นผ่านศูนย์กลาง	sên phàan sǒon-glaang
radius	เส้นรัศมี	sên rát-sà-měe
perimeter (circle's ~)	เส้นรอบวง	sên rôrp wong

center	กลาง	glaang
horizontal (adj)	แนวนอน	naew norn
vertical (adj)	แนวตั้ง	naew dtâng
parallel (n)	เส้นขนาน	sên khà-nǎan
parallel (as adj)	ขนาน	khà-nǎan

line	เส้น	sên
stroke	เส้น	sên
straight line	เส้นตรง	sên dtrorng
curve (curved line)	เส้นโค้ง	sên khóhng
thin (line, etc.)	บาง	baang
contour (outline)	เส้นขอบ	sâyn khòrp

intersection	เส้นตัด	sên dtàt
right angle	มุมฉาก	mum chàak
segment	เซกเมนต์	sâyk-mayn
sector (circular ~)	เซกเตอร์	sâyk-dtêr
side (of triangle)	ขาง	khâang
angle	มุม	mum

22. Units of measurement

weight	น้ำหนัก	nám nàk
length	ความยาว	khwaam yaao
width	ความกว้าง	khwaam gwâang
height	ความสูง	khwaam sǒong
depth	ความลึก	khwaam léuk
volume	ปริมาณ	bpà-rí-maan
area	บริเวณ	bor-rí-wayn

gram	กรัม	gram
milligram	มิลลิกรัม	min-lí gram
kilogram	กิโลกรัม	gì-loh gram
ton	ตัน	dtan
pound	ปอนด์	bporn
ounce	ออนซ์	orn

meter	เมตร	máyt
millimeter	มิลลิเมตร	min-lí mâyt
centimeter	เซ็นติเมตร	sen dtì mâyt
kilometer	กิโลเมตร	gì-loh máyt
mile	ไมล์	mai

inch	นิ้ว	níw
foot	ฟุต	fút
yard	หลา	lǎa

square meter	ตารางเมตร	dtaa-raang máyt
hectare	เฮกตาร์	hêek dtaa
liter	ลิตร	lít

degree	องศา	ong-săa
volt	โวลต์	wohn
ampere	แอมแปร์	aem-bpae
horsepower	แรงม้า	raeng máa

quantity	จำนวน	jam-nuan
a little bit of …	นิดหน่อย	nít nói
half	ครึ่ง	khrêung
dozen	โหล	lŏh
piece (item)	ส่วน	sùan

size	ขนาด	khà-nàat
scale (map ~)	มาตราส่วน	mâat-dtraa sùan

minimal (adj)	น้อยที่สุด	nói thêe sùt
the smallest (adj)	เล็กที่สุด	lék thêe sùt
medium (adj)	กลาง	glaang
maximal (adj)	สูงสุด	sŏong sùt
the largest (adj)	ใหญ่ที่สุด	yài têe sùt

23. Containers

canning jar (glass ~)	ขวดโหล	khùat lŏh
can	กระป๋อง	grà-bpŏrng
bucket	ถัง	thăng
barrel	ถัง	thăng

wash basin (e.g., plastic ~)	กะทะ	gà-thá
tank (100L water ~)	ถังเก็บน้ำ	thăng gèp nám
hip flask	กระติกน้ำ	grà-dtìk nám
jerrycan	ภาชนะ	phaa-chá-ná
tank (e.g., tank car)	ถังบรรจุ	thăng ban-jù

mug	แก้ว	gâew
cup (of coffee, etc.)	ถ้วย	thûay
saucer	จานรอง	jaan rorng
glass (tumbler)	แก้ว	gâew
wine glass	แก้วไวน์	gâew wai
stock pot (soup pot)	หม้อ	môr

bottle (~ of wine)	ขวด	khùat
neck (of the bottle, etc.)	ปาก	bpàak

carafe (decanter)	คนโท	khon-thoh
pitcher	เหยือก	yèuak
vessel (container)	ภาชนะ	phaa-chá-ná
pot (crock, stoneware ~)	หม้อ	môr
vase	แจกัน	jae-gan
flacon, bottle (perfume ~)	กระติก	grà-dtìk
vial, small bottle	ขวดเล็ก	khùat lék

tube (of toothpaste)	หลอด	lòrt
sack (bag)	ถุง	thŭng
bag (paper ~, plastic ~)	ถุง	thŭng
pack (of cigarettes, etc.)	ซอง	sorng

box (e.g., shoebox)	กล่อง	glòrng
crate	ลัง	lang
basket	ตะกร้า	dtà-grâa

24. Materials

material	วัสดุ	wát-sà-dù
wood (n)	ไม้	máai
wood-, wooden (adj)	ไม	máai

| glass (n) | แก้ว | gâew |
| glass (as adj) | แกว | gâew |

| stone (n) | หิน | hĭn |
| stone (as adj) | หิน | hĭn |

| plastic (n) | พลาสติก | pláat-dtìk |
| plastic (as adj) | พลาสติก | pláat-dtìk |

| rubber (n) | ยาง | yaang |
| rubber (as adj) | ยาง | yaang |

| cloth, fabric (n) | ผ้า | phâa |
| fabric (as adj) | ผา | phâa |

| paper (n) | กระดาษ | grà-dàat |
| paper (as adj) | กระดาษ | grà-dàat |

| cardboard (n) | กระดาษแข็ง | grà-dàat khăeng |
| cardboard (as adj) | กระดาษแข็ง | grà-dàat khăeng |

| polyethylene | โพลีเอทิลีน | phoh-lee-ay-thí-leen |
| cellophane | เซลโลเฟน | sayn loh-fayn |

| linoleum | เสื่อน้ำมัน | sèua náam man |
| plywood | ไม้อัด | máai àt |

porcelain (n)	เครื่องเคลือบ ดินเผา	khrêuang khlêuap din phăo
porcelain (as adj)	เครื่องเคลือบ ดินเผา	khrêuang khlêuap din phăo
clay (n)	ดินเหนียว	din nĭeow
clay (as adj)	ดินเหนียว	din nĭeow
ceramic (n)	เซรามิก	say-raa mík
ceramic (as adj)	เซรามิก	say-raa mík

25. Metals

metal (n)	โลหะ	loh-hà
metal (as adj)	โลหะ	loh-hà
alloy (n)	โลหะสัมฤทธิ์	loh-hà sǎm-rít

gold (n)	ทอง	thorng
gold, golden (adj)	ทอง	thorng
silver (n)	เงิน	ngern
silver (as adj)	เงิน	ngern

iron (n)	เหล็ก	lèk
iron-, made of iron (adj)	เหล็ก	lèk
steel (n)	เหล็กกล้า	lèk glâa
steel (as adj)	เหล็กกล้า	lèk glâa
copper (n)	ทองแดง	thorng daeng
copper (as adj)	ทองแดง	thorng daeng

aluminum (n)	อะลูมิเนียม	a-loo-mí-niam
aluminum (as adj)	อะลูมิเนียม	a-loo-mí-niam
bronze (n)	ทองบรอนซ์	thorng-bron
bronze (as adj)	ทองบรอนซ์	thorng-bron

brass	ทองเหลือง	thorng lĕuang
nickel	นิกเกิล	ník-gêrn
platinum	ทองคำขาว	thorng kham khăao
mercury	ปรอท	bpa -ròrt
tin	ดีบุก	dee-bùk
lead	ตะกั่ว	dtà-gùa
zinc	สังกะสี	sǎng-gà-sĕe

HUMAN BEING

Human being. The body

26. Humans. Basic concepts

human being	มนุษย์	má-nút
man (adult male)	ผู้ชาย	phôo chaai
woman	ผู้หญิง	phôo yǐng
child	เด็ก, ลูก	dèk, lôok
girl	เด็กผู้หญิง	dèk phôo yǐng
boy	เด็กผู้ชาย	dèk phôo chaai
teenager	วัยรุ่น	wai rûn
old man	ชายชรา	chaai chá-raa
old woman	หญิงชรา	yǐng chá-raa

27. Human anatomy

organism (body)	ร่างกาย	râang gaai
heart	หัวใจ	hǔa jai
blood	เลือด	lêuat
artery	เส้นเลือดแดง	sâyn lêuat daeng
vein	เส้นเลือดดำ	sâyn lêuat dam
brain	สมอง	sà-mǒrng
nerve	เส้นประสาท	sên bprà-sàat
nerves	เส้นประสาท	sên bprà-sàat
vertebra	กระดูกสันหลัง	grà-dòok sǎn-lǎng
spine (backbone)	สันหลัง	sǎn lǎng
stomach (organ)	กระเพาะอาหาร	grà phór aa-hǎan
intestines, bowels	ลำไส้	lam sâi
intestine (e.g., large ~)	ลำไส้	lam sâi
liver	ตับ	dtàp
kidney	ไต	dtai
bone	กระดูก	grà-dòok
skeleton	โครงกระดูก	khrohng grà-dòok
rib	ซี่โครง	sêe khrohng
skull	กะโหลก	gà-lòhk
muscle	กล้ามเนื้อ	glâam néua
biceps	กล้ามเนื้อไบเซ็ปส์	glâam néua bai-sép

triceps	กล้ามเนื้อไทรเซปส์	gglâam néua thrai-sâyp
tendon	เส้นเอ็น	sâyn en
joint	ข้อต่อ	khôr dtòr
lungs	ปอด	bpòrt
genitals	อวัยวะเพศ	a-wai-wá phâyt
skin	ผิวหนัง	phĭw nǎng

28. Head

head	หัว	hŭa
face	หน้า	nâa
nose	จมูก	jà-mòok
mouth	ปาก	bpàak

eye	ตา	dtaa
eyes	ตา	dtaa
pupil	รูม่านตา	roo mâan dtaa
eyebrow	คิ้ว	khíw
eyelash	ขนตา	khŏn dtaa
eyelid	เปลือกตา	bplèuak dtaa

tongue	ลิ้น	lín
tooth	ฟัน	fan
lips	ริมฝีปาก	rim fĕe bpàak
cheekbones	โหนกแก้ม	nòhk gâem
gum	เหงือก	ngèuak
palate	เพดานปาก	phay-daan bpàak

nostrils	รูจมูก	roo jà-mòok
chin	คาง	khaang
jaw	ขากรรไกร	khǎa gan-grai
cheek	แก้ม	gâem

forehead	หน้าผาก	nâa phàak
temple	ขมับ	khà-màp
ear	หู	hŏo
back of the head	หลังศีรษะ	lăng sĕe-sà
neck	คอ	khor
throat	ลำคอ	lam khor

hair	ผม	phŏm
hairstyle	ทรงผม	song phŏm
haircut	ทรงผม	song phŏm
wig	ผมปลอม	phŏm bplorm

mustache	หนวด	nùat
beard	เครา	krao
to have (a beard, etc.)	ลองไว้	lorng wái
braid	ผมเปีย	phŏm bpia
sideburns	จอน	jorn

red-haired (adj)	ผมแดง	phŏm daeng
gray (hair)	ผมหงอก	phŏm ngòrk
bald (adj)	หัวล้าน	hǔa láan
bald patch	หัวล้าน	hǔa láan
ponytail	ผมทูรงหางม้า	phŏm song hǎang máa
bangs	ผมม้า	phŏm máa

29. Human body

hand	มือ	meu
arm	แขน	khǎen
finger	นิ้ว	níw
toe	นิ้วเท้า	níw tháo
thumb	นิ้วโป้ง	níw bpôhng
little finger	นิ้วก้อย	níw gôi
nail	เล็บ	lép
fist	กำปั้น	gam bpân
palm	ฝ่ามือ	fàa meu
wrist	ข้อมือ	khôr meu
forearm	แขนช่วงล่าง	khǎen chûang lâang
elbow	ข้อศอก	khôr sòrk
shoulder	ไหล่	lài
leg	ขา	khǎa
foot	เท้า	tháo
knee	หัวเข่า	hǔa khào
calf (part of leg)	น่อง	nôrng
hip	สะโพก	sà-phôhk
heel	ส้นเท้า	sôn tháo
body	ร่างกาย	râang gaai
stomach	ท้อง	thórng
chest	อก	òk
breast	หน้าอก	nâa òk
flank	ข้าง	khâang
back	หลัง	lǎng
lower back	หลังส่วนล่าง	lǎng sùan lâang
waist	เอว	eo
navel (belly button)	สะดือ	sà-deu
buttocks	ก้น	gôn
bottom	ก้น	gôn
beauty mark	ไฝเสน่ห์	fǎi sà-này
birthmark (café au lait spot)	ปาน	bpaan
tattoo	รอยสัก	roi sàk
scar	แผลเป็น	phlǎe bpen

Clothing & Accessories

30. Outerwear. Coats

clothes	เสื้อผ้า	sêua phâa
outerwear	เสื้อนอก	sêua nôk
winter clothing	เสื้อกันหนาว	sêua gan năao
coat (overcoat)	เสื้อโค้ท	sêua khóht
fur coat	เสื้อโค้ทขนสัตว์	sêua khóht khŏn sàt
fur jacket	แจคเก็ตขนสัตว์	jáek-gèt khŏn sàt
down coat	แจ็คเก็ตกันหนาว	jàek-gèt gan năao
jacket (e.g., leather ~)	แจ๊คเก็ต	jáek-gèt
raincoat (trenchcoat, etc.)	เสื้อกันฝน	sêua gan fŏn
waterproof (adj)	ซึ่งกันน้ำได้	sêung gan náam dâai

31. Men's & women's clothing

shirt (button shirt)	เสื้อ	sêua
pants	กางเกง	gaang-gayng
jeans	กางเกงยีนส์	gaang-gayng yeen
suit jacket	แจ็คเก็ตสูท	jàek-gèt sòot
suit	ชุดสูท	chút sòot
dress (frock)	ชุดเดรส	chút draet
skirt	กระโปรง	grà bprohng
blouse	เสื้อ	sêua
knitted jacket (cardigan, etc.)	แจคเก็ตถัก	jáek-gèt thàk
jacket (of woman's suit)	แจ๊คเก็ต	jáek-gèt
T-shirt	เสื้อยืด	sêua yêut
shorts (short trousers)	กางเกงขาสั้น	gaang-gayng khăa sân
tracksuit	ชุดวอรม	chút wom
bathrobe	เสื้อคลุมอาบน้ำ	sêua khlum àap náam
pajamas	ชุดนอน	chút norn
sweater	เสื้อไหมพรม	sêua măi phrom
pullover	เสื้อกันหนาวแบบสวม	sêua gan năao bàep sŭam
vest	เสื้อกั๊ก	sêua gák
tailcoat	เสื้อเทลโค้ต	sêua thayn-khóht
tuxedo	ชุดทักซิโด	chút thák sí dôh

uniform	เครื่องแบบ	khrêuang bàep
workwear	ชุดทำงาน	chút tam ngaan
overalls	ชุดเอี๊ยม	chút íam
coat (e.g., doctor's smock)	เสื้อคลุม	sêua khlum

32. Clothing. Underwear

underwear	ชุดชั้นใน	chút chán nai
boxers, briefs	กางเกงในชาย	gaang-gayng nai chaai
panties	กางเกงในสตรี	gaang-gayng nai sàt-dtree
undershirt (A-shirt)	เสื้อชั้นใน	sêua chán nai
socks	ถุงเท้า	thǔng tháo

nightdress	ชุดนอนสตรี	chút norn sàt-dtree
bra	ยกทรง	yók song
knee highs (knee-high socks)	ถุงเท้ายาว	thǔng tháo yaao
pantyhose	ถุงน่องเต็มตัว	thǔng nôrng dtem dtua
stockings (thigh highs)	ถุงน่อง	thǔng nôrng
bathing suit	ชุดว่ายน้ำ	chút wâai náam

33. Headwear

hat	หมวก	mùak
fedora	หมวก	mùak
baseball cap	หมวกเบสบอล	mùak bàyt-bon
flatcap	หมวกติงลี่	mùak dting lêe

beret	หูมวกเบเร่ต์	mùak bay-rây
hood	ฮูด	hóot
panama hat	หมวกปานามา	mùak bpaa-naa-maa
knit cap (knitted hat)	หมวกไหมพรม	mùak mǎi phrom

headscarf	ผ้าโพกศีรษะ	phâa phôhk sěe-sà
women's hat	หมวกสตรี	mùak sàt-dtree
hard hat	หมวกนิรภัย	mùak ní-rá-phai
garrison cap	หมวกหนีบ	mùak nèep
helmet	หมวกกันน็อค	mùak ní-rá-phai

| derby | หมวกกลมทรงสูง | mùak glom song sǒong |
| top hat | หมวกทรงสูง | mùak song sǒong |

34. Footwear

| footwear | รองเท้า | rorng tháo |
| shoes (men's shoes) | รองเทา | rorng tháo |

shoes (women's shoes)	รองเท้า	rorng tháo
boots (e.g., cowboy ~)	รองเท้าบูท	rorng tháo bòot
slippers	รองเท้าแตะในบ้าน	rorng tháo dtàe nai bâan
tennis shoes (e.g., Nike ~)	รองเท้ากีฬา	rorng tháo gee-laa
sneakers (e.g., Converse ~)	รองเท้าผ้าใบ	rorng tháo phâa bai
sandals	รองเท้าแตะ	rorng tháo dtàe
cobbler (shoe repairer)	คนซ่อมรองเท้า	khon sôrm rorng tháo
heel	สันรองเทา	sôn rorng tháo
pair (of shoes)	คู่	khôo
shoestring	เชือกรองเท้า	chêuak rorng tháo
to lace (vt)	ผูกเชือกรองเทา	phòok chêuak rorng tháo
shoehorn	ที่ชอนรองเทา	thêe chón rorng tháo
shoe polish	ยาขัดรองเทา	yaa khàt rorng tháo

35. Textile. Fabrics

cotton (n)	ฝ้าย	fâai
cotton (as adj)	ฝ้าย	fâai
flax (n)	แฟลกซ์	fláek
flax (as adj)	แฟลกซ์	fláek
silk (n)	ไหม	măi
silk (as adj)	ไหม	măi
wool (n)	ขนสัตว์	khŏn sàt
wool (as adj)	ขนสัตว์	khŏn sàt
velvet	กำมะหยี่	gam-má-yèe
suede	หนังกลับ	năng glàp
corduroy	ผ้าลูกฟูก	phâa lôok fôok
nylon (n)	ไนลอน	nai-lorn
nylon (as adj)	ไนลอน	nai-lorn
polyester (n)	โพลีเอสเตอร์	poh-lee-àyt-dtêr
polyester (as adj)	โพลีเอสเตอร์	poh-lee-àyt-dtêr
leather (n)	หนัง	năng
leather (as adj)	หนัง	năng
fur (n)	ขนสัตว์	khŏn sàt
fur (e.g., ~ coat)	ขนสัตว์	khŏn sàt

36. Personal accessories

gloves	ถุงมือ	thŭng meu
mittens	ถุงมือ	thŭng meu

scarf (muffler)	ผ้าพันคอ	phâa phan khor
glasses (eyeglasses)	แว่นตา	wâen dtaa
frame (eyeglass ~)	กรอบแว่น	gròrp wâen
umbrella	ร่ม	rôm
walking stick	ไม้เท้า	máai tháo
hairbrush	แปรงหวีผม	bpraeng wěe phǒm
fan	พัด	phát
tie (necktie)	เนคไท	nâyk-thai
bow tie	โบว์หูกระต่าย	boh hǒo grà-dtàai
suspenders	สายเอี่ยม	sǎai íam
handkerchief	ผ้าเช็ดหน้า	phâa chét-nâa
comb	หวี	wěe
barrette	ที่หนีบผม	têe nèep phǒm
hairpin	กิ๊บ	gíp
buckle	หัวเข็มขัด	hǔa khěm khàt
belt	เข็มขัด	khěm khàt
shoulder strap	สายกระเป๋า	sǎai grà-bpǎo
bag (handbag)	กระเป๋า	grà-bpǎo
purse	กระเป๋าถือ	grà-bpǎo thěu
backpack	กระเป๋าสะพายหลัง	grà-bpǎo sà-phaai lǎng

37. Clothing. Miscellaneous

fashion	แฟชั่น	fae-chân
in vogue (adj)	คานิยม	khâa ní-yom
fashion designer	นักออกแบบแฟชั่น	nák òrk bàep fae-chân
collar	คอปกเสื้อ	khor bpòk sêua
pocket	กระเป๋า	grà-bpǎo
pocket (as adj)	กระเป๋า	grà-bpǎo
sleeve	แขนเสื้อ	khǎen sêua
hanging loop	ที่แขวนเสื้อ	thêe khwǎen sêua
fly (on trousers)	ซิปกางเกง	síp gaang-gayng
zipper (fastener)	ซิป	síp
fastener	ซิป	síp
button	กระดุม	grà dum
buttonhole	รูกระดุม	roo grà dum
to come off (ab. button)	หลุดออก	lùt òrk
to sew (vi, vt)	เย็บ	yép
to embroider (vi, vt)	ปัก	bpàk
embroidery	ลายปัก	laai bpàk
sewing needle	เข็มเย็บผ้า	khěm yép phâa
thread	เส้นด้าย	sây-dâai
seam	รอยเย็บ	roi yép

to get dirty (vi)	สกปรก	sòk-gà-bpròk
stain (mark, spot)	รอยเปื้อน	roi bpêuan
to crease, crumple (vi)	พับเป็นรอยย่น	pháp bpen roi yôn
to tear, to rip (vt)	ฉีก	chèek
clothes moth	แมลงกินผ้า	má-laeng gin phâa

38. Personal care. Cosmetics

toothpaste	ยาสีฟัน	yaa sĕe fan
toothbrush	แปรงสีฟัน	bpraeng sĕe fan
to brush one's teeth	แปรงฟัน	bpraeng fan
razor	มีดโกน	mêet gohn
shaving cream	ครีมโกนหนวด	khreem gohn nùat
to shave (vi)	โกน	gohn
soap	สบู่	sà-bòo
shampoo	แชมพู	chaem-phoo
scissors	กรรไกร	gan-grai
nail file	ตะไบเล็บ	dtà-bai lép
nail clippers	กรรไกรตัดเล็บ	gan-grai dtàt lép
tweezers	แหนบ	nàep
cosmetics	เครื่องสำอาง	khrêuang săm-aang
face mask	มาสกหน้า	mâak nâa
manicure	การแต่งเล็บ	gaan dtàeng lép
to have a manicure	แต่งเล็บ	dtàeng lép
pedicure	การแต่งเล็บเท้า	gaan dtàeng lép táo
make-up bag	กระเป๋าเครื่องสำอาง	grà-bpăo khrêuang săm-aang
face powder	แป้งฝุ่น	bpâeng-fùn
powder compact	ตลับแป้ง	dtà-làp bpâeng
blusher	แป้งทาแก้ม	bpâeng thaa gâem
perfume (bottled)	น้ำหอม	nám hŏrm
toilet water (lotion)	น้ำหอมอ่อนๆ	náam hŏrm òn òn
lotion	โลชั่น	loh-chân
cologne	โคโลญจ์	khoh-lohn
eyeshadow	อายแชโดว์	aai-chae-doh
eyeliner	อายไลเนอร์	aai lai-ner
mascara	มาสคารา	mâat-khaa-râa
lipstick	ลิปสติก	líp-sà-dtìk
nail polish, enamel	น้ำยาทาเล็บ	nám yaa-thaa lép
hair spray	สเปรย์ฉีดผม	sà-bpray chèet phŏm
deodorant	ยาดับกลิ่น	yaa dàp glìn
cream	ครีม	khreem

face cream	ครีมทาหน้า	khreem thaa nâa
hand cream	ครีมทามือ	khreem thaa meu
anti-wrinkle cream	ครีมลดริ้วรอย	khreem lót ríw roi
day cream	ครีมกลางวัน	khreem klaang wan
night cream	ครีมกลางคืน	khreem klaang kheun
day (as adj)	กลางวัน	glaang wan
night (as adj)	กลางคืน	glaang kheun
tampon	ผ้าอนามัยแบบสอด	phâa a-naa-mai bàep sòrt
toilet paper (toilet roll)	กระดาษชำระ	grà-dàat cham-rá
hair dryer	เครื่องเป่าผม	khrêuang bpào phŏm

39. Jewelry

jewelry, jewels	เครื่องเพชรพลอย	khrêuang phét phloi
precious (e.g., ~ stone)	เพชรพลอย	phét phloi
hallmark stamp	ตราฮอลมาร์ค	dtraa hon-mâak
ring	แหวน	wăen
wedding ring	แหวนแต่งงาน	wăen dtàeng ngaan
bracelet	กำไลขอมือ	gam-lai khôr meu
earrings	ตุ้มหู	dtûm hŏo
necklace (~ of pearls)	สร้อยคอ	sôi khor
crown	มงกุฎ	mong-gùt
bead necklace	สร้อยคอลูกปัด	sôi khor lôok bpàt
diamond	เพชร	phét
emerald	มรกต	mor-rá-gòt
ruby	พลอยสีทับทิม	phloi sĕe tháp-thim
sapphire	ไพลิน	phai-lin
pearl	ไข่มุก	khài múk
amber	อำพัน	am phan

40. Watches. Clocks

watch (wristwatch)	นาฬิกา	naa-lí-gaa
dial	หน้าปัด	nâa bpàt
hand (of clock, watch)	เข็ม	khĕm
metal watch band	สายนาฬิกาข้อมือ	săi naa-lí-gaa khôr meu
watch strap	สายรัดขอมือ	săi rát khôr meu
battery	แบตเตอรี่	bàet-dter-rêe
to be dead (battery)	หมด	mòt
to change a battery	เปลี่ยนแบตเตอรี่	bplìan bàet-dter-rêe
to run fast	เดินเร็วเกินไป	dern reo gern bpai
to run slow	เดินช้า	dern cháa
wall clock	นาฬิกา แขวนผนัง	naa-lí-gaa khwăen phà-năng

hourglass	นาฬิกาทราย	naa-lí-gaa saai
sundial	นาฬิกาแดด	naa-lí-gaa dàet
alarm clock	นาฬิกาปลุก	naa-lí-gaa bplùk
watchmaker	ช่างซ่อมนาฬิกา	châang sôrm naa-lí-gaa
to repair (vt)	ซ่อม	sôrm

Food. Nutricion

41. Food

meat	เนื้อ	néua
chicken	ไก่	gài
Rock Cornish hen (poussin)	เนื้อลูกไก่	néua lôok gài
duck	เป็ด	bpèt
goose	ห่าน	hàan
game	สัตว์ที่ล่า	sàt thêe lâa
turkey	ไก่งวง	gài nguang
pork	เนื้อหมู	néua mŏo
veal	เนื้อลูกวัว	néua lôok wua
lamb	เนื้อแกะ	néua gàe
beef	เนื้อวัว	néua wua
rabbit	เนื้อกระต่าย	néua grà-dtàai
sausage (bologna, etc.)	ไส้กรอก	sâi gròrk
vienna sausage (frankfurter)	ไสกรอกเวียนนา	sâi gròrk wian-naa
bacon	หมูเบคอน	mŏo bay-khorn
ham	แฮม	haem
gammon	แฮมแกมมอน	haem gaem-morn
pâté	ปาเต	bpaa dtay
liver	ตับ	dtàp
hamburger (ground beef)	เนื้อสับ	néua sàp
tongue	ลิ้น	lín
egg	ไข่	khài
eggs	ไข่	khài
egg white	ไข่ขาว	khài khăo
egg yolk	ไขแดง	khài daeng
fish	ปลา	bplaa
seafood	อาหารทะเล	aa hăan thá-lay
crustaceans	สัตว์พวกกุ้งกั้งปู	sàt phûak gûng gâng bpoo
caviar	ไขปลา	khài-bplaa
crab	ปู	bpoo
shrimp	กุ้ง	gûng
oyster	หอยนางรม	hŏi naang rom
spiny lobster	กุ้งมังกร	gûng mang-gon
octopus	ปลาหมึก	bplaa mèuk

squid	ปลาหมึกกล้วย	bplaa mèuk-glûay
sturgeon	ปลาสเตอรเจียน	bpláa sà-dtêr jian
salmon	ปลาแซลมอน	bplaa saen-morn
halibut	ปลาตาเดียว	bplaa dtaa-dieow

cod	ปลาค็อด	bplaa khót
mackerel	ปลาแม็คเคอเร็ล	bplaa máek-kay-a-rěn
tuna	ปลาทูนา	bplaa thoo-nâa
eel	ปลาไหล	bplaa lǎi

trout	ปลาเทราท์	bplaa thrau
sardine	ปลาซาร์ดีน	bplaa saa-deen
pike	ปลาไพค์	bplaa phai
herring	ปลาเฮอร์ริง	bplaa her-ring

bread	ขนมปัง	khà-nǒm bpang
cheese	เนยแข็ง	noie khǎeng
sugar	น้ำตาล	nám dtaan
salt	เกลือ	gleua

rice	ข้าว	khâao
pasta (macaroni)	พาสต้า	phâat-dtâa
noodles	กวยเตี๋ยว	gǔay-dtǐeow

butter	เนย	noie
vegetable oil	น้ำมันพืช	nám man phêut
sunflower oil	น้ำมันดอก ทานตะวัน	nám man dòrk thaan dtà-wan
margarine	เนยเทียม	noie thiam

| olives | มะกอก | má-gòrk |
| olive oil | น้ำมันมะกอก | nám man má-gòrk |

milk	นม	nom
condensed milk	นมข้น	nom khôn
yogurt	โยเกิร์ต	yoh-gèrt

| sour cream | ซาวร์ครีม | saao khreem |
| cream (of milk) | ครีม | khreem |

| mayonnaise | มาย็องเนส | maa-yorng-nâyt |
| buttercream | สวนผสมของเนย และน้ำตาล | sùan phà-sǒm khǒrng noie láe nám dtaan |

groats (barley ~, etc.)	เมล็ดธัญพืช	má-lét than-yá-phêut
flour	แป้ง	bpâeng
canned food	อาหารกระป๋อง	aa-hǎan grà-bpǒrng

cornflakes	คอร์นเฟลค	khorn-flâyk
honey	น้ำผึ้ง	nám phêung
jam	แยม	yaem
chewing gum	หมากฝรั่ง	màak fà-ràng

42. Drinks

water	น้ำ	nám
drinking water	น้ำดื่ม	nám dèum
mineral water	น้ำแร่	nám râe
still (adj)	ไม่มีฟอง	mâi mee forng
carbonated (adj)	น้ำอัดลม	nám àt lom
sparkling (adj)	มีฟอง	mee forng
ice	น้ำแข็ง	nám khǎeng
with ice	ใส่น้ำแข็ง	sài nám khǎeng
non-alcoholic (adj)	ไม่มีแอลกอฮอล์	mâi mee aen-gor-hor
soft drink	เครื่องดื่มที่	krêuang dèum têe
	ไม่มีแอลกอฮอล์	mâi mee aen-gor-hor
refreshing drink	เครื่องดื่มให้	khrêuang dèum hâi
	ความสดชื่น	khwaam sòt chêun
lemonade	น้ำเลมอนเนด	nám lay-morn-nâyt
liquors	เหล้า	lâu
wine	ไวน์	wai
white wine	ไวน์ขาว	wai khǎao
red wine	ไวน์แดง	wai daeng
liqueur	สุรา	sù-raa
champagne	แชมเปญ	chaem-bpayn
vermouth	เหล้าองุ่นขาว	lâo a-ngùn khǎao
	ซึ่งมีกลิ่นหอม	sêung mee glìn hǒrm
whiskey	เหล้าวิสกี้	lâu wít-sa -gêe
vodka	เหล้าวอดก้า	lâu wórt-gâa
gin	เหล้ายิน	lâu yin
cognac	เหล้าคอนยัก	lâu khorn yák
rum	เหล้ารัม	lâu ram
coffee	กาแฟ	gaa-fae
black coffee	กาแฟดำ	gaa-fae dam
coffee with milk	กาแฟใส่นม	gaa-fae sài nom
cappuccino	กาแฟคาปูชิโน	gaa-fae khaa bpoo chí noh
instant coffee	กาแฟสำเร็จรูป	gaa-fae sǎm-rèt rôop
milk	นม	nom
cocktail	ค็อกเทล	khók-tayn
milkshake	มิลค์เชค	min-châyk
juice	น้ำผลไม้	nám phǒn-lá-máai
tomato juice	น้ำมะเขือเทศ	nám má-khěua thâyt
orange juice	น้ำส้ม	nám sôm
freshly squeezed juice	น้ำผลไม้	nám phǒn-lá-máai
	คั้นสด	khán sòt
beer	เบียร์	bia

light beer	เบียร์ไลท์	bia lai
dark beer	เบียร์ดาร์ค	bia dàak
tea	ชา	chaa
black tea	ชาดำ	chaa dam
green tea	ชาเขียว	chaa khǐeow

43. Vegetables

vegetables	ผัก	phàk
greens	ผักใบเขียว	phàk bai khǐeow
tomato	มะเขือเทศ	má-khěua thâyt
cucumber	แตงกวา	dtaeng-gwaa
carrot	แครอท	khae-rót
potato	มันฝรั่ง	man fà-ràng
onion	หัวหอม	hǔa hǒrm
garlic	กระเทียม	grà-thiam
cabbage	กะหล่ำปลี	gà-làm bplee
cauliflower	ดอกกะหล่ำ	dòrk gà-làm
Brussels sprouts	กะหล่ำดาว	gà-làm-daao
broccoli	บร็อคโคลี่	bròrk-khoh-lêe
beet	บีทรูท	bee-trôot
eggplant	มะเขือยาว	má-khěua-yaao
zucchini	แตงซูคินี	dtaeng soo-khí-nee
pumpkin	ฟักทอง	fák-thorng
turnip	หัวผักกาด	hǔa-phàk-gàat
parsley	ผักชีฝรั่ง	phàk chee fà-ràng
dill	ผักชีลาว	phàk-chee-laao
lettuce	ผักกาดหอม	phàk gàat hǒrm
celery	คื่นฉ่าย	khêun-châai
asparagus	หน่อไม้ฝรั่ง	nòr máai fà-ràng
spinach	ผักขม	phàk khǒm
pea	ถั่วลันเตา	thùa-lan-dtao
beans	ถั่ว	thùa
corn (maize)	ข้าวโพด	khâao-phôht
kidney bean	ถั่วรูปไต	thùa rôop dtai
bell pepper	พริกหยวก	phrík-yùak
radish	หัวไชเท้า	hǔa chai tháo
artichoke	อาร์ติโชค	aa dtì chôhk

44. Fruits. Nuts

fruit	ผลไม้	phǒn-lá-máai
apple	แอปเปิ้ล	àep-bpêrn

pear	แพร์	phae
lemon	มะนาว	má-naao
orange	ส้ม	sôm
strawberry (garden ~)	สตรอว์เบอร์รี่	sà-dtror-ber-rêe

mandarin	ส้มแมนดาริน	sôm maen daa rin
plum	พลัม	phlam
peach	ลูกท้อ	lôok thór
apricot	แอปริคอท	ae-bprì-khôrt
raspberry	ราสเบอร์รี่	râat-ber-rêe
pineapple	สับปะรด	sàp-bpà-rót

banana	กล้วย	glûay
watermelon	แตงโม	dtaeng moh
grape	องุ่น	a-ngùn
sour cherry	เชอร์รี่	cher-rêe
sweet cherry	เชอร์รี่ป่า	cher-rêe bpàa
melon	เมลอน	may-lorn

grapefruit	ส้มโอ	sôm oh
avocado	อะโวคาโด	a-who-khaa-doh
papaya	มะละกอ	má-lá-gor
mango	มะม่วง	má-mûang
pomegranate	ทับทิม	tháp-thim

redcurrant	เรดเคอร์แรนท์	râyt-khêr-raen
blackcurrant	แบล็คเคอูรแรนท์	blàek khêr-raen
gooseberry	กูสเบอร์รี่	gòot-ber-rêe
bilberry	บิลเบอร์รี่	bil-ber-rêe
blackberry	แบล็คเบอร์รี่	blàek ber-rêe

raisin	ลูกเกด	lôok gàyt
fig	มะเดื่อฝรั่ง	má dèua fà-ràng
date	ลูกอินทผลัม	lôok in-thá-plăm

peanut	ถั่วลิสง	thùa-lí-sŏng
almond	อัลมอนด์	an-morn
walnut	วอลนัต	wor-lá-nát
hazelnut	เฮเซลนัท	hay sayn nát
coconut	มะพร้าว	má-phráao
pistachios	ถั่วพิสตาชิโอ	thùa phít dtaa chí oh

45. Bread. Candy

bakers' confectionery (pastry)	ขนม	khà-nŏm
bread	ขนมปัง	khà-nŏm bpang
cookies	คุกกี้	khúk-gêe
chocolate (n)	ช็อกโกแลต	chók-goh-láet
chocolate (as adj)	ช็อกโกแลต	chók-goh-láet

candy (wrapped)	ลูกกวาด	lôok gwàat
cake (e.g., cupcake)	ขนมเค้ก	khà-nŏm kháyk
cake (e.g., birthday ~)	ขนมเค้ก	khà-nŏm kháyk
pie (e.g., apple ~)	ขนมพาย	khà-nŏm phaai
filling (for cake, pie)	ไส้ในขนม	sâi nai khà-nŏm
jam (whole fruit jam)	แยม	yaem
marmalade	แยมผิวส้ม	yaem phĭw sôm
wafers	วาฟเฟิล	waaf-fern
ice-cream	ไอศกรีม	ai-sà-greem
pudding	พุดดิ้ง	phút-dîng

46. Cooked dishes

course, dish	มื้ออาหาร	méu aa-hăan
cuisine	อาหาร	aa-hăan
recipe	ตำราอาหาร	dtam-raa aa-hăan
portion	สวน	sùan
salad	สลัด	sà-làt
soup	ซุป	súp
clear soup (broth)	ซุปน้ำใส	súp nám-săi
sandwich (bread)	แซนด์วิช	saen-wít
fried eggs	ไข่ทอด	khài thôrt
hamburger (beefburger)	แฮมเบอร์เกอร์	haem-ber-gêr
beefsteak	สเต็กเนื้อ	sà-dtèk néua
side dish	เครื่องเคียง	khrêuang khiang
spaghetti	สปาเก็ตตี้	sà-bpaa-gèt-dtêe
mashed potatoes	มันฝรั่งบด	man fà-ràng bòt
pizza	พิซซ่า	phít-sâa
porridge (oatmeal, etc.)	ข้าวตม	khâao-dtôm
omelet	ไข่เจียว	khài jieow
boiled (e.g., ~ beef)	ต้ม	dtôm
smoked (adj)	รมควัน	rom khwan
fried (adj)	ทอด	thôrt
dried (adj)	ตากแห้ง	dtàak hâeng
frozen (adj)	แช่แข็ง	châe khăeng
pickled (adj)	ดอง	dorng
sweet (sugary)	หวาน	wăan
salty (adj)	เค็ม	khem
cold (adj)	เย็น	yen
hot (adj)	ร้อน	rórn
bitter (adj)	ขม	khŏm
tasty (adj)	อร่อย	à-ròi

to cook in boiling water	ต้ม	dtôm
to cook (dinner)	ทำอาหาร	tham aa-hǎan
to fry (vt)	ทอด	thôrt
to heat up (food)	อุ่น	ùn
to salt (vt)	ใส่เกลือ	sài gleua
to pepper (vt)	ใสพริกไทย	sài phrík thai
to grate (vt)	ขูด	khòot
peel (n)	เปลือก	bplèuak
to peel (vt)	ปอกเปลือก	bpòrk bplêuak

47. Spices

salt	เกลือ	gleua
salty (adj)	เค็ม	khem
to salt (vt)	ใสเกลือ	sài gleua
black pepper	พริกไทย	phrík thai
red pepper (milled ~)	พริกแดง	phrík daeng
mustard	มัสตารด	mát-dtàat
horseradish	ฮอสแรดิช	hórt rae dìt
condiment	เครื่องปรุงรส	khrêuang bprung rót
spice	เครื่องเทศ	khrêuang thâyt
sauce	ซู้อส	sós
vinegar	น้ำสมสายชู	nám sôm sǎai choo
anise	เทียนสัตตบุษย์	thian-sàt-dtà-bùt
basil	ใบโหระพา	bai hǒh rá phaa
cloves	กานพลู	gaan-phloo
ginger	ขิง	khǐng
coriander	ผักชีลา	pàk-chee-laa
cinnamon	อบเชย	òp-choie
sesame	งา	ngaa
bay leaf	ใบกระวาน	bai grà-waan
paprika	พริกปน	phrík bpòn
caraway	เทียนตากบ	thian dtaa gòp
saffron	หญาฝรั่น	yâa fà-ràn

48. Meals

food	อาหาร	aa-hǎan
to eat (vi, vt)	กิน	gin
breakfast	อาหารเช้า	aa-hǎan cháo
to have breakfast	ทานอาหารเช้า	thaan aa-hǎan cháo

lunch	ข้าวเที่ยง	khâao thîang
to have lunch	ทานอาหารเที่ยง	thaan aa-hǎan thîang
dinner	อาหารเย็น	aa-hǎan yen
to have dinner	ทานอาหารเย็น	thaan aa-hǎan yen

| appetite | ความอยากอาหาร | kwaam yàak aa hǎan |
| Enjoy your meal! | กินให้อร่อย! | gin hâi a-ròi |

to open (~ a bottle)	เปิด	bpèrt
to spill (liquid)	ทำหก	tham hòk
to spill out (vi)	ทำหกออกมา	tham hòk òrk maa

to boil (vi)	ต้ม	dtôm
to boil (vt)	ต้ม	dtôm
boiled (~ water)	ตม	dtôm
to chill, cool down (vt)	แช่เย็น	châe yen
to chill (vi)	แช่เย็น	châe yen

| taste, flavor | รสชาติ | rót châat |
| aftertaste | รส | rót |

to slim down (lose weight)	ลดน้ำหนัก	lót nám nàk
diet	อาหารพิเศษ	aa-hǎan phí-sàyt
vitamin	วิตามิน	wí-dtaa-min
calorie	แคลอรี่	khae-lor-rêe
vegetarian (n)	คนกินเจ	khon gin jay
vegetarian (adj)	มังสวิรัติ	mang-sà-wí-rát

fats (nutrient)	ไขมัน	khǎi man
proteins	โปรตีน	bproh-dteen
carbohydrates	คาร์โบไฮเดรต	kaa-boh-hai-dràyt

slice (of lemon, ham)	แผ่น	phàen
piece (of cake, pie)	ชิ้น	chín
crumb (of bread, cake, etc.)	เศษ	sàyt

49. Table setting

spoon	ช้อน	chórn
knife	มีด	mêet
fork	ส้อม	sôrm

| cup (e.g., coffee ~) | แก้ว | gâew |
| plate (dinner ~) | จาน | jaan |

saucer	จานรอง	jaan rorng
napkin (on table)	ผ้าเช็ดปาก	phâa chét bpàak
toothpick	ไม้จิ้มฟัน	máai jîm fan

50. Restaurant

restaurant	ร้านอาหาร	ráan aa-hăan
coffee house	ร้านกาแฟ	ráan gaa-fae
pub, bar	ร้านเหล้า	ráan lâo
tearoom	ร้านน้ำชา	ráan nám chaa
waiter	คนเสิร์ฟชาย	khon sèrf chaai
waitress	คนเสิร์ฟหญิง	khon sèrf yĭng
bartender	บาร์เทนเดอร์	baa-thayn-dêr
menu	เมนู	may-noo
wine list	รายการไวน์	raai gaan wai
to book a table	จองโต๊ะ	jorng dtó
course, dish	มื้ออาหาร	méu aa-hăan
to order (meal)	สั่ง	sàng
to make an order	สั่งอาหาร	sàng aa-hăan
aperitif	เครื่องดื่มเหล้า	khrêuang dèum lâo
	กอนอาหาร	gòrn aa-hăan
appetizer	ของกินเล่น	khŏrng gin lâyn
dessert	ของหวาน	khŏrng wăan
check	คิดเงิน	khít ngern
to pay the check	จ่วยคาอาหาร	jàai khâa aa hăan
to give change	ให้เงินทอน	hâi ngern thorn
tip	เงินทิป	ngern thíp

Family, relatives and friends

51. Personal information. Forms

name (first name)	ชื่อ	chêu
surname (last name)	นามสกุล	naam sà-gun
date of birth	วันเกิด	wan gèrt
place of birth	สถานที่เกิด	sà-thǎan thêe gèrt
nationality	สัญชาติ	sǎn-châat
place of residence	ที่อยู่อาศัย	thêe yòo aa-sǎi
country	ประเทศ	bprà-thâyt
profession (occupation)	อาชีพ	aa-chêep
gender, sex	เพศ	phâyt
height	ความสูง	khwaam sǒong
weight	น้ำหนัก	nám nàk

52. Family members. Relatives

mother	มารดา	maan-daa
father	บิดา	bì-daa
son	ลูกชาย	lôok chaai
daughter	ลูกสาว	lôok sǎao
younger daughter	ลูกสาวคนเล็ก	lôok sǎao khon lék
younger son	ลูกชายคนเล็ก	lôok chaai khon lék
eldest daughter	ลูกสาวคนโต	lôok sǎao khon dtoh
eldest son	ลูกชายคนโต	lôok chaai khon dtoh
elder brother	พี่ชาย	phêe chaai
younger brother	น้องชาย	nórng chaai
elder sister	พี่สาว	phêe sǎao
younger sister	น้องสาว	nórng sǎao
cousin (masc.)	ลูกพี่ลูกน้อง	lôok phêe lôok nórng
cousin (fem.)	ลูกพี่ลูกน้อง	lôok phêe lôok nórng
mom, mommy	แม่	mâe
dad, daddy	พ่อ	phôr
parents	พ่อแม่	phôr mâe
child	เด็ก, ลูก	dèk, lôok
children	เด็กๆ	dèk dèk
grandmother	ย่า, ยาย	yâa, yaai

grandfather	ปู่, ตา	bpòo, dtaa
grandson	หลานชาย	lǎan chaai
granddaughter	หลานสาว	lǎan sǎao
grandchildren	หลานๆ	lǎan

uncle	ลุง	lung
aunt	ป้า	bpâa
nephew	หลานชาย	lǎan chaai
niece	หลานสาว	lǎan sǎao
mother-in-law (wife's mother)	แม่ยาย	mâe yaai
father-in-law (husband's father)	พ่อสามี	phôr sǎa-mee
son-in-law (daughter's husband)	ลูกเขย	lôok khǒie
stepmother	แม่เลี้ยง	mâe líang
stepfather	พอเลี้ยง	phôr líang

infant	ทารก	thaa-rók
baby (infant)	เด็กเล็ก	dèk lék
little boy, kid	เด็ก	dèk

wife	ภรรยา	phan-rá-yaa
husband	สามี	sǎa-mee
spouse (husband)	สามี	sǎa-mee
spouse (wife)	ภรรยา	phan-rá-yaa

married (masc.)	แต่งงานแล้ว	dtàeng ngaan láew
married (fem.)	แตงงานแลว	dtàeng ngaan láew
single (unmarried)	เป็นโสด	bpen sòht
bachelor	ชายโสด	chaai sòht
divorced (masc.)	หย่าแล้ว	yàa láew
widow	แม่หม้าย	mâe mâai
widower	พอหม้าย	phôr mâai

relative	ญาติ	yâat
close relative	ญาติใกล้ชิด	yâat glâi chít
distant relative	ญาติหางๆ	yâat hàang hàang
relatives	ญาติๆ	yâat

orphan (boy)	เด็กชายกำพร้า	dèk chaai gam phráa
orphan (girl)	เด็กหญิงกำพรา	dèk yǐng gam phráa
guardian (of a minor)	ผูปกครอง	phôo bpòk khrorng
to adopt (a boy)	บุญธรรม	bun tham
to adopt (a girl)	บุญธรรม	bun tham

53. Friends. Coworkers

friend (masc.)	เพื่อน	phêuan
friend (fem.)	เพื่อน	phêuan

friendship	มิตรภาพ	mít-dtrà-phâap
to be friends	เป็นเพื่อน	bpen phêuan
buddy (masc.)	เพื่อนสนิท	phêuan sà-nìt
buddy (fem.)	เพื่อนสนิท	phêuan sà-nìt
partner	หุ้นส่วน	hûn sùan
chief (boss)	หัวหน้า	hǔa-nâa
superior (n)	ผู้บังคับบัญชา	phôo bang-kháp ban-chaa
owner, proprietor	เจ้าของ	jâo khǒrng
subordinate (n)	ลูกน้อง	lôok nórng
colleague	เพื่อนร่วมงาน	phêuan rûam ngaan
acquaintance (person)	ผู้คุ้นเคย	phôo khún khoie
fellow traveler	เพื่อนร่วมทาง	pêuan rûam thaang
classmate	เพื่อนรุ่น	phêuan rûn
neighbor (masc.)	เพื่อนบ้านผู้ชาย	phêuan bâan pôo chaai
neighbor (fem.)	เพื่อนบ้านผู้หญิง	phêuan bâan phôo yǐng
neighbors	เพื่อนบาน	phêuan bâan

54. Man. Woman

woman	ผู้หญิง	phôo yǐng
girl (young woman)	หญิงสาว	yǐng sǎao
bride	เจ้าสาว	jâo sǎao
beautiful (adj)	สวย	sǔay
tall (adj)	สูง	sǒong
slender (adj)	ผอม	phǒrm
short (adj)	เตี้ย	dtîa
blonde (n)	ผมสีทอง	phǒm sěe thorng
brunette (n)	ผมสีคล้ำ	phǒm sěe khlám
ladies' (adj)	สตรี	sàt-dtree
virgin (girl)	บริสุทธิ์	bor-rí-sùt
pregnant (adj)	ตั้งครรภ์	dtâng khan
man (adult male)	ผู้ชาย	phôo chaai
blond (n)	ผมสีทอง	phǒm sěe thorng
brunet (n)	ผมสีคล้ำ	phǒm sěe khlám
tall (adj)	สูง	sǒong
short (adj)	เตี้ย	dtîa
rude (rough)	หยาบคาย	yàap kaai
stocky (adj)	แข็งแรง	khǎeng raeng
robust (adj)	กำยำ	gam-yam
strong (adj)	แข็งแรง	khǎeng raeng
strength	ความแข็งแรง	khwaam khǎeng raeng

stout, fat (adj)	ท้วม	thúam
swarthy (adj)	ผิวดำ	phǐw dam
slender (well-built)	ผอม	phǒrm
elegant (adj)	สง่า	sà-ngàa

55. Age

age	อายุ	aa-yú
youth (young age)	วัยเยาว์	wai yao
young (adj)	หนุ่ม	nùm
younger (adj)	อายุน้อยกว่า	aa-yú nói gwàa
older (adj)	อายุสูงกว่า	aa-yú sǒong gwàa
young man	ชายหนุ่ม	chaai nùm
teenager	วัยรุ่น	wai rûn
guy, fellow	คนหนุ่ม	khon nùm
old man	ชายชรา	chaai chá-raa
old woman	หญิงชรา	yǐng chá-raa
adult (adj)	ผู้ใหญ่	phôo yài
middle-aged (adj)	วัยกลาง	wai glaang
elderly (adj)	วัยชรา	wai chá-raa
old (adj)	แก่	gàe
retirement	การเกษียณอายุ	gaan gà-sĭan aa-yú
to retire (from job)	เกษียณ	gà-sĭan
retiree	ผู้เกษียณอายุ	phôo gà-sĭan aa-yú

56. Children

child	เด็ก, ลูก	dèk, lôok
children	เด็กๆ	dèk dèk
twins	แฝด	fàet
cradle	เปล	bplay
rattle	ของเล่นกุ๊งกิ๋ง	khǒrng lên gúng-gîng
diaper	ผ้าอ้อม	phâa ôrm
pacifier	จุกนม	jùk-nom
baby carriage	รถเข็นเด็ก	rót khěn dèk
kindergarten	โรงเรียนอนุบาล	rohng rian a-nú-baan
babysitter	คนเฝ้าเด็ก	khon fâo dèk
childhood	วัยเด็ก	wai dèk
doll	ตุ๊กตา	dtúk-dtaa
toy	ของเล่น	khǒrng lên

construction set (toy)	ชุดของเล่นก่อสร้าง	chút khǒrng lên gòr sâang
well-bred (adj)	มีกิริยา	mee gì-rí-yaa
	มารยาทดี	maa-rá-yâat dee
ill-bred (adj)	ไม่มีมารยาท	mâi mee maa-rá-yâat
spoiled (adj)	เสียคน	sǐa khon

to be naughty	ซน	son
mischievous (adj)	ซน	son
mischievousness	ความเกเร	kwaam gay-ray
mischievous child	เด็กเกเร	dèk gay-ray

| obedient (adj) | ที่เชื่อฟัง | thêe chêua fang |
| disobedient (adj) | ที่ไม่เชื่อฟัง | thêe mâi chêua fang |

docile (adj)	ที่เชื่อฟังผู้ใหญ่	thée chêua fang phôo yài
clever (smart)	ฉลาด	chà-làat
child prodigy	เด็กมีพรสวรรค์	dèk mee phon sà-wǎn

57. Married couples. Family life

to kiss (vt)	จูบ	jòop
to kiss (vi)	จูบ	jòop
family (n)	ครอบครัว	khrôrp khrua
family (as adj)	ครอบครัว	khrôrp khrua
couple	ผัวเมีย	phǔa mia
marriage (state)	การแต่งงาน	gaan dtàeng ngaan
hearth (home)	บ้าน	bâan
dynasty	วงศ์ตระกูล	wong dtrà-goon

| date | การออกเดท | gaan òrk dàyt |
| kiss | การจูบ | gaan jòop |

love (for sb)	ความรัก	khwaam rák
to love (sb)	รัก	rák
beloved	ที่รัก	thêe rák

tenderness	ความละเมียดละไม	khwaam lá-mîat lá-mai
tender (affectionate)	ละเมียดละไม	lá-mîat lá-mai
faithfulness	ความซื่อ	khwaam sêu
faithful (adj)	ซื่อ	sêu
care (attention)	การดูแล	gaan doo lae
caring (~ father)	ชอบดูแล	chôrp doo lae
newlyweds	ดูแต่งงานใหม่	khôo dtàeng ngaan mài
honeymoon	ฮันนีมูน	han-nee-moon
to get married (ab. woman)	แต่งงาน	dtàeng ngaan
to get married (ab. man)	แต่งงาน	dtàeng ngaan
wedding	การสมรส	gaan sǒm rót
golden wedding	การสมรสครบรอบ50ปี	gaan sǒm rót khróp rôrp hâa-sìp bpee

anniversary	วันครบรอบ	wan khróp rôrp
lover (masc.)	ชู้รัก	khôo rák
mistress (lover)	เมียน้อย	mia nói

adultery	การคบชู้	gaan khóp chóo
to cheat on … (commit adultery)	คบชู้	khóp chóo
jealous (adj)	หึงหวง	hĕung hŭang
to be jealous	หึง	hĕung
divorce	การหย่าร้าง	gaan yàa ráang
to divorce (vi)	หย่า	yàa

to quarrel (vi)	ทะเลาะ	thá-lór
to be reconciled (after an argument)	ประนีประนอม	bprà-nee-bprà-nom
together (adv)	ด้วยกัน	dûay gan
sex	เพศสัมพันธ์	phâyt săm-phan

happiness	ความสุข	khwaam sùk
happy (adj)	มีความสุข	mee khwaam sùk
misfortune (accident)	เหตุราย	hàyt ráai
unhappy (adj)	ไม่มีความสุข	mâi mee khwaam sùk

Character. Feelings. Emotions

58. Feelings. Emotions

feeling (emotion)	ความรู้สึก	khwaam róo sèuk
feelings	ความรู้สึก	khwaam róo sèuk
to feel (vt)	รู้สึก	róo sèuk
hunger	ความหิว	khwaam hĭw
to be hungry	หิว	hĭw
thirst	ความกระหาย	khwaam grà-hăai
to be thirsty	กระหาย	grà-hăai
sleepiness	ความง่วง	khwaam ngûang
to feel sleepy	ง่วง	ngûang
tiredness	ความเหนื่อย	khwaam nèuay
tired (adj)	เหนื่อย	nèuay
to get tired	เหนื่อย	nèuay
mood (humor)	อารมณ์	aa-rom
boredom	ความเบื่อ	khwaam bèua
to be bored	เบื่อ	bèua
seclusion	ความเหงา	khwaam ngăo
to seclude oneself	ปลีกวิเวก	bplèek wí-wâyk
to worry (make anxious)	ทำให้...เป็นห่วง	tham hâi...bpen hùang
to be worried	กังวล	gang-won
worrying (n)	ความเป็นห่วง	khwaam bpen hùang
anxiety	ความวิตกกังวล	khwaam wí-dtòk gang-won
preoccupied (adj)	เป็นห่วงใหญ่	bpen hùang yài
to be nervous	กระวนกระวาย	grà won grà waai
to panic (vi)	ตื่นตระหนก	dtèun dtrà-nòk
hope	ความหวัง	khwaam wăng
to hope (vi, vt)	หวัง	wăng
certainty	ความแน่ใจ	khwaam nâe jai
certain, sure (adj)	แน่ใจ	nâe jai
uncertainty	ความไม่มั่นใจ	khwaam mâi mân jai
uncertain (adj)	ไม่มั่นใจ	mâi mân jai
drunk (adj)	เมา	mao
sober (adj)	ไม่เมา	mâi mao
weak (adj)	อ่อนแอ	òrn ae
happy (adj)	มีความสุข	mee khwaam sùk
to scare (vt)	ทำให้...กลัว	tham hâi...glua

| fury (madness) | ความโกรธเคือง | khwaam gròht kheuang |
| rage (fury) | ความเดือดดาล | khwaam dèuat daan |

depression	ความหดหู่	khwaam hòt-hòo
discomfort (unease)	อึดอัด	èut àt
comfort	สบาย	sà-baai
to regret (be sorry)	เสียดาย	sĭa daai
regret	ความเสียดาย	khwaam sĭa daai
bad luck	โชคร้าย	chôhk rái
sadness	ความเศร้า	khwaam sâo

shame (remorse)	ความละอายใจ	khwaam lá-aai jai
gladness	ความปิติ	khwaam bpì-dtì
enthusiasm, zeal	ความกระตือรือร้น	khwaam grà-dteu-reu-rón
enthusiast	คนที่กระตือรือร้น	khon thêe grà-dteu-reu-rón
to show enthusiasm	แสดงความ กระตือรือร้น	sà-daeng khwaam grà-dteu-reu-rón

59. Character. Personality

character	นิสัย	ní-sǎi
character flaw	ขอเสีย	khôr sĭa
mind	สติ	sà-dtì
reason	สติ	sà-dtì

conscience	มโนธรรม	má-noh tham
habit (custom)	นิสัย	ní-sǎi
ability (talent)	ความสามารถ	khwaam sǎa-mâat
can (e.g., ~ swim)	สามารถ	sǎa-mâat

patient (adj)	อดทน	òt thon
impatient (adj)	ใจร้อนใจเร็ว	jai rórn jai reo
curious (inquisitive)	อยากรู้อยากเห็น	yàak róo yàak hĕn
curiosity	ความอยาก รู้อยากเห็น	khwaam yàak róo yàak hĕn

modesty	ความถ่อมตน	khwaam thòrm dton
modest (adj)	ถ่อมตน	thòrm dton
immodest (adj)	หยาบโลน	yàap lohn

laziness	ความขี้เกียจ	khwaam khêe gìat
lazy (adj)	ขี้เกียจ	khêe gìat
lazy person (masc.)	คนขี้เกียจ	khon khêe gìat

cunning (n)	ความเจ้าเล่ห์	khwaam jâo lây
cunning (as adj)	เจ้าเลห	jâo lây
distrust	ความหวาดระแวง	khwaam wàat rá-waeng
distrustful (adj)	เคลือบแคลง	khlêuap-khlaeng
generosity	ความเอื้อเฟื้อ	khwaam êua féua
generous (adj)	มีน้ำใจ	mee nám jai

talented (adj)	มีพรสวรรค์	mee phon sà-wǎn
talent	พรสวรรค์	phon sà-wǎn
courageous (adj)	กล้าหาญ	glâa hǎan
courage	ความกล้าหาญ	khwaam glâa hǎan
honest (adj)	ซื่อสัตย์	sêu sàt
honesty	ความซื่อสัตย์	khwaam sêu sàt
careful (cautious)	ระมัดระวัง	rá mát rá-wang
brave (courageous)	กล้า	glâa
serious (adj)	เอาจริงเอาจัง	ao jing ao jang
strict (severe, stern)	เข้มงวด	khêm ngûat
decisive (adj)	เด็ดเดี่ยว	dèt dìeow
indecisive (adj)	ไม่เด็ดขาด	mâi dèt khàat
shy, timid (adj)	อาย	aai
shyness, timidity	ความขวยอาย	khwaam khǔay aai
confidence (trust)	ความไว้ใจ	khwaam wái jai
to believe (trust)	ไว้เนื้อเชื่อใจ	wái néua chêua jai
trusting (credulous)	เชื่อใจ	chêua jai
sincerely (adv)	อย่างจริงใจ	yàang jing jai
sincere (adj)	จริงใจ	jing jai
sincerity	ความจริงใจ	khwaam jing jai
open (person)	เปิดเผย	bpèrt phǒie
calm (adj)	ใจเย็น	jai yen
frank (sincere)	จริงใจ	jing jai
naïve (adj)	หลงเชื่อ	lǒng chêua
absent-minded (adj)	ใจลอย	jai loi
funny (odd)	ตลก	dtà-lòk
greed, stinginess	ความโลภ	khwaam lôhp
greedy, stingy (adj)	โลภ	lôhp
stingy (adj)	ขี้เหนียว	khêe nǐeow
evil (adj)	เลว	leo
stubborn (adj)	ดื้อ	dêu
unpleasant (adj)	ไม่น่าพึงพอใจ	mâi nâa pheung phor jai
selfish person (masc.)	คนที่เห็นแก่ตัว	khon thêe hěn gàe dtua
selfish (adj)	เห็นแก่ตัว	hěn gàe dtua
coward	คนขี้ขลาด	khon khêe khlàat
cowardly (adj)	ขี้ขลาด	khêe khlàat

60. Sleep. Dreams

to sleep (vi)	นอน	norn
sleep, sleeping	ความนอน	khwaam norn
dream	ความฝัน	khwaam fǎn

| to dream (in sleep) | ฝัน | făn |
| sleepy (adj) | ง่วง | ngûang |

bed	เตียง	dtiang
mattress	ฟูกนอน	fôok norn
blanket (comforter)	ผ้าห่ม	phâa hòm
pillow	หมอน	mŏrn
sheet	ผ้าปูที่นอน	phâa bpoo thêe norn

insomnia	อาการนอนไม่หลับ	aa-gaan norn mâi làp
sleepless (adj)	นอนไม่หลับ	norn mâi làp
sleeping pill	ยานอนหลับ	yaa-norn-làp
to take a sleeping pill	กินยานอนหลับ	gin yaa-norn-làp

to feel sleepy	ง่วง	ngûang
to yawn (vi)	หาว	hăao
to go to bed	ไปนอน	bpai norn
to make up the bed	ปูที่นอน	bpoo thêe norn
to fall asleep	หลับ	làp

nightmare	ฝันร้าย	făn ráai
snore, snoring	การกรน	gaan-kron
to snore (vi)	กรน	gron

alarm clock	นาฬิกาปลุก	naa-lí-gaa bplùk
to wake (vt)	ปลุก	bplùk
to wake up	ตื่น	dtèun
to get up (vi)	ลุกขึ้น	lúk khêun
to wash up (wash face)	ล้างหน้าล้างตา	láang nâa láang dtaa

61. Humour. Laughter. Gladness

humor (wit, fun)	อารมณ์ขัน	aa-rom khăn
sense of humor	อารมณ์	aa-rom
to enjoy oneself	เริงรื่น	rerng rêun
cheerful (merry)	เริงรื่น	rerng rêun
merriment (gaiety)	ความรื่นเริง	khwaam rêun-rerng

smile	รอยยิ้ม	roi yím
to smile (vi)	ยิ้ม	yím
to start laughing	เริ่มหัวเราะ	rêrm hŭa rór
to laugh (vi)	หัวเราะ	hŭa rór
laugh, laughter	การหัวเราะ	gaan hŭa rór

anecdote	เรื่องขำขัน	rêuang khăm khăn
funny (anecdote, etc.)	ตลก	dtà-lòk
funny (odd)	ขบขัน	khòp khăn

| to joke (vi) | ล้อเล่น | lór lên |
| joke (verbal) | ตลก | dtà-lòk |

joy (emotion)	ความสุขสันต์	khwaam sùk-săn
to rejoice (vi)	โมทนา	moh-thá-naa
joyful (adj)	ยินดี	yin dee

62. Discussion, conversation. Part 1

| communication | การสื่อสาร | gaan sèu săan |
| to communicate | สื่อสาร | sèu săan |

conversation	การสนทนา	gaan sŏn-thá-naa
dialog	บทสนทนา	bòt sŏn-thá-naa
discussion (discourse)	การหารือ	gaan hăa-reu
dispute (debate)	การโต้แย้ง	gaan dtôh yáeng
to dispute	โต้แย้ง	dtôh yáeng

interlocutor	คู่สนทนา	khôo sŏn-tá-naa
topic (theme)	หัวข้อ	hŭa khôr
point of view	แง่คิด	ngâe khít
opinion (point of view)	ความคิดเห็น	khwaam khít hĕn
speech (talk)	สุนทรพจน์	sŭn tha ra phót

discussion (of report, etc.)	การหารือ	gaan hăa-reu
to discuss (vt)	หารือ	hăa-reu
talk (conversation)	การสนทนา	gaan sŏn-thá-naa
to talk (to chat)	คุยกัน	khui gan
meeting (encounter)	การพบกัน	gaan phóp gan
to meet (vi, vt)	พบ	phóp

proverb	สุภาษิต	sù-phaa-sìt
saying	คำกล่าว	kham glàao
riddle (poser)	ปริศนา	bprìt-sà-năa
to pose a riddle	ถามปริศนา	thăam bprìt-sà-năa
password	รหัสผ่าน	rá-hàt phàan
secret	ความลับ	khwaam láp

oath (vow)	คำสาบาน	kham săa-baan
to swear (an oath)	สาบาน	săa baan
promise	คำสัญญา	kham săn-yaa
to promise (vt)	สัญญา	săn-yaa

advice (counsel)	คำแนะนำ	kham náe nam
to advise (vt)	แนะนำ	náe nam
to follow one's advice	ทำตาม คำแนะนำ	tham dtaam kham náe nam
to listen to ... (obey)	เชื่อฟัง	chêua fang

news	ข่าว	khàao
sensation (news)	ข่าวดัง	khàao dang
information (report)	ข้อมูล	khôr moon
conclusion (decision)	ข้อสรุป	khôr sà-rùp

voice	เสียง	sĭang
compliment	คำชมเชย	kham chom choie
kind (nice)	ใจดี	jai dee

word	คำ	kham
phrase	วลี	wá-lee
answer	คำตอบ	kham dtòrp

| truth | ความจริง | khwaam jing |
| lie | การโกหก | gaan goh-hòk |

thought	ความคิด	khwaam khít
idea (inspiration)	ความคิด	khwaam khít
fantasy	จินตนาการ	jin-dtà-naa gaan

63. Discussion, conversation. Part 2

respected (adj)	ที่นับถือ	thêe náp thĕu
to respect (vt)	นับถือ	náp thĕu
respect	ความนับถือ	khwaam náp thĕu
Dear ... (letter)	ทาน	thâan

| to introduce (sb to sb) | แนะนำ | náe nam |
| to make acquaintance | รู้จัก | róo jàk |

intention	ความตั้งใจ	khwaam dtâng jai
to intend (have in mind)	ตั้งใจ	dtâng jai
wish	การขอพร	gaan khŏr phon
to wish (~ good luck)	ขอ	khŏr

surprise (astonishment)	ความประหลาดใจ	khwaam bprà-làat jai
to surprise (amaze)	ทำให้...ประหลาดใจ	tham hâi...bprà-làat jai
to be surprised	ประหลาดใจ	bprà-làat jai

to give (vt)	ให้	hâi
to take (get hold of)	รับ	ráp
to give back	ให้คืน	hâi kheun
to return (give back)	เอาคืน	ao kheun

to apologize (vi)	ขอโทษ	khŏr thôht
apology	คำขอโทษ	kham khŏr thôht
to forgive (vt)	ให้อภัย	hâi a-phai

to talk (speak)	คุยกัน	khui gan
to listen (vi)	ฟัง	fang
to hear out	ฟังจนจบ	fang jon jòp
to understand (vt)	เข้าใจ	khâo jai

| to show (to display) | แสดง | sà-daeng |
| to look at ... | ดู | doo |

to call (yell for sb)	เรียก	rîak
to distract (disturb)	รบกวน	róp guan
to disturb (vt)	รบกวน	róp guan
to pass (to hand sth)	ส่ง	sòng

demand (request)	ข้อร้องขอ	khôr rórng khŏr
to request (ask)	ร้องขอ	rórng khŏr
demand (firm request)	ขอเรียกร้อง	khôr rîak rórng
to demand (request firmly)	เรียกร้อง	rîak rórng

to tease (call names)	แซว	saew
to mock (make fun of)	ล้อเลียน	lór lian
mockery, derision	ขอล้อเลียน	khôr lór lian
nickname	ชื่อเล่น	chêu lên

insinuation	การพูดเป็นนัย	gaan phôot bpen nai
to insinuate (imply)	พูดเป็นนัย	phôot bpen nai
to mean (vt)	หมายความว่า	măai khwaam wâa

description	คำพรรณนา	kham phan-ná-naa
to describe (vt)	พรรณนา	phan-ná-naa
praise (compliments)	คำชม	kham chom
to praise (vt)	ชม	chom

disappointment	ความผิดหวัง	khwaam phìt wăng
to disappoint (vt)	ทำให้...ผิดหวัง	tham hâi...phìt wăng
to be disappointed	ผิดหวัง	phìt wăng

supposition	ข้อสมมุติ	khôr sŏm mút
to suppose (assume)	สมมุติ	sŏm mút
warning (caution)	คำเตือน	kham dteuan
to warn (vt)	เตือน	dteuan

64. Discussion, conversation. Part 3

| to talk into (convince) | เกลี้ยกล่อม | glîak-glôrm |
| to calm down (vt) | ทำให้...สงบ | tham hâi...sà-ngòp |

silence (~ is golden)	ความเงียบ	khwaam ngîap
to be silent (not speaking)	เงียบ	ngîap
to whisper (vi, vt)	กระซิบ	grà síp
whisper	เสียงกระซิบ	sĭang grà síp

frankly, sincerely (adv)	พูดตรงๆ	phôot dtrorng dtrorng
in my opinion ...	ในสายตาของ	nai săai dtaa-kŏrng
	ผม/ฉัน...	phŏm/chăn...

detail (of the story)	รายละเอียด	raai lá-ìat
detailed (adj)	โดยละเอียด	doi lá-ìat
in detail (adv)	อย่างละเอียด	yàang lá-ìat

| hint, clue | คำบอกใบ้ | kham bòrk bâi |
| to give a hint | บอกใบ้ | bòrk bâi |

look (glance)	การมอง	gaan morng
to have a look	มอง	morng
fixed (look)	จอง	jôrng
to blink (vi)	กระพริบตา	grà phríp dtaa
to wink (vi)	ขยิบตา	khà-yìp dtaa
to nod (in assent)	พยักหน้า	phá-yák nâa

sigh	การถอนหายใจ	gaan thŏrn hăai jai
to sigh (vi)	ถอนหายใจ	thŏrn hăai-jai
to shudder (vi)	สั่น	sàn
gesture	อิริยาบถ	i-rí-yaa-bòt
to touch (one's arm, etc.)	สัมผัส	săm-phàt
to seize	จับ	jàp
(e.g., ~ by the arm)		
to tap (on the shoulder)	แตะ	dtàe

Look out!	ระวัง!	rá-wang
Really?	จริงหรือ?	jing rĕu
Are you sure?	คุณแน่ใจหรือ?	khun nâe jai rĕu
Good luck!	ขอให้โชคดี!	khŏr hâi chôhk dee
I see!	ฉันเข้าใจ!	chăn khâo jai
What a pity!	น่าเสียดาย!	nâa sĭa-daai

65. Agreement. Refusal

consent	การยินยอม	gaan yin yorm
to consent (vi)	ยินยอม	yin yorm
approval	คำอนุมัติ	kham a-nú-mát
to approve (vt)	อนุมัติ	a-nú-mát
refusal	คำปฏิเสธ	kham bpà-dtì-sàyt
to refuse (vi, vt)	ปฏิเสธ	bpà-dtì-sàyt

Great!	เยี่ยม!	yîam
All right!	ดีเลย!	dee loie
Okay! (I agree)	โอเค!	oh-khay

forbidden (adj)	ไม่ได้รับอนุญาต	mâi dâai ráp a-nú-yâat
it's forbidden	ห้าม	hâam
it's impossible	มันเป็นไปไม่ได้	man bpen bpai mâi dâai
incorrect (adj)	ไม่ถูกต้อง	mâi thòok dtôrng

to reject (~ a demand)	ปฏิเสธ	bpà-dtì-sàyt
to support (cause, idea)	สนับสนุน	sà-nàp-sà-nŭn
to accept (~ an apology)	ยอมรับ	yorm ráp

| to confirm (vt) | ยืนยัน | yeun yan |
| confirmation | คำยืนยัน | kham yeun yan |

permission	คำอนุญาต	kham a-nú-yâat
to permit (vt)	อนุญาต	a-nú-yâat
decision	การตัดสินใจ	gaan dtàt sĭn jai
to say nothing (hold one's tongue)	ไม่พูดอะไร	mâi phôot a-rai
condition (term)	เงื่อนไข	ngêuan khăi
excuse (pretext)	ข้ออาง	khôr âang
praise (compliments)	คำชม	kham chom
to praise (vt)	ชม	chom

66. Success. Good luck. Failure

success	ความสำเร็จ	khwaam săm-rèt
successfully (adv)	ให้เป็นผลสำเร็จ	hâi bpen phŏn săm-rèt
successful (adj)	ที่สำเร็จ	thêe săm-rèt
luck (good luck)	โชค	chôhk
Good luck!	ขอให้โชคดี!	khŏr hâi chôhk dee
lucky (e.g., ~ day)	มีโชค	mee chôhk
lucky (fortunate)	มีโชคดี	mee chôhk dee
failure	ความล้มเหลว	khwaam lóm lĕo
misfortune	โชคร้าย	chôhk ráai
bad luck	โชคร้าย	chôhk ráai
unsuccessful (adj)	ไม่ประสบความสำเร็จ	mâi bprà-sòp khwaam săm-rèt
catastrophe	ความล้มเหลว	khwaam lóm lĕo
pride	ความภาคภูมิใจ	khwaam phâak phoom jai
proud (adj)	ภูมิใจ	phoom jai
to be proud	ภูมิใจ	phoom jai
winner	ผู้ชนะ	phôo chá-ná
to win (vi)	ชนะ	chá-ná
to lose (not win)	แพ้	pháe
try	ความพยายาม	khwaam phá-yaa-yaam
to try (vi)	พยายาม	phá-yaa-yaam
chance (opportunity)	โอกาส	oh-gàat

67. Quarrels. Negative emotions

shout (scream)	เสียงตะโกน	sĭang dtà-gohn
to shout (vi)	ตะโกน	dtà-gohn
to start to cry out	เริ่มตะโกน	rêrm dtà-gohn
quarrel	การทะเลาะ	gaan thá-lór
to quarrel (vi)	ทะเลาะ	thá-lór

fight (squabble)	ความทะเลาะ	khwaam thá-lór
to make a scene	ตีโพยตีพาย	dtee phoi dtee phaai
conflict	ความขัดแย้ง	khwaam khàt yáeng
misunderstanding	การเขาใจผิด	gaan khâo jai phìt
insult	คำดูถูก	kham doo thòok
to insult (vt)	ดูถูก	doo thòok
insulted (adj)	โดนดูถูก	dohn doo thòok
resentment	ความเคียดแค้น	khwaam khîat-kháen
to offend (vt)	ลวงเกิน	lûang gern
to take offense	ถือสา	thěu sǎa
indignation	ความโกรธแค้น	khwaam gròht kháen
to be indignant	ขุนเคือง	khùn kheuang
complaint	คำร้อง	kham rórng
to complain (vi, vt)	บน	bòn
apology	คำขอโทษ	kham khǒr thôht
to apologize (vi)	ขอโทษ	khǒr thôht
to beg pardon	ขออภัย	khǒr a-phai
criticism	คำวิจารณ์	kham wí-jaan
to criticize (vt)	วิจารณ์	wí-jaan
accusation (charge)	การกลาวหา	gaan glàao hǎa
to accuse (vt)	กลาวหา	glàao hǎa
revenge	การแก้แค้น	gaan gâe kháen
to avenge (get revenge)	แก้แค้น	gâe kháen
to pay back	แก้แค้น	gâe kháen
disdain	ความดูหมิ่น	khwaam doo mìn
to despise (vt)	ดูหมิ่น	doo mìn
hatred, hate	ความเกลียดชัง	khwaam glìat chang
to hate (vt)	เกลียด	glìat
nervous (adj)	กระวนกระวาย	grà won grà waai
to be nervous	กระวนกระวาย	grà won grà waai
angry (mad)	โกรธ	gròht
to make angry	ทำให้...โกรธ	tham hâi...gròht
humiliation	ความเสียดเย้ย	khwaam sìat yóie
to humiliate (vt)	ฉีกหน้า	chèek nâa
to humiliate oneself	ฉีกหน้าตนเอง	chèek nâa dton ayng
shock	ความตกตะลึง	khwaam dtòk dtà-leung
to shock (vt)	ทำให้...ตกตะลึง	tham hâi...dtòk dtà-leung
trouble (e.g., serious ~)	ปัญหา	bpan-hǎa
unpleasant (adj)	ไมนาพึงพอใจ	mâi nâa pheung phor jai
fear (dread)	ความกลัว	khwaam glua
terrible (storm, heat)	แย	yâe

scary (e.g., ~ story)	น่ากลัว	nâa glua
horror	ความกลัว	khwaam glua
awful (crime, news)	แย่มาก	yâe mâak
to begin to tremble	เริ่มตัวสั่น	rêrm dtua sàn
to cry (weep)	ร้องไห้	rórng hâi
to start crying	เริ่มร้องไห้	rêrm rórng hâi
tear	น้ำตา	nám dtaa
fault	ความผิด	khwaam phìt
guilt (feeling)	ผิด	phìt
dishonor (disgrace)	เสียเกียรติ	sĭa gìat
protest	การประท้วง	gaan bprà-thúang
stress	ความวาวุ่นใจ	khwaam wáa-wûn-jai
to disturb (vt)	รบกวน	róp guan
to be furious	โกรธจัด	gròht jàt
mad, angry (adj)	โกรธ	gròht
to end (~ a relationship)	ยุติ	yút-dtì
to swear (at sb)	ดุด่า	dù dàa
to scare (become afraid)	ตกใจ	dtòk jai
to hit (strike with hand)	ตี	dtee
to fight (street fight, etc.)	สู้	sôo
to settle (a conflict)	ยุติ	yút-dtì
discontented (adj)	ไม่พอใจ	mâi phor jai
furious (adj)	โกรธจัด	gròht jàt
It's not good!	มันไม่ค่อยดี	man mâi khôi dee
It's bad!	มันไม่ดีเลย	man mâi dee loie

Medicine

68. Diseases

sickness	โรค	rôhk
to be sick	ป่วย	bpùay
health	สุขภาพ	sùk-khà-phâap
runny nose (coryza)	น้ำมูกไหล	nám môok lǎi
tonsillitis	ตอมทอนซิลอักเสบ	dtòm thorn-sin àk-sàyp
cold (illness)	หวัด	wàt
to catch a cold	เป็นหวัด	bpen wàt
bronchitis	โรคหลอดลมอักเสบ	rôhk lòrt lom àk-sàyp
pneumonia	โรคปอดบวม	rôhk bpòrt-buam
flu, influenza	ไขหวัดใหญ	khâi wàt yài
nearsighted (adj)	สายตาสั้น	sǎai dtaa sân
farsighted (adj)	สายตายาว	sǎai dtaa yaao
strabismus (crossed eyes)	ตาเหล	dtaa lày
cross-eyed (adj)	เป็นตาเหล	bpen dtaa kǎy rěu lày
cataract	ตอกระจก	dtôr grà-jòk
glaucoma	ตอหิน	dtôr hǐn
stroke	โรคหลอดเลือดสมอง	rôhk lòrt lêuat sà-mǒrng
heart attack	อาการหัวใจวาย	aa-gaan hǔa jai waai
myocardial infarction	กลามเนื้อหัวใจตายเหตุขาดเลือด	glâam néua hǔa jai dtaai hàyt khàat lêuat
paralysis	อัมพาต	am-má-phâat
to paralyze (vt)	ทำใหเป็นอัมพาต	tham hâi bpen am-má-phâat
allergy	ภูมิแพ้	phoom pháe
asthma	โรคหืด	rôhk hèut
diabetes	โรคเบาหวาน	rôhk bao wǎan
toothache	อาการปวดฟัน	aa-gaan bpùat fan
caries	ฟันผุ	fan phù
diarrhea	อาการทองเสีย	aa-gaan thórng sǐa
constipation	อาการทองผูก	aa-gaan thórng phòok
stomach upset	อาการปวดทอง	aa-gaan bpùat thórng
food poisoning	ภาวะอาหารเป็นพิษ	phaa-wá aa hǎan bpen pít
to get food poisoning	กินอาหารเป็นพิษ	gin aa hǎan bpen phít
arthritis	โรคขออักเสบ	rôhk khôr àk-sàyp
rickets	โรคกระดูกออน	rôhk grà-dòok òrn

rheumatism	โรครูมาติก	rôhk roo-maa-dtìk
atherosclerosis	ภาวะหลอดเลือดแข็ง	phaa-wá lòrt lêuat khǎeng
gastritis	โรคกระเพาะอาหาร	rôhk grà-phór aa-hǎan
appendicitis	ไส้ติ่งอักเสบ	sâi dtìng àk-sàyp
cholecystitis	โรคถุงน้ำดี อักเสบ	rôhk thǔng nám dee àk-sàyp
ulcer	แผลเปื่อย	phlǎe bpèuay
measles	โรคหัด	rôhk hàt
rubella (German measles)	โรคหัดเยอรมัน	rôhk hàt yer-rá-man
jaundice	โรคดีซาน	rôhk dee sâan
hepatitis	โรคตับอักเสบ	rôhk dtàp àk-sàyp
schizophrenia	โรคจิตเภท	rôhk jìt-dtà-phâyt
rabies (hydrophobia)	โรคพิษสุนัขบ้า	rôhk phít sù-nák bâa
neurosis	โรคประสาท	rôhk bprà-sàat
concussion	สมองกระทบ กระเทือน	sà-mǒrng grà-thóp grà-theuan
cancer	มะเร็ง	má-reng
sclerosis	กูารแข็งตัวของ เนื้อเยื่อรางกาย	gaan kǎeng dtua kǒng néua yêua râang gaai
multiple sclerosis	โรคปลอกประสาท เสื่อมแข็ง	rôhk bplòk bprà-sàat sèuam kǎeng
alcoholism	โรคพิษสุราเรื้อรัง	rôhk phít sù-raa réua rang
alcoholic (n)	คนขี้เหล้า	khon khêe lâo
syphilis	โรคซิฟิลิส	rôhk sí-fí-lít
AIDS	โรคเอดส์	rôhk àyt
tumor	เนื้องอก	néua ngôk
malignant (adj)	ร้าย	ráai
benign (adj)	ไมราย	mâi ráai
fever	ไข้	khâi
malaria	ไข้มาลาเรีย	kâi maa-laa-ria
gangrene	เนื้อตายเน่า	néua dtaai nâo
seasickness	ภาวะเมาคลื่น	phaa-wá mao khlêun
epilepsy	โรคลมบ้าหมู	rôhk lom bâa-mǒo
epidemic	โรคระบาด	rôhk rá-bàat
typhus	โรครากสาดใหญ่	rôhk râak-sàat yài
tuberculosis	วัณโรค	wan-ná-rôhk
cholera	อหิวาตกโรค	a-hì-wâat-gà-rôhk
plague (bubonic ~)	กาฬโรค	gaan-lá-rôhk

69. Symptoms. Treatments. Part 1

symptom	อาการ	aa-gaan
temperature	อุณหภูมิ	un-hà-phoom

| high temperature (fever) | อุณหภูมิสูง | un-hà-phoom sŏong |
| pulse (heartbeat) | ชีพจร | chêep-phá-jon |

dizziness (vertigo)	อาการเวียนหัว	aa-gaan wian hŭa
hot (adj)	ร้อน	rórn
shivering	หนาวสั่น	năao sàn
pale (e.g., ~ face)	หน้าเชียว	nâa sieow

cough	การไอ	gaan ai
to cough (vi)	ไอ	ai
to sneeze (vi)	จาม	jaam
faint	การเป็นลม	gaan bpen lom
to faint (vi)	เป็นลม	bpen lom

bruise (hématome)	ฟกช้ำ	fók chám
bump (lump)	บวม	buam
to bang (bump)	ชน	chon
contusion (bruise)	รอยฟกช้ำ	roi fók chám
to get a bruise	ได้รอยช้ำ	dâai roi chám

to limp (vi)	กะโผลกกะเผลก	gà-phlòhk-gà-phlàyk
dislocation	ขอหลุด	khôr lùt
to dislocate (vt)	ทำขอหลุด	tham khôr lùt
fracture	กระดูกหัก	grà-dòok hàk
to have a fracture	หักกระดูก	hàk grà-dòok

cut (e.g., paper ~)	รอยบาด	roi bàat
to cut oneself	ทำบาด	tham bàat
bleeding	การเลือดไหล	gaan lêuat lăi

| burn (injury) | แผลไฟไหม้ | phlăe fai mâi |
| to get burned | ได้รับแผลไฟไหม้ | dâai ráp phlăe fai mâi |

to prick (vt)	ตำ	dtam
to prick oneself	ตำตัวเอง	dtam dtua ayng
to injure (vt)	ทำให้บาดเจ็บ	tham hâi bàat jèp
injury	การบาดเจ็บ	gaan bàat jèp
wound	แผล	phlăe
trauma	แผลบาดเจ็บ	phlăe bàat jèp

to be delirious	คลุ้มคลั่ง	khlúm khlâng
to stutter (vi)	พูดตะกุกตะกัก	phôot dtà-gùk-dtà-gàk
sunstroke	โรคลมแดด	rôhk lom dàet

70. Symptoms. Treatments. Part 2

pain, ache	ความเจ็บปวด	khwaam jèp bpùat
splinter (in foot, etc.)	เสี้ยน	sîan
sweat (perspiration)	เหงื่อ	ngèua
to sweat (perspire)	เหงื่อออก	ngèua òrk

vomiting	การอาเจียน	gaan aa-jian
convulsions	การชัก	gaan chák
pregnant (adj)	ตั้งครรภ์	dtâng khan
to be born	เกิด	gèrt
delivery, labor	การคลอด	gaan khlôrt
to deliver (~ a baby)	คลอดบุตร	khlôrt bùt
abortion	การแท้งบุตร	gaan tháeng bùt
breathing, respiration	การหายใจ	gaan hăai-jai
in-breath (inhalation)	การหายใจเข้า	gaan hăai-jai khâo
out-breath (exhalation)	การหายใจออก	gaan hăai-jai òrk
to exhale (breathe out)	หายใจออก	hăai-jai òrk
to inhale (vi)	หายใจเข้า	hăai-jai khâo
disabled person	คนพิการ	khon phí-gaan
cripple	พิการ	phí-gaan
drug addict	ผู้ติดยาเสพติด	phôo dtìt yaa-sàyp-dtìt
deaf (adj)	หูหนวก	hŏo nùak
mute (adj)	เป็นใบ้	bpen bâi
deaf mute (adj)	หูหนวกเป็นใบ้	hŏo nùak bpen bâi
mad, insane (adj)	บ้า	bâa
madman (demented person)	คนบ้า	khon bâa
madwoman	คนบ้า	khon bâa
to go insane	เสียสติ	sĭa sà-dtì
gene	ยีน	yeun
immunity	ภูมิคุ้มกัน	phoom khúm gan
hereditary (adj)	เป็นกรรมพันธุ์	bpen gam-má-phan
congenital (adj)	แต่กำเนิด	dtàe gam-nèrt
virus	เชื้อไวรัส	chéua wai-rát
microbe	จุลินทรีย์	jù-lin-see
bacterium	แบคทีเรีย	bàek-tee-ria
infection	การติดเชื้อ	gaan dtìt chéua

71. Symptoms. Treatments. Part 3

hospital	โรงพยาบาล	rohng phá-yaa-baan
patient	ผู้ป่วย	phôo bpùay
diagnosis	การวินิจฉัยโรค	gaan wí-nít-chăi rôhk
cure	การรักษา	gaan rák-săa
medical treatment	การรักษา ทางการแพทย์	gaan rák-săa thaang gaan phâet
to get treatment	รับการรักษา	ráp gaan rák-săa
to treat (~ a patient)	รักษา	rák-săa

to nurse (look after)	รักษา	rák-sǎa
care (nursing ~)	การดูแลรักษา	gaan doo lae rák-sǎa
operation, surgery	การผ่าตัด	gaan phàa dtàt
to bandage (head, limb)	พันแผล	phan phlǎe
bandaging	การพันแผล	gaan phan phlǎe
vaccination	การฉีดวัคซีน	gaan chèet wák-seen
to vaccinate (vt)	ฉีดวัคซีน	chèet wák-seen
injection, shot	การฉีดยา	gaan chèet yaa
to give an injection	ฉีดยา	chèet yaa
attack	มีอาการเฉียบพลัน	mee aa-gaan chìap phlan
amputation	การตัดอวัยวะออก	gaan dtàt a-wai-wá òrk
to amputate (vt)	ตัด	dtàt
coma	อาการโคม่า	aa-gaan khoh-mâa
to be in a coma	อยู่ในอาการโคม่า	yòo nai aa-gaan khoh-mâa
intensive care	หน่วยอภิบาล	nùay à-phí-baan
to recover (~ from flu)	ฟื้นตัว	féun dtua
condition (patient's ~)	อาการ	aa-gaan
consciousness	สติสัมปชัญญะ	sà-dtì sǎm-bpà-chan-yá
memory (faculty)	ความทรงจำ	khwaam song jam
to pull out (tooth)	ถอน	thǒrn
filling	การอุด	gaan ùt
to fill (a tooth)	อุด	ùt
hypnosis	การสะกดจิต	gaan sà-gòt jìt
to hypnotize (vt)	สะกดจิต	sà-gòt jìt

72. Doctors

doctor	แพทย์	phâet
nurse	พยาบาล	phá-yaa-baan
personal doctor	แพทย์สวนตัว	phâet sùan dtua
dentist	ทันตแพทย์	than-dtà phâet
eye doctor	จักษุแพทย์	jàk-sù phâet
internist	อายุรแพทย์	aa-yú-rá-phâet
surgeon	ศัลยแพทย์	sǎn-yá-phâet
psychiatrist	จิตแพทย์	jìt-dtà-phâet
pediatrician	กุมารแพทย์	gù-maan phâet
psychologist	นักจิตวิทยา	nák jìt wít-thá-yaa
gynecologist	นรีแพทย์	ná-ree phâet
cardiologist	หทัยแพทย์	hà-thai phâet

73. Medicine. Drugs. Accessories

medicine, drug	ยา	yaa
remedy	ยา	yaa
to prescribe (vt)	จ่ายยา	jàai yaa
prescription	ใบสั่งยา	bai sàng yaa
tablet, pill	ยาเม็ด	yaa mét
ointment	ยาทา	yaa thaa
ampule	หลอดยา	lòrt yaa
mixture, solution	ยาส่วนผสม	yaa sùan phà-sǒm
syrup	น้ำเชื่อม	nám chêuam
capsule	ยาเม็ด	yaa mét
powder	ยาผง	yaa phǒng
gauze bandage	ผ้าพันแผล	phâa phan phlǎe
cotton wool	สำลี	sǎm-lee
iodine	ไอโอดีน	ai oh-deen
Band-Aid	พลาสเตอร์	phláat-dtêr
eyedropper	ที่หยอดตา	thêe yòrt dtaa
thermometer	ปรอท	bpa -ròrt
syringe	เข็มฉีดยา	khěm chèet-yaa
wheelchair	รถเข็นคนพิการ	rót khěn khon phí-gaan
crutches	ไม้ค้ำยัน	máai khám yan
painkiller	ยาแก้ปวด	yaa gâe bpùat
laxative	ยาระบาย	yaa rá-baai
spirits (ethanol)	เอธานอล	ay-thaa-norn
medicinal herbs	สมุนไพร ทางการแพทย์	sà-mǔn phrai thaang gaan phâet
herbal (~ tea)	สมุนไพร	sà-mǔn phrai

74. Smoking. Tobacco products

tobacco	ยาสูบ	yaa sòop
cigarette	บุหรี่	bù rèe
cigar	ซิการ์	sí-gâa
pipe	ไปป์	bpai
pack (of cigarettes)	ซอง	sorng
matches	ไม้ขีด	máai khèet
matchbox	กล่องไม้ขีด	glòrng máai khèet
lighter	ไฟแช็ก	fai cháek
ashtray	ที่เขี่ยบุหรี่	thêe khìa bù rèe
cigarette case	กล่องใส่บุหรี่	glòrng sài bù rèe
cigarette holder	ที่ตอบุหรี่	thêe dtòr bù rèe
filter (cigarette tip)	ตัวกรองบุหรี่	dtua grorng bù rèe

to smoke (vi, vt)	สูบ	sòop
to light a cigarette	จุดบุหรี่	jùt bù rèe
smoking	การสูบบุหรี่	gaan sòop bù rèe
smoker	ผู้สูบบุหรี่	pôo sòop bù rèe
stub, butt (of cigarette)	ก้นบุหรี่	gôn bù rèe
smoke, fumes	ควันบุหรี่	khwan bù rèe
ash	ขี้บุหรี่	khêe bù rèe

HUMAN HABITAT

City

city, town	เมือง	meuang
capital city	เมืองหลวง	meuang lǔang
village	หมู่บ้าน	mòo bâan
city map	แผนที่เมือง	phǎen thêe meuang
downtown	ใจกลางเมือง	jai glaang-meuang
suburb	ชานเมือง	chaan meuang
suburban (adj)	ชานเมือง	chaan meuang
outskirts	รอบนอกเมือง	rôrp nôrk meuang
environs (suburbs)	เขตรอบเมือง	khàyt rôrp-meuang
city block	บล็อกผังเมือง	blòrk phǎng meuang
residential block (area)	บล็อกที่อยู่อาศัย	blòrk thêe yòo aa-sǎi
traffic	การจราจร	gaan jà-raa-jon
traffic lights	ไฟจราจร	fai jà-raa-jon
public transportation	ขนส่งมวลชน	khǒn sòng muan chon
intersection	สี่แยก	sèe yâek
crosswalk	ทางม้าลาย	thaang máa laai
pedestrian underpass	อุโมงค์คนเดิน	u-mohng kon dern
to cross (~ the street)	ข้าม	khâam
pedestrian	คนเดินเท้า	khon dern tháo
sidewalk	ทางเท้า	thaang tháo
bridge	สะพาน	sà-phaan
embankment (river walk)	ทางเลียบแม่น้ำ	thaang lîap mâe náam
fountain	น้ำพุ	nám phú
allée (garden walkway)	ทางเลียบสวน	thaang lîap sǔan
park	สวน	sǔan
boulevard	ถนนกว้าง	thà-nǒn gwâang
square	จัตุรัส	jàt-dtù-ràt
avenue (wide street)	ถนนใหญ่	thà-nǒn yài
street	ถนน	thà-nǒn
side street	ซอย	soi
dead end	ทางตัน	thaang dtan
house	บ้าน	bâan
building	อาคาร	aa-khaan

skyscraper	ตึกระฟ้า	dtèuk rá-fáa
facade	ด้านหน้าอาคาร	dâan-nâa aa-khaan
roof	หลังคา	lǎng khaa
window	หน้าต่าง	nâa dtàang
arch	ซุ้มประตู	súm bprà-dtoo
column	เสา	sǎo
corner	มุม	mum
store window	หน้าต่างร้านค้า	nâa dtàang ráan kháa
signboard (store sign, etc.)	ป้ายร้าน	bpâai ráan
poster (e.g., playbill)	โปสเตอร์	bpòht-dtêr
advertising poster	ป้ายโฆษณา	bpâai khôht-sà-naa
billboard	กระดานปิดประกาศ	grà-daan bpìt bprà-gàat
	โฆษณา	khôht-sà-naa
garbage, trash	ขยะ	khà-yà
trash can (public ~)	ถังขยะ	thǎng khà-yà
to litter (vi)	ทิ้งขยะ	thíng khà-yà
garbage dump	ที่ทิ้งขยะ	thêe thíng khà-yà
phone booth	ตู้โทรศัพท์	dtôo thoh-rá-sàp
lamppost	เสาโคม	sǎo khohm
bench (park ~)	ม้านั่ง	máa nâng
police officer	เจ้าหน้าที่ตำรวจ	jâo nâa-thêe dtam-rùat
police	ตำรวจ	dtam-rùat
beggar	ขอทาน	khǒr thaan
homeless (n)	คนไร้บ้าน	khon rái bâan

76. Urban institutions

store	ร้านค้า	ráan kháa
drugstore, pharmacy	ร้านขายยา	ráan khǎai yaa
eyeglass store	ร้านตัดแว่น	ráan dtàt wâen
shopping mall	ศูนย์การค้า	sǒon gaan kháa
supermarket	ซูเปอร์มาร์เก็ต	soo-bper-maa-gèt
bakery	ร้านขนมปัง	ráan khà-nǒm bpang
baker	คนอบขนมปัง	khon òp khà-nǒm bpang
pastry shop	ร้านขนม	ráan khà-nǒm
grocery store	ร้านขายของชำ	ráan khǎai khǒrng cham
butcher shop	ร้านขายเนื้อ	ráan khǎai néua
produce store	ร้านขายผัก	ráan khǎai phàk
market	ตลาด	dtà-làat
coffee house	ร้านกาแฟ	ráan gaa-fae
restaurant	ร้านอาหาร	ráan aa-hǎan
pub, bar	บาร์	baa
pizzeria	ร้านพิชซ่า	ráan phís-sâa

hair salon	ร้านทำผม	ráan tham phŏm
post office	โรงไปรษณีย์	rohng bprai-sà-nee
dry cleaners	ร้านซักแห้ง	ráan sák hâeng
photo studio	ห้องถ่ายภาพ	hôrng thàai phâap

shoe store	ร้านขายรองเท้า	ráan khăai rorng táo
bookstore	ร้านขายหนังสือ	ráan khăai năng-sĕu
sporting goods store	ร้านขาย อุปกรณ์กีฬา	ráan khăai u-bpà-gon gee-laa

clothes repair shop	ร้านซ่อมเสื้อผ้า	ráan sôrm sêua phâa
formal wear rental	ร้านเช่าเสื้อออกงาน	ráan châo sêua òrk ngaan
video rental store	ร้านเช่าวิดีโอ	ráan châo wí-dee-oh

circus	โรงละครสัตว์	rohng lá-khon sàt
zoo	สวนสัตว์	sŭan sàt
movie theater	โรงภาพยนตร์	rohng phâap-phá-yon
museum	พิพิธภัณฑ์	phí-phítha phan
library	ห้องสมุด	hôrng sà-mùt

theater	โรงละคร	rohng lá-khon
opera (opera house)	โรงอุปรากร	rohng ù-bpà-raa-gon
nightclub	ไนท์คลับ	nai-khláp
casino	คาสิโน	khaa-sì-noh

mosque	สุเหร่า	sù-rào
synagogue	โบสถ์ยิว	bòht yiw
cathedral	อาสนวิหาร	aa sŏn wí-hăan
temple	วิหาร	wí-hăan
church	โบสถ์	bòht

college	วิทยาลัย	wít-thá-yaa-lai
university	มหาวิทยาลัย	má-hăa wít-thá-yaa-lai
school	โรงเรียน	rohng rian

prefecture	ศาลากลางจังหวัด	săa-laa glaang jang-wàt
city hall	ศาลาเทศบาล	săa-laa thâyt-sà-baan
hotel	โรงแรม	rohng raem
bank	ธนาคาร	thá-naa-khaan

| embassy | สถานทูต | sà-thăan thôot |
| travel agency | บริษัททัวร์ | bor-rí-sàt thua |

| information office | สำนักงาน ศูนย์ข้อมูล | săm-nák ngaan sŏon khôr moon |
| currency exchange | ร้านแลกเงิน | ráan lâek ngern |

| subway | รถไฟใต้ดิน | rót fai dtâi din |
| hospital | โรงพยาบาล | rohng phá-yaa-baan |

| gas station | ปั๊มน้ำมัน | bpám náam man |
| parking lot | ลานจอดรถ | laan jòrt rót |

77. Urban transportation

bus	รถเมล์	rót may
streetcar	รถราง	rót raang
trolley bus	รถโดยสารประจำ	rót doi săan bprà-jam
	ทางไฟฟ้า	thaang fai fáa
route (of bus, etc.)	เส้นทาง	sên thaang
number (e.g., bus ~)	หมายเลข	măai lâyk
to go by …	ไปด้วย	bpai dûay
to get on (~ the bus)	ขึ้น	khêun
to get off …	ลง	long
stop (e.g., bus ~)	ป้าย	bpâai
next stop	ป้ายถัดไป	bpâai thàt bpai
terminus	ป้ายสุดท้าย	bpâai sùt tháai
schedule	ตารางเวลา	dtaa-raang way-laa
to wait (vt)	รอ	ror
ticket	ตั๋ว	dtŭa
fare	ค่าตั๋ว	khâa dtŭa
cashier (ticket seller)	คนขายตั๋ว	khon khăai dtŭa
ticket inspection	การตรวจตั๋ว	gaan dtrùat dtŭa
ticket inspector	พนักงานตรวจตั๋ว	phá-nák ngaan dtrùat dtŭa
to be late (for …)	ไปสาย	bpai săai
to miss (~ the train, etc.)	พลาด	phlâat
to be in a hurry	รีบเร่ง	rêep râyng
taxi, cab	แท็กซี่	tháek-sêe
taxi driver	คนขับแท็กซี่	khon khàp tháek-sêe
by taxi	โดยแท็กซี่	doi tháek-sêe
taxi stand	ป้ายจอดแท็กซี่	bpâai jòrt tháek sêe
to call a taxi	เรียกแท็กซี่	rîak tháek sêe
to take a taxi	ขึ้นรถแท็กซี่	khêun rót tháek-sêe
traffic	การจราจร	gaan jà-raa-jon
traffic jam	การจราจรติดขัด	gaan jà-raa-jon dtìt khàt
rush hour	ชั่วโมงเร่งด่วน	chûa mohng râyng dùan
to park (vi)	จอด	jòrt
to park (vt)	จอด	jòrt
parking lot	ลานจอดรถ	laan jòrt rót
subway	รถไฟใต้ดิน	rót fai dtâi din
station	สถานี	sà-thăa-nee
to take the subway	ขึ้นรถไฟใต้ดิน	khêun rót fai dtâi din
train	รถไฟ	rót fai
train station	สถานีรถไฟ	sà-thăa-nee rót fai

78. Sightseeing

monument	อนุสาวรีย์	a-nú-sǎa-wá-ree
fortress	ป้อม	bpôrm
palace	วัง	wang
castle	ปราสาท	bpraa-sàat
tower	หอ	hǒr
mausoleum	สุสาน	sù-sǎan
architecture	สถาปัตยกรรม	sà-thǎa-bpàt-dtà-yá-gam
medieval (adj)	ยุคกลาง	yúk glaang
ancient (adj)	โบราณ	boh-raan
national (adj)	แห่งชาติ	hàeng châat
famous (monument, etc.)	ที่มีชื่อเสียง	thêe mee chêu-sǐang
tourist	นักท่องเที่ยว	nák thôrng thîeow
guide (person)	มัคคุเทศก์	mák-khú-thâyt
excursion, sightseeing tour	ทัศนศึกษา	thát-sà-ná-sèuk-sǎa
to show (vt)	แสดง	sà-daeng
to tell (vt)	เล่า	lâo
to find (vt)	หาพบ	hǎa phóp
to get lost (lose one's way)	หลงทาง	lǒng thaang
map (e.g., subway ~)	แผนที่	phǎen thêe
map (e.g., city ~)	แผนที่	phǎen thêe
souvenir, gift	ของที่ระลึก	khǒrng thêe rá-léuk
gift shop	ร้านขาย	ráan khǎai
	ของที่ระลึก	khǒrng thêe rá-léuk
to take pictures	ถ่ายภาพ	thàai phâap
to have one's picture taken	ได้รับการ	dâai ráp gaan
	ถ่ายภาพให้	thàai phâap hâi

79. Shopping

to buy (purchase)	ซื้อ	séu
purchase	ของซื้อ	khǒrng séu
to go shopping	ไปซื้อของ	bpai séu khǒrng
shopping	การชอปปิง	gaan chóp bping
to be open (ab. store)	เปิด	bpèrt
to be closed	ปิด	bpìt
footwear, shoes	รองเท้า	rorng tháo
clothes, clothing	เสื้อผ้า	sêua phâa
cosmetics	เครื่องสำอาง	khrêuang sǎm-aang
food products	อาหาร	aa-hǎan
gift, present	ของขวัญ	khǒrng khwǎn
salesman	พนักงานขาย	phá-nák ngaan khǎai

saleswoman	พนักงานขาย	phá-nák ngaan khǎai
check out, cash desk	ที่จ่ายเงิน	thêe jàai ngern
mirror	กระจก	grà-jòk
counter (store ~)	เคาน์เตอร์	khao-dtêr
fitting room	ห้องลองเสื้อผ้า	hôrng lorng sêua phâa
to try on	ลอง	lorng
to fit (ab. dress, etc.)	เหมาะ	mò
to like (I like …)	ชอบ	chôrp
price	ราคา	raa-khaa
price tag	ป้ายราคา	bpâai raa-khaa
to cost (vt)	ราคา	raa-khaa
How much?	ราคาเท่าไหร่?	raa-khaa thâo rài
discount	ลดราคา	lót raa-khaa
inexpensive (adj)	ไม่แพง	mâi phaeng
cheap (adj)	ถูก	thòok
expensive (adj)	แพง	phaeng
It's expensive	มันราคาแพง	man raa-khaa phaeng
rental (n)	การเช่า	gaan châo
to rent (~ a tuxedo)	เช่า	châo
credit (trade credit)	สินเชื่อ	sǐn chêua
on credit (adv)	ซื้อเงินเชื่อ	séu ngern chêua

80. Money

money	เงิน	ngern
currency exchange	การแลกเปลี่ยน สกุลเงิน	gaan lâek bplìan sà-gun ngern
exchange rate	อัตราแลกเปลี่ยน สกุลเงิน	àt-dtraa lâek bplìan sà-gun ngern
ATM	เอทีเอ็ม	ay-thee-em
coin	เหรียญ	rǐan
dollar	ดอลลาร์	dorn-lâa
euro	ยูโร	yoo-roh
lira	ลีราอิตาลี	lee-raa ì-dtaa-lee
Deutschmark	มาร์ค	mâak
franc	ฟรังค์	frang
pound sterling	ปอนด์สเตอร์ลิง	bporn sà-dtêr-ling
yen	เยน	yayn
debt	หนี้	nêe
debtor	ลูกหนี้	lôok nêe
to lend (money)	ให้ยืม	hâi yeum
to borrow (vi, vt)	ขอยืม	khǒr yeum
bank	ธนาคาร	thá-naa-khaan

account	บัญชี	ban-chee
to deposit (vt)	ฝาก	fàak
to deposit into the account	ฝากเงินเข้าบัญชี	fàak ngern khâo ban-chee
to withdraw (vt)	ถอน	thǒrn

credit card	บัตรเครดิต	bàt khray-dìt
cash	เงินสด	ngern sòt
check	เช็ค	chék
to write a check	เขียนเช็ค	khǐan chék
checkbook	สมุดเช็ค	sà-mùt chék

wallet	กระเป๋าเงิน	grà-bpǎo ngern
change purse	กระเป๋าสตางค์	grà-bpǎo sà-dtaang
safe	ตู้เซฟ	dtôo sâyf

heir	ทายาท	thaa-yâat
inheritance	มรดก	mor-rá-dòrk
fortune (wealth)	เงินจำนวนมาก	ngern jam-nuan mâak

lease	สัญญาเช่า	sǎn-yaa châo
rent (money)	ค่าเช่า	kâa châo
to rent (sth from sb)	เช่า	châo

price	ราคา	raa-khaa
cost	ราคา	raa-khaa
sum	จำนวนเงินรวม	jam-nuan ngern ruam

to spend (vt)	จ่าย	jàai
expenses	ค่าจ่าย	khâa jàai
to economize (vi, vt)	ประหยัด	bprà-yàt
economical	ประหยัด	bprà-yàt

to pay (vi, vt)	จ่าย	jàai
payment	การจ่ายเงิน	gaan jàai ngern
change (give the ~)	เงินทอน	ngern thorn

tax	ภาษี	phaa-sěe
fine	ค่าปรับ	khâa bpràp
to fine (vt)	ปรับ	bpràp

81. Post. Postal service

post office	โรงไปรษณีย์	rohng bprai-sà-nee
mail (letters, etc.)	จดหมาย	jòt mǎai
mailman	บุรุษไปรษณีย์	bù-rùt bprai-sà-nee
opening hours	เวลาทำการ	way-laa tham gaan

letter	จดหมาย	jòt mǎai
registered letter	จดหมายลงทะเบียน	jòt mǎai long thá-bian
postcard	ไปรษณียบัตร	bprai-sà-nee-yá-bàt

telegram	โทรเลข	thoh-rá-lâyk
package (parcel)	พัสดุ	phát-sà-dù
money transfer	การโอนเงิน	gaan ohn ngern

to receive (vt)	รับ	ráp
to send (vt)	ฝาก	fàak
sending	การฝาก	gaan fàak

address	ที่อยู่	thêe yòo
ZIP code	รหัสไปรษณีย์	rá-hàt bprai-sà-nee
sender	ผู้ฝาก	phôo fàak
receiver	ผู้รับ	phôo ráp

name (first name)	ชื่อ	chêu
surname (last name)	นามสกุล	naam sà-gun

postage rate	อัตราค่าส่งไปรษณีย์	àt-dtraa khâa sòng bprai-sà-nee
standard (adj)	มาตรฐาน	mâat-dtrà-thǎan
economical (adj)	ประหยัด	bprà-yàt

weight	น้ำหนัก	nám nàk
to weigh (~ letters)	มีน้ำหนัก	mee nám nàk
envelope	ซอง	sorng
postage stamp	แสตมป์ไปรษณีย์	sà-dtaem bprai-sà-nee
to stamp an envelope	แสตมป์ตราประทับบนซอง	sà-dtaem dtraa bprà-tháp bon song

Dwelling. House. Home

82. House. Dwelling

house	บ้าน	bâan
at home (adv)	ที่บ้าน	thêe bâan
yard	สนาม	sà-nǎam
fence (iron ~)	รั้ว	rúa
brick (n)	อิฐ	ìt
brick (as adj)	อิฐ	ìt
stone (n)	หิน	hǐn
stone (as adj)	หิน	hǐn
concrete (n)	คอนกรีต	khorn-grèet
concrete (as adj)	คอนกรีต	khorn-grèet
new (new-built)	ใหม่	mài
old (adj)	เก่า	gào
decrepit (house)	เสื่อมสภาพ	sèuam sà-phâap
modern (adj)	ทันสมัย	than sà-mǎi
multistory (adj)	ที่มีหลายชั้น	thêe mee lǎai chán
tall (~ building)	สูง	sǒong
floor, story	ชั้น	chán
single-story (adj)	ชั้นเดียว	chán dieow
1st floor	ชั้นล่าง	chán lâang
top floor	ชั้นบนสุด	chán bon sùt
roof	หลังคา	lǎng khaa
chimney	ปล่องควัน	bplòrng khwan
roof tiles	กระเบื้องหลังคา	grà-bêuang lǎng khaa
tiled (adj)	กระเบื้อง	grà-bêuang
attic (storage place)	ห้องใต้หลังคา	hôrng dtâi lǎng-khaa
window	หน้าต่าง	nâa dtàang
glass	แก้ว	gâew
window ledge	ชั้นติดผนัง	chán dtìt phà-nǎng
	ใต้หน้าต่าง	dtâi nâa dtàang
shutters	ชัตเตอร์	chát-dtêr
wall	ฝาผนัง	fǎa phà-nǎng
balcony	ระเบียง	rá-biang
downspout	รางน้ำ	raang náam
upstairs (to be ~)	ชั้นบน	chán bon
to go upstairs	ขึ้นไปข้างบน	khêun bpai khâang bon

| to come down (the stairs) | ลง | long |
| to move (to new premises) | ย้ายไป | yáai bpai |

83. House. Entrance. Lift

entrance	ทางเข้า	thaang khâo
stairs (stairway)	บันได	ban-dai
steps	ขั้นบันได	khân ban-dai
banister	ราวบันได	raao ban-dai
lobby (hotel ~)	ห้องโถง	hông thŏhng
mailbox	ตู้จดหมาย	dtôo jòt măai
garbage can	ถังขยะ	thăng khà-yà
trash chute	ช่องทิ้งขยะ	chông thíng khà-yà
elevator	ลิฟต์	líf
freight elevator	ลิฟต์ขนของ	líf khŏn khŏrng
elevator cage	กรงลิฟต์	grorng líf
to take the elevator	ขึ้นลิฟต์	khêun líf
apartment	อพาร์ตเมนต์	a-phâat-mayn
residents (~ of a building)	ผู้อาศัย	phôo aa-săi
neighbor (masc.)	เพื่อนบ้าน	phêuan bâan
neighbor (fem.)	เพื่อนบ้าน	phêuan bâan
neighbors	เพื่อนบ้าน	phêuan bâan

84. House. Doors. Locks

door	ประตู	bprà-dtoo
gate (vehicle ~)	ประตูรั้ว	bprà-dtoo rúa
handle, doorknob	ลูกบิดประตู	lôok bìt bprà-dtoo
to unlock (unbolt)	ไข	khăi
to open (vt)	เปิด	bpèrt
to close (vt)	ปิด	bpìt
key	ลูกกุญแจ	lôok gun-jae
bunch (of keys)	พวง	phuang
to creak (door, etc.)	ออดแอ๊ด	órt-áet
creak	เสียงออดแอ๊ด	sĭang órt-áet
hinge (door ~)	บานพับ	baan pháp
doormat	ที่เช็ดเท้า	thêe chét tháo
door lock	แม่กุญแจ	mâe gun-jae
keyhole	รูกุญแจ	roo gun-jae
crossbar (sliding bar)	ไม้ที่วางขวาง	máai thêe waang khwăang
door latch	กลอนประตู	glorn bprà-dtoo
padlock	ดอกกุญแจ	dòrk gun-jae
to ring (~ the door bell)	กดออด	gòt òrt

ringing (sound)	เสียงดัง	sĭang dang
doorbell	กระดิ่งประตู	grà-dìng bprà-dtoo
doorbell button	ปุ่มออดหน้าประตู	bpùm òrt nâa bprà-dtoo
knock (at the door)	เสียงเคาะ	sĭang khór
to knock (vi)	เคาะ	khór

code	รหัส	rá-hàt
combination lock	กุญแจรหัส	gun-jae rá-hàt
intercom	อินเตอรคอม	in-dtêr-khom
number (on the door)	เลข	lâyk
doorplate	ป้ายหน้าประตู	bpâai nâa bprà-dtoo
peephole	ช่องตาแมว	chôrng dtaa maew

85. Country house

village	หมู่บ้าน	mòo bâan
vegetable garden	สวนผัก	sŭan phàk
fence	รั้ว	rúa
picket fence	รั้วปักดิน	rúa bpàk din
wicket gate	ประตูรั้วเล็กๆ	bprà-dtoo rúa lék lék

granary	ยุ้งฉาง	yúng chăang
root cellar	ห้องใต้ดิน	hôrng dtâi din
shed (garden ~)	โรงนา	rohng naa
water well	บอน้ำ	bòr náam

stove (wood-fired ~)	เตา	dtao
to stoke the stove	จุดไฟ	jùt fai
firewood	ฟืน	feun
log (firewood)	ทอน	thôrn

veranda	เฉลียงหน้าบ้าน	chà-lĭang nâa bâan
deck (terrace)	ระเบียง	rá-biang
stoop (front steps)	บันไดทางเข้าบ้าน	ban-dai thaang khâo bâan
swing (hanging seat)	ชิงช้า	ching cháa

86. Castle. Palace

castle	ปราสาท	bpraa-sàat
palace	วัง	wang
fortress	ป้อม	bpôrm

wall (round castle)	กำแพง	gam-phaeng
tower	หอ	hŏr
keep, donjon	หอกลาง	hŏr klaang

| portcullis | ประตูชักรอก | bprà-dtoo chák rôrk |
| underground passage | ทางใต้ดิน | taang dtâi din |

moat	ดูเมือง	khoo meuang
chain	โซ่	sôh
arrow loop	ช่องยิงธนู	chôrng ying thá-noo

magnificent (adj)	ภัทร	phát
majestic (adj)	โอ่โถง	òh thŏhng
impregnable (adj)	ที่ไม่สวมารถ	thêe mâi sǎa-mâat
	เจาะเขาไปถึง	jòr khăo bpai thĕung
medieval (adj)	ยุคกลาง	yúk glaang

87. Apartment

apartment	อพาร์ตเมนต์	a-phâat-mayn
room	ห้อง	hôrng
bedroom	ห้องนอน	hôrng norn
dining room	ห้องรับประทาน	hôrng ráp bprà-thaan
	อาหาร	aa-hǎan
living room	ห้องนั่งเล่น	hôrng nâng lên
study (home office)	ห้องทำงาน	hôrng tham ngaan

entry room	ห้องเข้า	hôrng khâo
bathroom (room with a bath or shower)	ห้องน้ำ	hôrng náam
half bath	ห้องส้วม	hôrng sûam

ceiling	เพดาน	phay-daan
floor	พื้น	phéun
corner	มุม	mum

88. Apartment. Cleaning

| to clean (vi, vt) | ทำความสะอาด | tham khwaam sà-àat |
| to put away (to stow) | เก็บ | gèp |

dust	ฝุ่น	fùn
dusty (adj)	มีฝุ่นเยอะ	mee fùn yúh
to dust (vt)	ปัดกวาด	bpàt gwàat
vacuum cleaner	เครื่องดูดฝุ่น	khrêuang dòot fùn
to vacuum (vt)	ดูดฝุ่น	dòot fùn
to sweep (vi, vt)	กวาด	gwàat
sweepings	ฝุ่นกวาด	fùn gwàat
order	ความสะอาด	khwaam sà-àat
disorder, mess	ความไม่เป็นระเบียบ	khwaam mâi bpen rá-bìap

mop	ไม้ถูพื้น	mái thŏo phéun
dust cloth	ผ้าเช็ดพื้น	phâa chét phéun
short broom	ไม้กวาดสั้น	máai gwàat sân
dustpan	ที่ตักผง	têe dtàk phŏng

89. Furniture. Interior

furniture	เครื่องเรือน	khrêuang reuan
table	โต๊ะ	dtó
chair	เก้าอี้	gâo-êe
bed	เตียง	dtiang
couch, sofa	โซฟา	soh-faa
armchair	เก้าอี้เท้าแขน	gâo-êe tháo khǎen
bookcase	ตู้หนังสือ	dtôo nǎng-sěu
shelf	ชั้นวาง	chán waang
wardrobe	ตู้เสื้อผ้า	dtôo sêua phâa
coat rack (wall-mounted ~)	ที่แขวนเสื้อ	thêe khwǎen sêua
coat stand	ไม้แขวนเสื้อ	mái khwǎen sêua
bureau, dresser	ตู้ลิ้นชัก	dtôo lín chák
coffee table	โต๊ะกาแฟ	dtó gaa-fae
mirror	กระจก	grà-jòk
carpet	พรม	phrom
rug, small carpet	พรมเช็ดเท้า	phrom chét tháo
fireplace	เตาผิง	dtao phǐng
candle	เทียน	thian
candlestick	เชิงเทียน	cherng thian
drapes	ผ้าแขวน	phâa khwǎen
wallpaper	วอลเปเปอร์	worn-bpay-bper
blinds (jalousie)	บานเกล็ดหน้าต่าง	baan glèt nâa dtàang
table lamp	โคมไฟตั้งโต๊ะ	khohm fai dtâng dtó
wall lamp (sconce)	ไฟติดผนัง	fai dtìt phà-nǎng
floor lamp	โคมไฟตั้งพื้น	khohm fai dtâng phéun
chandelier	โคมระย้า	khohm rá-yáa
leg (of chair, table)	ขา	khǎa
armrest	ที่พักแขน	thêe phák khǎen
back (backrest)	พนักพิง	phá-nák phing
drawer	ลิ้นชัก	lín chák

90. Bedding

bedclothes	ชุดผ้าปูที่นอน	chút phâa bpoo thêe norn
pillow	หมอน	mǒrn
pillowcase	ปลอกหมอน	bplòk mǒrn
duvet, comforter	ผ้านวม	phâa phǔay
sheet	ผ้าปู	phâa bpoo
bedspread	ผ้าคลุมเตียง	phâa khlum dtiang

91. Kitchen

kitchen	ห้องครัว	hôrng khrua
gas	แก๊ส	gáet
gas stove (range)	เตาแก๊ส	dtao gàet
electric stove	เตาไฟฟ้า	dtao fai-fáa
oven	เตาอบ	dtao òp
microwave oven	เตาอบไมโครเวฟ	dtao òp mai-khroh-we p
refrigerator	ตู้เย็น	dtôo yen
freezer	ตู้แช่แข็ง	dtôo châe khǎeng
dishwasher	เครื่องล้างจาน	khrêuang láang jaan
meat grinder	เครื่องบดเนื้อ	khrêuang bòt néua
juicer	เครื่องคั้นน้ำผลไม้	khrêuang khán náam phǒn-lá-mái
toaster	เครื่องปิ้งขนมปัง	khrêuang bpîng khà-nǒm bpang
mixer	เครื่องปั่น	khrêuang bpàn
coffee machine	เครื่องชงกาแฟ	khrêuang chong gaa-fae
coffee pot	หม้อกาแฟ	môr gaa-fae
coffee grinder	เครื่องบดกาแฟ	khrêuang bòt gaa-fae
kettle	กาน้ำ	gaa náam
teapot	กาน้ำชา	gaa náam chaa
lid	ฝา	fǎa
tea strainer	ที่กรองชา	thêe grorng chaa
spoon	ช้อน	chórn
teaspoon	ช้อนชา	chórn chaa
soup spoon	ช้อนซุป	chórn súp
fork	ส้อม	sôrm
knife	มีด	mêet
tableware (dishes)	ถ้วยชาม	thûay chaam
plate (dinner ~)	จาน	jaan
saucer	จานรอง	jaan rorng
shot glass	แก้วช็อต	gâew chórt
glass (tumbler)	แก้ว	gâew
cup	ถ้วย	thûay
sugar bowl	โถน้ำตาล	thǒh náam dtaan
salt shaker	กระปุกเกลือ	grà-bpùk gleua
pepper shaker	กระปุกพริกไท	grà-bpùk phrík thai
butter dish	ที่ใส่เนย	thêe sài noie
stock pot (soup pot)	หม้อต้ม	môr dtôm
frying pan (skillet)	กระทะ	grà-thá
ladle	กระบวย	grà-buay

colander	กระชอน	grà chorn
tray (serving ~)	ถาด	thàat
bottle	ขวด	khùat
jar (glass)	ขวดโหล	khùat lŏh
can	กระป๋อง	grà-bpŏrng
bottle opener	ที่เปิดขวด	thêe bpèrt khùat
can opener	ที่เปิดกระป๋อง	thêe bpèrt grà-bpŏrng
corkscrew	ที่เปิดจุก	thêe bpèrt jùk
filter	ที่กรอง	thêe grorng
to filter (vt)	กรอง	grorng
trash, garbage (food waste, etc.)	ขยะ	khà-yà
trash can (kitchen ~)	ถังขยะ	thăng khà-yà

92. Bathroom

bathroom	ห้องน้ำ	hôrng náam
water	น้ำ	nám
faucet	ก๊อกน้ำ	gòk náam
hot water	น้ำร้อน	nám rórn
cold water	น้ำเย็น	nám yen
toothpaste	ยาสีฟัน	yaa sĕe fan
to brush one's teeth	แปรงฟัน	bpraeng fan
toothbrush	แปรงสีฟัน	bpraeng sĕe fan
to shave (vi)	โกน	gohn
shaving foam	โฟมโกนหนวด	fohm gohn nùat
razor	มีดโกน	mêet gohn
to wash (one's hands, etc.)	ล้าง	láang
to take a bath	อาบ	àap
shower	ฝักบัว	fàk bua
to take a shower	อาบน้ำฝักบัว	àap náam fàk bua
bathtub	อ่างอาบน้ำ	àang àap náam
toilet (toilet bowl)	โถชักโครก	thŏh chák khrôhk
sink (washbasin)	อางลางหนา	àang láang-nâa
soap	สบู่	sà-bòo
soap dish	ที่ใส่สบู่	thêe sài sà-bòo
sponge	ฟองน้ำ	forng náam
shampoo	แชมพู	chaem-phoo
towel	ผ้าเช็ดตัว	phâa chét dtua
bathrobe	เสื้อคลุมอาบน้ำ	sêua khlum àap náam
laundry (laundering)	การซักผ้า	gaan sák phâa

washing machine	เครื่องซักผ้า	khrêuang sák phâa
to do the laundry	ซักผ้า	sák phâa
laundry detergent	ผงซักฟอก	phŏng sák-fôrk

93. Household appliances

TV set	ทีวี	thee-wee
tape recorder	เครื่องบันทึกเทป	khrêuang ban-théuk thâyp
VCR (video recorder)	เครื่องบันทึก วีดีโอ	khrêuang ban-théuk wí-dee-oh
radio	วิทยุ	wít-thá-yú
player (CD, MP3, etc.)	เครื่องเล่น	khrêuang lên

video projector	โปรเจ็คเตอร์	bproh-jèk-dtêr
home movie theater	เครื่องฉาย ภาพยนตร์ที่บ้าน	khhrêuang chăai phâap-phá yon thêe bâan
DVD player	เครื่องเล่น DVD	khrêuang lên dee-wee-dee
amplifier	เครื่องขยายเสียง	khrêuang khà-yăai sĭang
video game console	เครื่องเกม คอนโซล	khrêuang gaym khorn sohn

video camera	กล้องถ่ายวิดีโอ	glôrng thàai wí-dee-oh
camera (photo)	กล้องถ่ายรูป	glôrng thàai rôop
digital camera	กลองดิจิตอล	glôrng dì-jì-dton

vacuum cleaner	เครื่องดูดฝุ่น	khrêuang dòot fùn
iron (e.g., steam ~)	เตารีด	dtao rêet
ironing board	กระดานรองรีด	grà-daan rorng rêet

telephone	โทรศัพท์	thoh-rá-sàp
cell phone	มือถือ	meu thĕu
typewriter	เครื่องพิมพ์ดีด	khrêuang phim dèet
sewing machine	จักรเย็บผ้า	jàk yép phâa

microphone	ไมโครโฟน	mai-khroh-fohn
headphones	หูฟัง	hŏo fang
remote control (TV)	รีโมตทีวี	ree môht thee wee

CD, compact disc	CD	see-dee
cassette, tape	เทป	thâyp
vinyl record	จานเสียง	jaan sĭang

94. Repairs. Renovation

renovations	การซ่อมแซม	gaan sôrm saem
to renovate (vt)	ซ่อมแซม	sôrm saem
to repair, to fix (vt)	ซ่อมแซม	sôrm saem
to put in order	สะสาง	sà-săang

to redo (do again)	ทำใหม่	tham mài
paint	สี	sĕe
to paint (~ a wall)	ทาสี	thaa sĕe
house painter	ช่างทาสีบ้าน	châang thaa sĕe bâan
paintbrush	แปรงทาสี	bpraeng thaa sĕe

whitewash	สารฟอกขาว	săan fôrk khăao
to whitewash (vt)	ฟอกขาว	fôrk khăao

wallpaper	วอลเปเปอร์	worn-bpay-bper
to wallpaper (vt)	ติดวอลเปเปอร์	dtìt wor lá-bpay-bper
varnish	น้ำมันชักเงา	náam man chák ngao
to varnish (vt)	เคลือบ	khlêuap

95. Plumbing

water	น้ำ	nám
hot water	น้ำร้อน	nám rórn
cold water	น้ำเย็น	nám yen
faucet	ก๊อกน้ำ	gòk náam

drop (of water)	หยด	yòt
to drip (vi)	ตก	dtòk
to leak (ab. pipe)	รั่ว	rûa
leak (pipe ~)	การรั่ว	gaan rûa
puddle	หลมน้ำ	lòm nám

pipe	ท่อ	thôr
valve (e.g., ball ~)	วาลว์	waao
to be clogged up	อุดตัน	ùt dtan

tools	เครื่องมือ	khrêuang meu
adjustable wrench	ประแจคอม้า	bprà-jae kor máa
to unscrew (lid, filter, etc.)	คลายเกลียวออก	khlaai glieow òrk
to screw (tighten)	ขันให้แน่น	khăn hâi nâen

to unclog (vt)	แก้การอุดตัน	gâe gaan ùt dtan
plumber	ช่างประปา	châang bprà-bpaa
basement	ชั้นใต้ดิน	chán dtâi din
sewerage (system)	ระบบท่อน้ำทิ้ง	rá-bòp thôr náam thíng

96. Fire. Conflagration

fire (accident)	ไฟไหม้	fai mâi
flame	เปลวไฟ	bpleo fai
spark	ประกายไฟ	bprà-gaai fai
smoke (from fire)	ควัน	khwan
torch (flaming stick)	คบเพลิง	khóp phlerng

campfire	กองไฟ	gorng fai
gas, gasoline	น้ำมันเชื้อเพลิง	nám man chéua phlerng
kerosene (type of fuel)	น้ำมันก๊าด	nám man gáat
flammable (adj)	ติดไฟได้	dtìt fai dâai
explosive (adj)	ที่ระเบิดได้	thêe rá-bèrt dâai
NO SMOKING	ห้ามสูบบุหรี่	hâam sòop bù rèe
safety	ความปลอดภัย	khwaam bplòrt phai
danger	อันตราย	an-dtà-raai
dangerous (adj)	อันตราย	an-dtà-raai
to catch fire	ติดไฟ	dtìt fai
explosion	การระเบิด	gaan rá-bèrt
to set fire	เผา	phǎo
arsonist	ผู้ลอบวางเพลิง	phôo lôp waang phlerng
arson	การลอบวางเพลิง	gaan lôp waang phlerng
to blaze (vi)	ไฟลุกโชน	fai lúk-chohn
to burn (be on fire)	ไหม้	mâi
to burn down	เผาให้ราบ	phǎo hâi râap
to call the fire department	เรียกนักดับเพลิง	rîak nák dàp phlerng
firefighter, fireman	นักดับเพลิง	nák dàp phlerng
fire truck	รถดับเพลิง	rót dàp phlerng
fire department	สถานีดับเพลิง	sà-thǎa-nee dàp phlerng
fire truck ladder	บันไดรถดับเพลิง	ban-dai rót dàp phlerng
fire hose	ท่อดับเพลิง	thôr dàp phlerng
fire extinguisher	ที่ดับเพลิง	thêe dàp phlerng
helmet	หมวกนิรภัย	mùak ní-rá-phai
siren	สัญญาณเตือนภัย	sǎn-yaan dteuan phai
to cry (for help)	ร้อง	rórng
to call for help	ขอช่วย	khǒr chûay
rescuer	นักกู้ภัย	nák gôo phai
to rescue (vt)	ช่วยชีวิต	chûay chee-wít
to arrive (vi)	มา	maa
to extinguish (vt)	ดับเพลิง	dàp phlerng
water	น้ำ	nám
sand	ทราย	saai
ruins (destruction)	ซาก	sâak
to collapse (building, etc.)	ถล่ม	thà-lòm
to fall down (vi)	ถล่มทลาย	thà-lòm thá-laai
to cave in (ceiling, floor)	ถล่ม	thà-lòm
piece of debris	ส่วนสะเก็ด	sùan sà-gèt
ash	ขี้เถ้า	khêe thâo
to suffocate (die)	ขาดอากาศตาย	khàat aa-gàat dtaai
to be killed (perish)	เสียชีวิต	sǐa chee-wít

HUMAN ACTIVITIES

Job. Business. Part 1

97. Banking

bank	ธนาคาร	thá-naa-khaan
branch (of bank, etc.)	สาขา	săa-khăa
bank clerk, consultant	พนักงาน	phá-nák ngaan
	ธนาคาร	thá-naa-khaan
manager (director)	ผู้จัดการ	phôo jàt gaan
bank account	บัญชีธนาคาร	ban-chee thá-naa-kaan
account number	หมายเลขบัญชี	măai lâyk ban-chee
checking account	กระแสรายวัน	grà-săe raai wan
savings account	บัญชีออมทรัพย์	ban-chee orm sáp
to open an account	เปิดบัญชี	bpèrt ban-chee
to close the account	ปิดบัญชี	bpìt ban-chee
to deposit into the account	ฝากเงินเข้าบัญชี	fàak ngern khâo ban-chee
to withdraw (vt)	ถอน	thŏrn
deposit	การฝาก	gaan fàak
to make a deposit	ฝาก	fàak
wire transfer	การโอนเงิน	gaan ohn ngern
to wire, to transfer	โอนเงิน	ohn ngern
sum	จำนวนเงินรวม	jam-nuan ngern ruam
How much?	เท่าไหร่?	thâo rài
signature	ลายมือชื่อ	laai meu chêu
to sign (vt)	ลงนาม	long naam
credit card	บัตรเครดิต	bàt khray-dìt
code (PIN code)	รหัส	rá-hàt
credit card number	หมายเลขบัตรเครดิต	măai lâyk bàt khray-dìt
ATM	เอทีเอ็ม	ay-thee-em
check	เช็ค	chék
to write a check	เขียนเช็ค	khĭan chék
checkbook	สมุดเช็ค	sà-mùt chék
loan (bank ~)	เงินกู้	ngern gôo
to apply for a loan	ขอสินเชื่อ	khŏr sĭn chêua

to get a loan	กู้เงิน	gôo ngern
to give a loan	ให้กู้เงิน	hâi gôo ngern
guarantee	การรับประกัน	gaan ráp bprà-gan

98. Telephone. Phone conversation

telephone	โทรศัพท์	thoh-rá-sàp
cell phone	มือถือ	meu thĕu
answering machine	เครื่องพูดตอบ	khrêuang phôot dtòp

| to call (by phone) | โทรศัพท์ | thoh-rá-sàp |
| phone call | การโทรศัพท์ | gaan thoh-rá-sàp |

to dial a number	หมุนหมายเลขโทรศัพท์	mŭn măai lâyk thoh-rá-sàp
Hello!	สวัสดี!	sà-wàt-dee
to ask (vt)	ถาม	thăam
to answer (vi, vt)	รับสาย	ráp săai

to hear (vt)	ได้ยิน	dâai yin
well (adv)	ดี	dee
not well (adv)	ไม่ดี	mâi dee
noises (interference)	เสียงรบกวน	sĭang róp guan

receiver	ตัวรับสัญญาณ	dtua ráp săn-yaan
to pick up (~ the phone)	รับสาย	ráp săai
to hang up (~ the phone)	วางสาย	waang săai

busy (engaged)	ไม่ว่าง	mâi wâang
to ring (ab. phone)	ดัง	dang
telephone book	สมุดโทรศัพท์	sà-mùt thoh-rá-sàp

local (adj)	ในประเทศ	nai bprà-thâyt
local call	โทรในประเทศ	thoh nai bprà-thâyt
long distance (~ call)	ระยะไกล	rá-yá glai
long-distance call	โทรระยะไกล	thoh-rá-yá glai
international (adj)	ต่างประเทศ	dtàang bprà-thâyt
international call	โทรต่างประเทศ	thoh dtàang bprà-thâyt

99. Cell phone

cell phone	มือถือ	meu thĕu
display	หน้าจอ	nâa jor
button	ปุ่ม	bpùm
SIM card	ซิมการ์ด	sím gàat

battery	แบตเตอรี่	bàet-dter-rêe
to be dead (battery)	หมด	mòt
charger	ที่ชาร์จ	thêe châat

menu	เมนู	may-noo
settings	การตั้งค่า	gaan dtâng khâa
tune (melody)	เสียงเพลง	sĭang phlayng
to select (vt)	เลือก	lêuak

calculator	เครื่องคิดเลข	khrêuang khít lâyk
voice mail	ขอความเสียง	khôr khwaam sĭang
alarm clock	นาฬิกาปลูก	naa-lí-gaa bplùk
contacts	รายชื่อผู้ติดต่อ	raai chêu phôo dtìt dtòr

SMS (text message)	SMS	es-e-mes
subscriber	ผู้สมัครรับ	phôo sà-màk ráp
	บริการ	bor-rí-gaan

100. Stationery

| ballpoint pen | ปากกาลูกลื่น | bpàak gaa lôok lêun |
| fountain pen | ปากกาหมึกซึม | bpàak gaa mèuk seum |

pencil	ดินสอ	din-sŏr
highlighter	ปากกาเน้น	bpàak gaa náyn
felt-tip pen	ปากกาเมจิค	bpàak gaa may jìk

| notepad | สมุดจด | sà-mùt jòt |
| agenda (diary) | สมุดบันทึกรายวัน | sà-mùt ban-théuk raai wan |

ruler	ไม้บรรทัด	máai ban-thát
calculator	เครื่องคิดเลข	khrêuang khít lâyk
eraser	ยางลบ	yaang lóp
thumbtack	เป๊ก	bpáyk
paper clip	ลวดหนีบกระดาษ	lûat nèep grà-dàat

glue	กาว	gaao
stapler	ที่เย็บกระดาษ	thêe yép grà-dàat
hole punch	ที่เจาะรูกระดาษ	thêe jòr roo grà-dàat
pencil sharpener	ที่เหลาดินสอ	thêe lăo din-sŏr

Job. Business. Part 2

101. Mass Media

newspaper	หนังสือพิมพ์	năng-sěu phim
magazine	นิตยสาร	nít-dtà-yá-sǎan
press (printed media)	สื่อสิ่งพิมพ์	sèu sìng phim
radio	วิทยุ	wít-thá-yú
radio station	สถานีวิทยุ	sà-thǎa-nee wít-thá-yú
television	โทรทัศน์	thoh-rá-thát
presenter, host	ผู้ประกาศข่าว	phôo bprà-gàat khàao
newscaster	ผู้ประกาศขาว	phôo bprà-gàat khàao
commentator	ผู้อธิบาย	phôo à-thí-baai
journalist	นักข่าว	nák khàao
correspondent (reporter)	ผู้รายงานข่าว	phôo raai ngaan khàao
press photographer	ช่างภาพ หนังสือพิมพ์	châang phâap năng-sěu phim
reporter	ผู้รายงาน	phôo raai ngaan
editor	บรรณาธิการ	ban-naa-thí-gaan
editor-in-chief	หัวหน้าบรรณาธิการ	hŭa nâa ban-naa-thí-gaan
to subscribe (to ...)	รับ	ráp
subscription	การรับ	gaan ráp
subscriber	ผู้รับ	phôo ráp
to read (vi, vt)	อ่าน	àan
reader	ผู้อาน	phôo àan
circulation (of newspaper)	การเผยแพร่	gaan phŏie-phrâe
monthly (adj)	รายเดือน	raai deuan
weekly (adj)	รายสัปดาห์	raai sàp-daa
issue (edition)	ฉบับ	chà-bàp
new (~ issue)	ใหม่	mài
headline	ข่าวพาดหัว	khàao phâat hŭa
short article	บทความสั้นๆ	bòt khwaam sân sân
column (regular article)	คอลัมน์	khor lam
article	บทความ	bòt khwaam
page	หน้า	nâa
reportage, report	การรายงานข่าว	gaan raai ngaan khàao
event (happening)	เหตุการณ์	hàyt gaan
sensation (news)	ข่าวดัง	khàao dang
scandal	เรื่องอื้อฉาว	rêuang êu chǎao

| scandalous (adj) | อื้อฉาว | êu chǎao |
| great (~ scandal) | ใหญ | yài |

show (e.g., cooking ~)	รายการ	raai gaan
interview	การสัมภาษณ์	gaan sǎm-phâat
live broadcast	ถ่ายทอดสด	thàai thôrt sòt
channel	ช่อง	chôrng

102. Agriculture

agriculture	เกษตรกรรม	gà-sàyt-dtra -gam
peasant (masc.)	ชาวนาผู้ชาย	chaao naa phôo chaai
peasant (fem.)	ชาวนาผู้หญิง	chaao naa phôo yǐng
farmer	ชาวนา	chaao naa

| tractor (farm ~) | รถแทร็คเตอร์ | rót tráek-dtêr |
| combine, harvester | เครื่องเก็บเกี่ยว | khrêuang gèp gìeow |

plow	คันไถ	khan thǎi
to plow (vi, vt)	ไถ	thǎi
plowland	ที่ดินที่ไถพรวน	thêe din thêe thǎi phruan
furrow (in field)	ร่องดิน	rôrng din

to sow (vi, vt)	หว่าน	wàan
seeder	เครื่องหว่านเมล็ด	khrêuang wàan má-lét
sowing (process)	การหว่าน	gaan wàan

| scythe | เคียว | khieow |
| to mow, to scythe | ถาง | thǎang |

| spade (tool) | พลั่ว | phlûa |
| to till (vt) | ขุด | khùt |

hoe	จอบ	jòrp
to hoe, to weed	ถาก	thàak
weed (plant)	วัชพืช	wát-chá-phêut

watering can	กระป๋องรดน้ำ	grà-bpǒrng rót náam
to water (plants)	รดน้ำ	rót náam
watering (act)	การรดน้ำ	gaan rót nám

| pitchfork | ส้อมเสียบ | sôrm sìap |
| rake | คราด | khrâat |

fertilizer	ปุ๋ย	bpǔi
to fertilize (vt)	ใส่ปุ๋ย	sài bpǔi
manure (fertilizer)	ปุ๋ยคอก	bpǔi khôrk

| field | ทุ่งนา | thûng naa |
| meadow | ทุ่งหญ้า | thûng yâa |

| vegetable garden | สวนผัก | sŭan phàk |
| orchard (e.g., apple ~) | สวนผลไม้ | sŭan phŏn-lá-máai |

to graze (vt)	เล็มหญ้า	lem yâa
herder (herdsman)	คนเลี้ยงสัตว์	khon líang sàt
pasture	ทุ่งเลี้ยงสัตว์	thûng líang sàt

| cattle breeding | การขยายพันธุ์สัตว์ | gaan khà-yăai phan sàt |
| sheep farming | การขยายพันธุ์แกะ | gaan khà-yăai phan gàe |

plantation	ที่เพาะปลูก	thêe phór bplòok
row (garden bed ~s)	แถว	thăe
hothouse	เรือนกระจกร้อน	reuan grà-jòk rón

| drought (lack of rain) | ภัยแล้ง | phai láeng |
| dry (~ summer) | แลง | láeng |

grain	ธัญพืช	than-yá-phêut
cereal crops	ผลผลิตธัญพืช	phŏn phà-lìt than-yá-phêut
to harvest, to gather	เก็บเกี่ยว	gèp gìeow

miller (person)	เจ้าของโรงโม่	jâo khŏrng rohng môh
mill (e.g., gristmill)	โรงสี	rohng sĕe
to grind (grain)	โม่	môh
flour	แป้ง	bpâeng
straw	ฟาง	faang

103. Building. Building process

construction site	สถานที่ก่อสร้าง	sà-thăan thêe gòr sâang
to build (vt)	สร้าง	sâang
construction worker	คนงานก่อสร้าง	khon ngaan gòr sâang

project	โครงการ	khrohng gaan
architect	สถาปนิก	sà-thăa-bpà-ník
worker	คนงาน	khon ngaan

foundation (of a building)	รากฐาน	râak thăan
roof	หลังคา	lăng khaa
foundation pile	เสาเข็ม	săo khĕm
wall	กำแพง	gam-phaeng

| reinforcing bars | เหล็กเส้นเสริมแรง | lèk sên sĕrm raeng |
| scaffolding | นั่งราน | nâng ráan |

concrete	คอนกรีต	khorn-grèet
granite	หินแกรนิต	hĭn grae-nít
stone	หิน	hĭn
brick	อิฐ	ìt
sand	ทราย	saai

cement	ปูนซีเมนต์	bpoon see-mayn
plaster (for walls)	พลาสเตอร์	phláat-dtêr
to plaster (vt)	ฉาบ	chàap

paint	สี	sĕe
to paint (~ a wall)	ทาสี	thaa sĕe
barrel	ถัง	thăng

crane	ปั้นจั่น	bpân jàn
to lift, to hoist (vt)	ยก	yók
to lower (vt)	ลด	lót

bulldozer	รถดันดิน	rót dan din
excavator	รถขุด	rót khùt
scoop, bucket	ช้อนขุด	chórn khùt
to dig (excavate)	ขุด	khùt
hard hat	หมวกนิรภัย	mùak ní-rá-phai

Professions and occupations

104. Job search. Dismissal

job	งาน	ngaan
staff (work force)	พนักงาน	phá-nák ngaan
personnel	พนักงาน	phá-nák ngaan
career	อาชีพ	aa-chêep
prospects (chances)	โอกาส	oh-gàat
skills (mastery)	ทักษะ	thák-sà
selection (screening)	การคัดเลือก	gaan khát lêuak
employment agency	สำนักงาน	sǎm-nák ngaan
	จัดหางาน	jàt hǎa ngaan
résumé	ประวัติย่อ	bprà-wàt yôr
job interview	สัมภาษณ์งาน	sǎm-phâat ngaan
vacancy, opening	ตำแหน่งว่าง	dtam-nàeng wâang
salary, pay	เงินเดือน	ngern deuan
fixed salary	เงินเดือน	ngern deuan
pay, compensation	คาแรง	khâa raeng
position (job)	ตำแหน่ง	dtam-nàeng
duty (of employee)	หน้าที่	nâa thêe
range of duties	หน้าที่	nâa thêe
busy (I'm ~)	ไม่ว่าง	mâi wâang
to fire (dismiss)	ไล่ออก	lâi òrk
dismissal	การไล่ออก	gaan lâi òrk
unemployment	การว่างงาน	gaan wâang ngaan
unemployed (n)	คนว่างงาน	khon wâang ngaan
retirement	การเกษียณอายุ	gaan gà-sĭan aa-yú
to retire (from job)	เกษียณ	gà-sĭan

105. Business people

director	ผู้อำนวยการ	phôo am-nuay gaan
manager (director)	ผู้จัดการ	phôo jàt gaan
boss	หัวหน้า	hǔa-nâa
superior	ผู้บังคับบัญชา	phôo bang-kháp ban-chaa
superiors	คณะผู้บังคับ	khá-ná phôo bang-kháp
	บัญชา	ban-chaa

| president | ประธานาธิปดี | bprà-thaa-naa-thí-bor-dee |
| chairman | ประธาน | bprà-thaan |

deputy (substitute)	รอง	rorng
assistant	ผู้ช่วย	phôo chûay
secretary	เลขา	lay-khǎa
personal assistant	ผู้ช่วยส่วน	phôo chûay sùan
	บุคคล	bùk-khon

businessman	นักธุรกิจ	nák thú-rá-gìt
entrepreneur	ผู้ประกอบการ	phôo bprà-gòp gaan
founder	ผู้ก่อตั้ง	phôo gòr dtâng
to found (vt)	ก่อตั้ง	gòr dtâng

incorporator	ผู้ก่อตั้ง	phôo gòr dtâng
partner	หุ้นส่วน	hûn sùan
stockholder	ผู้ถือหุ้น	phôo thěu hûn

millionaire	เศรษฐีเงินล้าน	sàyt-thěe ngern láan
billionaire	มหาเศรษฐี	má-hǎa sàyt-thěe
owner, proprietor	เจ้าของ	jâo khǒrng
landowner	เจ้าของที่ดิน	jâo khǒrng thêe din

client	ลูกค้า	lôok kháa
regular client	ลูกค้าประจำ	lôok kháa bprà-jam
buyer (customer)	ลูกค้า	lôok kháa
visitor	ผู้เข้าร่วม	phôo khâo rûam

professional (n)	ผู้เป็นมืออาชีพ	phôo bpen meu aa-chêep
expert	ผู้เชี่ยวชาญ	phôo chîeow-chaan
specialist	ผู้ชำนาญ	phôo cham-naan
	เฉพาะทาง	chà-phó thaang

banker	พนักงาน	phá-nák ngaan
	ธนาคาร	thá-naa-khaan
broker	นายหน้า	naai nâa

cashier, teller	แคชเชียร์	khâet chia
accountant	นักบัญชี	nák ban-chee
security guard	ยาม	yaam

investor	ผู้ลงทุน	phôo long thun
debtor	ลูกหนี้	lôok nêe
creditor	เจ้าหนี้	jâo nêe
borrower	ผู้ยืม	phôo yeum

| importer | ผู้นำเข้า | phôo nam khâo |
| exporter | ผู้ส่งออก | phôo sòng òrk |

manufacturer	ผู้ผลิต	phôo phà-lìt
distributor	ผู้จัดจำหน่าย	phôo jàt jam-nàai
middleman	คนกลาง	khon glaang

consultant	ที่ปรึกษา	thêe bprèuk-săa
sales representative	พนักงานขาย	phá-nák ngaan khăai
agent	ตัวแทน	dtua thaen
insurance agent	ตัวแทนประกัน	dtua thaen bprà-gan

106. Service professions

cook	ดูนครัว	khon khrua
chef (kitchen chef)	กุก	gúk
baker	ช่างอบขนมปัง	châang òp khà-nŏm bpang

bartender	บาร์เทนเดอร์	baa-thayn-dêr
waiter	พนักงานเสิร์ฟชาย	phá-nák ngaan sèrf chaai
waitress	พนักงานเสิร์ฟหญิง	phá-nák ngaan sèrf yĭng

lawyer, attorney	ทนายความ	thá-naai khwaam
lawyer (legal expert)	นักกฎหมาย	nák gòt măai
notary public	พนักงานจดทะเบียน	phá-nák ngaan jòt thá-bian

electrician	ช่างไฟฟ้า	châang fai-fáa
plumber	ช่างประปา	châang bprà-bpaa
carpenter	ช่างไม้	châang máai

masseur	หมอนวดชาย	mŏr nûat chaai
masseuse	หมอนวดหญิง	mŏr nûat yĭng
doctor	แพทย์	phâet

taxi driver	คนขับแท็กซี่	khon khàp tháek-sêe
driver	คนขับ	khon khàp
delivery man	คนส่งของ	khon sòng khŏrng

chambermaid	แม่บ้าน	mâe bâan
security guard	ยาม	yaam
flight attendant (fem.)	พนักงวนต้อนรับบนเครื่องบิน	phá-nák ngaan dtôrn ráp bon khrêuang bin

schoolteacher	อาจารย์	aa-jaan
librarian	บรรณารักษ์	ban-naa-rák
translator	นักแปล	nák bplae
interpreter	ลาม	lâam
guide	มัคคุเทศก์	mák-khú-thâyt

hairdresser	ช่างทำผม	châang tham phŏm
mailman	บุรุษไปรษณีย์	bù-rùt bprai-sà-nee
salesman (store staff)	คนขายของ	khon khăai khŏrng

gardener	ชาวสวน	chaao sŭan
domestic servant	คนใช้	khon chái
maid (female servant)	สาวใช้	săo chái
cleaner (cleaning lady)	คนทำความสะอาด	khon tham khwaam sà-àat

107. Military professions and ranks

private	พลทหาร	phon-thá-hǎan
sergeant	สิบเอก	sìp àyk
lieutenant	ร้อยโท	rói thoh
captain	ร้อยเอก	rói àyk

major	พลตรี	phon-dtree
colonel	พันเอก	phan àyk
general	นายพล	naai phon
marshal	จอมพล	jorm phon
admiral	พลเรือเอก	phon reua àyk

military (n)	ทางทหาร	thaang thá-hǎan
soldier	ทหาร	thá-hǎan
officer	นายทหาร	naai thá-hǎan
commander	ผู้บัญชาการ	phôo ban-chaa gaan

border guard	ยามเฝ้าชายแดน	yaam fâo chaai daen
radio operator	พลวิทยุ	phon wít-thá-yú
scout (searcher)	ทหารพราน	thá-hǎan phraan
pioneer (sapper)	ทหารช่าง	thá-hǎan châang
marksman	พลแมนปืน	phon mâen bpeun
navigator	ตนหน	dtôn hǒn

108. Officials. Priests

king	กษัตริย์	gà-sàt
queen	ราชินี	raa-chí-nee

prince	เจ้าชาย	jâo chaai
princess	เจาหญิง	jâo yǐng

czar	ซาร์	saa
czarina	ซารีนา	saa-ree-naa

president	ประธานาธิบดี	bprà-thaa-naa-thí-bor-dee
Secretary (minister)	รัฐมนตรี	rát-thà-mon-dtree
prime minister	นายกรัฐมนตรี	naa-yók rát-thà-mon-dtree
senator	สมาชิกวุฒิสภา	sà-maa-chík wút-thí sà-phaa

diplomat	นักการทูต	nák gaan thôot
consul	กงสุล	gong-sǔn
ambassador	เอกอัครราชทูต	àyk-gà-àk-krá-râat-chá-tôot

counselor (diplomatic officer)	เจ้าหน้าที่การทูต	jâo nâa-thêe gaan thôot
official, functionary (civil servant)	ข้าราชการ	khâa râat-chá-gaan

prefect	เจ้าหน้าที่	jâo nâa-thêe
mayor	นายกเทศ มนตรี	naa-yók thâyt-sà-mon-dtree
judge	ผู้พิพากษา	phôo phí-phâak-sǎa
prosecutor (e.g., district attorney)	อัยการ	ai-yá-gaan
missionary	ผู้สอนศาสนา	phôo sǒrn sàat-sà-nǎa
monk	พระ	phrá
abbot	เจ้าอาวาส	jâo aa-wâat
rabbi	พระในศาสนายิว	phrá nai sàat-sà-nǎa yiw
vizier	วีซีร์	wee see
shah	กษัตริย์อิหร่าน	gà-sàt i-ràan
sheikh	หัวหน้าเผ่าอาหรับ	hǔa nâa phào aa-ràp

109. Agricultural professions

beekeeper	คนเลี้ยงผึ้ง	khon líang phêung
herder, shepherd	คนเลี้ยงปศุสัตว์	khon líang bpà-sù-sàt
agronomist	นักปฐพี วิทยา	nák bpà-tà-phee wít-thá-yaa
cattle breeder	ผู้ขยายพันธุ์สัตว์	phôo khà-yǎai phan sàt
veterinarian	สัตวแพทย์	sàt phâet
farmer	ชาวนา	chaao naa
winemaker	ผู้ผลิตไวน์	phôo phà-lìt wai
zoologist	นักสัตววิทยา	nák sàt wít-thá-yaa
cowboy	โคบาล	khoh-baan

110. Art professions

actor	นักแสดงชาย	nák sà-daeng chaai
actress	นักแสดงหญิง	nák sà-daeng yǐng
singer (masc.)	นักร้องชาย	nák rórng chaai
singer (fem.)	นักร้องหญิง	nák rórng yǐng
dancer (masc.)	นักเต้นชาย	nák dtên chaai
dancer (fem.)	นักเต้นหญิง	nák dtên yǐng
performer (masc.)	นักแสดงชาย	nák sà-daeng chaai
performer (fem.)	นักแสดงหญิง	nák sà-daeng yǐng
musician	นักดนตรี	nák don-dtree
pianist	นักเปียโน	nák bpia noh
guitar player	ผู้เล่นกีตาร์	phôo lên gee-dtâa

conductor (orchestra ~)	ผู้ควบคุม วงดนตรี	phôo khûap khum wong don-dtree
composer	นักแต่งเพลง	nák dtàeng phlayng
impresario	ผู้ควบคุม การแสดง	phôo khûap khum gaan sà-daeng
film director	ผู้กำกับ ภาพยนตร์	phôo gam-gàp phâap-phá-yon
producer	ผู้อำนวยการสร้าง	phôo am-nuay gaan sâang
scriptwriter	คนเขียนบท ภาพยนตร์	khon khĭan bòt phâap-phá-yon
critic	นักวิจารณ์	nák wí-jaan
writer	นักเขียน	nák khĭan
poet	นักกวี	nák gà-wee
sculptor	ช่างสลัก	châang sà-làk
artist (painter)	ช่างวาดรูป	châang wâat rôop
juggler	นักมายากล โยนของ	nák maa-yaa gon yohn khŏrng
clown	ตัวตลก	dtua dtà-lòk
acrobat	นักกายกรรม	nák gaai-yá-gam
magician	นักเล่นกล	nák lên gon

111. Various professions

doctor	แพทย์	phâet
nurse	พยาบาล	phá-yaa-baan
psychiatrist	จิตแพทย์	jìt-dtà-phâet
dentist	ทันตแพทย์	than-dtà phâet
surgeon	ศัลยแพทย์	săn-yá-phâet
astronaut	นักบินอวกาศ	nák bin a-wá-gàat
astronomer	นักดาราศาสตร์	nák daa-raa sàat
pilot	นักบิน	nák bin
driver (of taxi, etc.)	คนขับ	khon khàp
engineer (train driver)	คุนขับรถไฟ	khon khàp rót fai
mechanic	ช่างเครื่อง	châang khrêuang
miner	คนงานเหมือง	khon ngaan mĕuang
worker	คุนงาน	khon ngaan
locksmith	ช่างโลหะ	châang loh-hà
joiner (carpenter)	ช่างไม้	châang máai
turner (lathe operator)	ช่างกลึง	châang gleung
construction worker	คุนงานก่อสร้าง	khon ngaan gòr sâang
welder	ช่างเชื่อม	châang chêuam
professor (title)	ศาสตราจารย์	sàat-sà-dtraa-jaan
architect	สถาปนิก	sà-thăa-bpà-ník

historian	นักประวัติศาสตร์	nák bprà-wàt sàat
scientist	นักวิทยาศาสตร	nák wít-thá-yaa sàat
physicist	นักฟิสิกส	nák fí-sìk
chemist (scientist)	นักเคมี	nák khay-mee
archeologist	นักโบราณคดี	nák boh-raan-ná-khá-dee
geologist	นักธรณี	nák thor-rá-nee
	วิทยา	wít-thá-yaa
researcher (scientist)	ผู้วิจัย	phôo wí-jai
babysitter	พี่เลี้ยงเด็ก	phêe líang dèk
teacher, educator	อาจารย	aa-jaan
editor	บรรณาธิการ	ban-naa-thí-gaan
editor-in-chief	หัวหน้าบรรณาธิการ	hǔa nâa ban-naa-thí-gaan
correspondent	ผู้สื่อข่าว	phôo sèu khàao
typist (fem.)	พนักงานพิมพ์ดีด	phá-nák ngaan phim dèet
designer	นักออกแบบ	nák òrk bàep
computer expert	ผู้เชี่ยวชาญด้าน	pôo chîeow-chaan dâan
	คอมพิวเตอร์	khorm-piw-dtêr
programmer	นักเขียนโปรแกรม	nák khĭan bproh-graem
engineer (designer)	วิศวกร	wít-sà-wá-gon
sailor	กะลาสี	gà-laa-sěe
seaman	คนเรือ	khon reua
rescuer	นักกู้ภัย	nák gôo phai
fireman	เจ้าหน้าที่ดับเพลิง	jâo nâa-thêe dàp phlerng
police officer	เจาหนาที่ตำรวจ	jâo nâa-thêe dtam-rùat
watchman	คนยาม	khon yaam
detective	นักสืบ	nák sèup
customs officer	เจ้าหน้าที่	jâo nâa-thêe
	ศุลกากร	sǔn-lá-gaa-gon
bodyguard	ผู้คุมกัน	phôo khúm gan
prison guard	ผู้คุม	phôo khum
inspector	ผู้ตรวจการ	phôo dtrùat gaan
sportsman	นักกีฬา	nák gee-laa
trainer, coach	โค้ช	khóht
butcher	คนขายเนื้อ	khon khǎai néua
cobbler (shoe repairer)	คนซอมรองเท้า	khon sôrm rorng tháo
merchant	คนค้า	khon kháa
loader (person)	คนงานยกของ	khon ngaan yók khǒrng
fashion designer	นักออกแบบแฟชั่น	nák òrk bàep fae-chân
model (fem.)	นางแบบ	naang bàep

112. Occupations. Social status

schoolboy	นักเรียน	nák rian
student (college ~)	นักศึกษา	nák sèuk-săa
philosopher	นักปราชญ์	nák bpràat
economist	นักเศรษฐศาสตร์	nák sàyt-thà-sàat
inventor	นักประดิษฐ์	nák bprà-dìt
unemployed (n)	คนว่างงาน	khon wâang ngaan
retiree	ผู้เกษียณอายุ	phôo gà-sĭan aa-yú
spy, secret agent	สายลับ	săai láp
prisoner	นักโทษ	nák thôht
striker	คนนัดหยุดงาน	kon nát yùt ngaan
bureaucrat	อำมาตย์	am-màat
traveler (globetrotter)	นักเดินทาง	nák dern-thaang
gay, homosexual (n)	ผู้รักเพศเดียวกัน	phôo rák phâyt dieow gan
hacker	แฮ็กเกอร์	háek-gêr
hippie	ฮิปปี้	híp-bpêe
bandit	โจร	john
hit man, killer	นักฆ่า	nák khâa
drug addict	ผู้ติดยาเสพติด	phôo dtìt yaa-sàyp-dtìt
drug dealer	ผู้ค้ายาเสพติด	phôo kháa yaa-sàyp-dtìt
prostitute (fem.)	โสเภณี	sŏh-phay-nee
pimp	แมงดา	maeng-daa
sorcerer	พ่อมด	phôr mót
sorceress (evil ~)	แม่มด	mâe mót
pirate	โจรสลัด	john sà-làt
slave	ทาส	thâat
samurai	ซามูไร	saa-moo-rai
savage (primitive)	คนป่าเถื่อน	khon bpàa thèuan

Sports

113. Kinds of sports. Sportspersons

sportsman	นักกีฬา	nák gee-laa
kind of sports	ประเภทกีฬา	bprà-phâyt gee-laa
basketball	บาสเก็ตบอล	bàat-gèt-bon
basketball player	ผู้เลนบาสเก็ตบอล	phôo lâyn bàat-gèt-bon
baseball	เบสบอล	bàyt-bon
baseball player	ผู้เลนเบสบอล	phôo lâyn bàyt bon
soccer	ฟุตบอล	fút bon
soccer player	นักฟุตบอล	nák fút-bon
goalkeeper	ผู้รักษาประตู	phôo rák-sǎa bprà-dtoo
hockey	ฮอกกี้	hôk-gêe
hockey player	ผู้เลนฮอกกี้	phôo lâyn hôk-gêe
volleyball	วอลเลย์บอล	won-lây-bon
volleyball player	ผู้เลนวอลเลย์บอล	phôo lâyn won-lây-bon
boxing	การชกมวย	gaan chók muay
boxer	นักมวย	nák muay
wrestling	การมวยปล้ำ	gaan muay bplâm
wrestler	นักมวยปล้ำ	nák muay bplâm
karate	คาราเต้	khaa-raa-dtây
karate fighter	นักคาราเต้	nák khaa-raa-dtây
judo	ยูโด	yoo-doh
judo athlete	นักยูโด	nák yoo-doh
tennis	เทนนิส	then-nít
tennis player	นักเทนนิส	nák then-nít
swimming	กีฬาว่ายน้ำ	gee-laa wâai náam
swimmer	นักวายน้ำ	nák wâai náam
fencing	กีฬาฟันดาบ	gee-laa fan dàap
fencer	นักฟันดาบ	nák fan dàap
chess	หมากรุก	màak rúk
chess player	ผู้เลนหมากรุก	phôo lên màak rúk

alpinism	การปีนเขา	gaan bpeen khǎo
alpinist	นักปีนเขา	nák bpeen khǎo

running	การวิ่ง	gaan wîng
runner	นักวิ่ง	nák wîng

athletics	กรีฑา	gree thaa
athlete	นักกรีฑา	nák gree thaa

horseback riding	กีฬาขี่ม้า	gee-laa khèe máa
horse rider	นักขี่ม้า	nák khèe máa

figure skating	สเก็ตลีลา	sà-gèt lee-laa
figure skater (masc.)	นักสเก็ตสเดง	nák sà-daeng
	สเก็ตลีลา	sà-gèt lee-laa
figure skater (fem.)	นักสเก็ตสเดง	nák sà-daeng
	สเก็ตลีลา	sà-gèt lee-laa

powerlifting	กีฬายกน้ำหนัก	gee-laa yók náam nàk
powerlifter	นักยกน้ำหนัก	nák yók nám nàk

car racing	การแข่งรถ	gaan khàeng rót
racer (driver)	นักแข่งรถ	nák khàeng rót

cycling	การแข่งจักรยาน	gaan khàeng jàk-grà-yaan
cyclist	นักแขงจักรยาน	nák khàeng jàk-grà-yaan

broad jump	กีฬากระโดดไกล	gee-laa grà-dòht glai
pole vault	กีฬากระโดด	gee-laa grà dòht
	ค้ำถอ	khám thòr
jumper	นักกระโดด	nák grà dòht

114. Kinds of sports. Miscellaneous

football	อเมริกันฟุตบอล	a-may-rí-gan fút bon
badminton	แบดมินตัน	bàet-min-dtân
biathlon	ไบแอธลอน	bpai-oht-lon
billiards	บิลเลียด	bin-lîat

bobsled	การขับเลื่อน	gaan khàp lêuan
	น้ำแข็ง	náam khǎeng
bodybuilding	การเพาะกาย	gaan phór gaai
water polo	กีฬาโปโลน้ำ	gee-laa bpoh loh nám
handball	แฮนด์บอล	haen-bon
golf	กอล์ฟ	góf

rowing, crew	การพายเรือ	gaan phaai reua
scuba diving	การดำน้ำ	gaan dam náam
cross-country skiing	การแข่งสกี	gaan khàeng sà-gee
	ตามเส้นทาง	dtaam sên thaang

table tennis (ping-pong)	กีฬาปิงปอง	gee-laa bping-bpong
sailing	การแล่นเรือใบ	gaan lâen reua bai
rally racing	การแข่งแรลลี่	gaan khàeng rae lá-lêe
rugby	รักบี้	rák-bêe
snowboarding	สโนว์บอร์ด	sà-nŏh bòt
archery	การยิงธนู	gaan ying thá-noo

115. Gym

barbell	บาร์เบลล์	baa bayn
dumbbells	ที่ยกน้ำหนัก	thêe yók nám nàk
training machine	เครื่องออกกำลังกาย	khrêuang òk gam-lang gaai
exercise bicycle	จักรยานออกกำลังกาย	jàk-grà-yaan òk gam-lang gaai
treadmill	ลู่วิ่งออกกำลังกาย	lôo wîng òk gam-lang gaai
horizontal bar	บาร์เดี่ยว	baa dìeow
parallel bars	บาร์คู่	baa khôo
vault (vaulting horse)	ม้าขวาง	máa khwăang
mat (exercise ~)	เสื่อออกกำลังกาย	sèua òrk gam-lang gaai
jump rope	กระโดดเชือก	grà dòht chêuak
aerobics	แอโรบิก	ae-roh-bìk
yoga	โยคะ	yoh-khá

116. Sports. Miscellaneous

Olympic Games	กีฬาโอลิมปิก	gee-laa oh-lim-bpìk
winner	ผู้ชนะ	phôo chá-ná
to be winning	ชนะ	chá-ná
to win (vi)	ชนะ	chá-ná
leader	ผู้นำ	phôo nam
to lead (vi)	นำ	nam
first place	อันดับที่หนึ่ง	an-dàp thêe nèung
second place	อันดับที่สอง	an-dàp thêe sŏrng
third place	อันดับที่สาม	an-dàp thêe săam
medal	เหรียญรางวัล	rĭan raang-wan
trophy	ถ้วยรางวัล	thûay raang-wan
prize cup (trophy)	เวท	wâyt
prize (in game)	รางวัล	raang-wan
main prize	รางวัลหลัก	raang-wan làk
record	สถิติ	sà-thì-dtì
to set a record	ทำสถิติ	tham sà-thì-dtì

final	รอบสุดท้าย	rôrp sùt tháai
final (adj)	สุดท้าย	sùt tháai
champion	แชมเปี้ยน	chaem-bpîan
championship	ชิงแชมป์	ching chaem
stadium	สนาม	sà-nǎam
stand (bleachers)	อัฒจันทร์	àt-tá-jan
fan, supporter	แฟน	faen
opponent, rival	คู่ต่อสู้	khôo dtòr sôo
start (start line)	เส้นเริ่ม	sên rêrm
finish line	เส้นชัย	sên chai
defeat	ความพ่ายแพ้	khwaam phâai pháe
to lose (not win)	แพ้	pháe
referee	กรรมฎาร	gam-má-gaan
jury (judges)	คณะผู้ตัดสิน	khá-ná phôo dtàt sǐn
score	คะแนน	khá-naen
tie	เสมอ	sà-měr
to tie (vi)	ได้คะแนนเท่ากัน	dâai khá-naen thâo gan
point	แต้ม	dtâem
result (final score)	ผลลัพธ์	phǒn láp
period	ช่วง	chûang
half-time	ช่วงพักครึ่ง	chûang phák khrêung
doping	การใช้สารต้องห้ามทางการกีฬา	gaan chái sǎan dtôrng hâam thaang gaan gee-laa
to penalize (vt)	ทำโทษ	tham thôht
to disqualify (vt)	ตัดสิทธิ์	dtàt sìt
apparatus	อุปกรณ์	ù-bpà-gon
javelin	แหลน	lǎen
shot (metal ball)	ลูกเหล็ก	lôok lèk
ball (snooker, etc.)	ลูก	lôok
aim (target)	เล็งเป้า	leng bpâo
target	เป้านิ่ง	bpâo nîng
to shoot (vi)	ยิง	ying
accurate (~ shot)	แม่นยำ	mâen yam
trainer, coach	โค้ช	khóht
to train (sb)	ฝึก	fèuk
to train (vi)	ฝึกหัด	fèuk hàt
training	การฝึกหัด	gaan fèuk hàt
gym	โรงยิม	rohng-yim
exercise (physical)	การออกกำลัง	gaan òrk gam-lang
warm-up (athlete ~)	การอบอุ่นรางกาย	gaan òp ùn râang gaai

Education

117. School

school	โรงเรียน	rohng rian
principal (headmaster)	อาจารย์ใหญ่	aa-jaan yài
pupil (boy)	นักเรียน	nák rian
pupil (girl)	นักเรียน	nák rian
schoolboy	เด็กนักเรียนชาย	dèk nák rian chaai
schoolgirl	เด็กนักเรียนหญิง	dèk nák rian yĭng
to teach (sb)	สอน	sŏrn
to learn (language, etc.)	เรียน	rian
to learn by heart	ท่องจำ	thôrng jam
to learn (~ to count, etc.)	เรียน	rian
to be in school	ไปโรงเรียน	bpai rohng rian
to go to school	ไปโรงเรียน	bpai rohng rian
alphabet	ตัวอักษร	dtua àk-sŏn
subject (at school)	วิชา	wí-chaa
classroom	ห้องเรียน	hôrng rian
lesson	ชั่วโมงเรียน	chûa mohng rian
recess	ช่วงพัก	chûang phák
school bell	สัญญาณหมดเรียน	săn-yaan mòt rian
school desk	โต๊ะนักเรียน	dtó nák rian
chalkboard	กระดานดำ	grà-daan dam
grade	เกรด	gràyt
good grade	เกรดดี	gràyt dee
bad grade	เกรดแย่	gràyt yâe
to give a grade	ให้เกรด	hâi gràyt
mistake, error	ข้อผิดพลาด	khôr phìt phlâat
to make mistakes	ทำผิดพลาด	tham phìt phlâat
to correct (an error)	แก้ไข	gâe khăi
cheat sheet	โพย	phoi
homework	การบ้าน	gaan bâan
exercise (in education)	แบบฝึกหัด	bàep fèuk hàt
to be present	มาเรียน	maa rian
to be absent	ขาด	khàat
to miss school	ขาดเรียน	khàat rian

to punish (vt)	ลงโทษ	long thôht
punishment	การลงโทษ	gaan long thôht
conduct (behavior)	ความประพฤติ	khwaam bprà-préut

report card	สมุดพก	sà-mùt phók
pencil	ดินสอ	din-sŏr
eraser	ยางลบ	yaang lóp
chalk	ชอล์ค	chôrk
pencil case	กล่องดินสอ	glòrng din-sŏr

schoolbag	กระเป๋า	grà-bpăo
pen	ปากกา	bpàak gaa
school notebook	สมุดจด	sà-mùt jòt
textbook	หนังสือเรียน	năng-sěu rian
drafting compass	วงเวียน	wong wian

| to make technical drawings | ร่างภาพ ทางเทคนิค | râang phâap thaang thék-nìk |
| technical drawing | ภาพร่าง ทางเทคนิค | phâap-râang thaang thék-nìk |

poem	กลอน	glorn
by heart (adv)	โดยท่องจำ	doi thôrng jam
to learn by heart	ท่องจำ	thôrng jam

school vacation	เวลาปิดเทอม	way-laa bpìt therm
to be on vacation	หยุดปิดเทอม	yùt bpìt therm
to spend one's vacation	ใช้เวลาหยุดปิดเทอม	chái way-laa yùt bpìt therm

test (written math ~)	การทดสอบ	gaan thót sòrp
essay (composition)	ความเรียง	khwaam riang
dictation	การเขียนตาม คำบอก	gaan khǐan dtaam kam bòrk
exam (examination)	การสอบ	gaan sòrp
to take an exam	สอบไล	sòrp lâi
experiment (e.g., chemistry ~)	การทดลอง	gaan thót lorng

118. College. University

academy	โรงเรียน	rohng rian
university	มหาวิทยาลัย	má-hăa wít-thá-yaa-lai
faculty (e.g., ~ of Medicine)	คณะ	khá-ná

student (masc.)	นักศึกษา	nák sèuk-săa
student (fem.)	นักศึกษา	nák sèuk-săa
lecturer (teacher)	อาจารย์	aa-jaan
lecture hall, room	ห้องบรรยาย	hôrng ban-yaai
graduate	บัณฑิต	ban-dìt

| diploma | อนุปริญญา | a-nú bpà-rin-yaa |
| dissertation | ปริญญานิพนธ์ | bpà-rin-yaa ní-phon |

| study (report) | การวิจัย | gaan wí-jai |
| laboratory | หองปฏิบัติการ | hôrng bpà-dtì-bàt gaan |

lecture	การบรรยาย	gaan ban-yaai
coursemate	เพื่อนรวมชั้น	phêuan rûam chán
scholarship	ทุน	thun
academic degree	วุฒิการศึกษา	wút-thí gaan sèuk-săa

119. Sciences. Disciplines

mathematics	คณิตศาสตร์	khá-nít sàat
algebra	พีชคณิต	phee-chá-khá-nít
geometry	เรขาคณิต	ray-khăa khá-nít

astronomy	ดาราศาสตร์	daa-raa sàat
biology	ชีววิทยา	chee-wá-wít-thá-yaa
geography	ภูมิศาสตร์	phoo-mí-sàat
geology	ธรณีวิทยา	thor-rá-nee wít-thá-yaa
history	ประวัติศาสตร์	bprà-wàt sàat

medicine	แพทยศาสตร์	phâet-tha-ya-sàat
pedagogy	ครุศาสตร์	khrú sàat
law	ธรรมศาสตร์	tham-ma -sàat

physics	ฟิสิกส์	fí-sìk
chemistry	เคมี	khay-mee
philosophy	ปรัชญา	bpràt-yaa
psychology	จิตวิทยา	jìt-wít-thá-yaa

120. Writing system. Orthography

grammar	ไวยากรณ์	wai-yaa-gon
vocabulary	คำศัพท	kham sàp
phonetics	การออกเสียง	gaan òrk sĭang

noun	นาม	naam
adjective	คำคุณศัพท์	kham khun-ná-sàp
verb	กริยา	grì-yaa
adverb	คำวิเศษณ์	kham wí-sàyt

pronoun	คำสรรพนาม	kham sàp-phá-naam
interjection	คำอุทาน	kham u-thaan
preposition	คำบุพบท	kham bùp-phá-bòt
root	รากศัพท	râak sàp
ending	คำลงทาย	kham long tháai

prefix	คำนำหน้า	kham nam nâa
syllable	พยางค์	phá-yaang
suffix	คำเสริมท้าย	kham sěrm tháai
stress mark	เครื่องหมายเน้น	khrêuang măai náyn
apostrophe	อะพอสทรอฟี	à-phor-sòt-ror-fee
period, dot	จุด	jùt
comma	จุลภาค	jun-lá-phâak
semicolon	อัฒภาค	àt-thá-phâak
colon	ทวิภาค	thá-wí phâak
ellipsis	การละไว้	gaan lá wái
question mark	เครื่องหมายปรัศนี	khrêuang măai bpràt-nee
exclamation point	เครื่องหมาย อัศเจรีย์	khrêuang măai àt-sà-jay-ree
quotation marks	อัญประกาศ	an-yá-bprà-gàat
in quotation marks	ในอัญประกาศ	nai an-yá-bprà-gàat
parenthesis	วงเล็บ	wong lép
in parenthesis	ในวงเล็บ	nai wong lép
hyphen	ยัติภังค์	yát-dtì-phang
dash	ขีดคั่น	khèet khân
space (between words)	ช่องไฟ	chôrng fai
letter	ตัวอักษร	dtua àk-sŏn
capital letter	อักษรตัวใหญ่	àk-sŏn dtua yài
vowel (n)	สระ	sà-ra
consonant (n)	พยัญชนะ	phá-yan-chá-ná
sentence	ประโยค	bprà-yòhk
subject	ภาคประธาน	phâak bprà-thaan
predicate	ภาคแสดง	phâak sà-daeng
line	บรรทัด	ban-thát
on a new line	ที่บรรทัดใหม่	têe ban-thát mài
paragraph	วรรค	wák
word	คำ	kham
group of words	กลุ่มคำ	glùm kham
expression	วลี	wá-lee
synonym	คำพ้องความหมาย	kham phóng khwaam măai
antonym	คำตรงกันข้าม	kham dtrorng gan khâam
rule	กฎ	gòt
exception	ข้อยกเว้น	khôr yok-wâyn
correct (adj)	ถูก	thòok
conjugation	คอนจูเกชัน	khorn joo gay chan
declension	การกระจายคำ	gaan grà-jaai kham

nominal case	การก	gaa-rók
question	คำถาม	kham thǎam
to underline (vt)	ขีดเส้นใต้	khèet sên dtâi
dotted line	เส้นประ	sên bprà

121. Foreign languages

language	ภาษา	phaa-sǎa
foreign (adj)	ต่างชาติ	dtàang châat
foreign language	ภาษาต่างชาติ	phaa-sǎa dtàang châat
to study (vt)	เรียน	rian
to learn (language, etc.)	เรียน	rian
to read (vi, vt)	อ่าน	àan
to speak (vi, vt)	พูด	phôot
to understand (vt)	เข้าใจ	khâo jai
to write (vt)	เขียน	khǐan
fast (adv)	รวดเร็ว	rûat reo
slowly (adv)	อย่างช้า	yàang cháa
fluently (adv)	อย่างคล่อง	yàang khlôrng
rules	กฎ	gòt
grammar	ไวยากรณ์	wai-yaa-gon
vocabulary	คำศัพท์	kham sàp
phonetics	การออกเสียง	gaan òrk sǐang
textbook	หนังสือเรียน	nǎng-sěu rian
dictionary	พจนานุกรม	phót-jà-naa-nú-grom
teach-yourself book	หนังสือแบบเรียน	nǎng-sěu bàep rian
	ด้วยตนเอง	dûay dton ayng
phrasebook	เฟรสบุก	frayt bùk
cassette, tape	เทปคาสเซ็ตต์	thâyp khaas-sét
videotape	วิดีโอ	wí-dee-oh
CD, compact disc	CD	see-dee
DVD	DVD	dee-wee-dee
alphabet	ตัวอักษร	dtua àk-sǒn
to spell (vt)	สะกด	sà-gòt
pronunciation	การออกเสียง	gaan òrk sǐang
accent	สำเนียง	sǎm-niang
with an accent	มีสำเนียง	mee sǎm-niang
without an accent	ไม่มีสำเนียง	mâi mee sǎm-niang
word	คำ	kham
meaning	ความหมาย	khwaam mǎai
course (e.g., a French ~)	หลักสูตร	làk sòot
to sign up	สมัคร	sà-màk

teacher	อาจารย์	aa-jaan
translation (process)	การแปล	gaan bplae
translation (text, etc.)	คำแปล	kham bplae
translator	นักแปล	nák bplae
interpreter	ล่าม	lâam
polyglot	ผู้รู้หลายภาษา	phôo róo lăai paa-săa
memory	ความทรงจำ	khwaam song jam

122. Fairy tale characters

Santa Claus	ซานตาคลอส	saan-dtaa-khlôrt
Cinderella	ซินเดอเรลลา	sín-day-rayn-lâa
mermaid	เงือก	ngêuak
Neptune	เนปจูน	nâyp-joon
magician, wizard	พ่อมด	phôr mót
fairy	แม่มด	mâe mót
magic (adj)	วิเศษ	wí-sàyt
magic wand	ไม้กายสิทธิ์	mái gaai-yá-sìt
fairy tale	เทพนิยาย	thâyp ní-yaai
miracle	ปาฏิหาริย์	bpaa dtì-hăan
dwarf	คนแคระ	khon khráe
to turn into …	กลายเป็น...	glaai bpen...
ghost	ผี	phěe
phantom	ภูตผีปีศาจ	phôot phěe bpee-sàat
monster	สัตว์ประหลาด	sàt bprà-làat
dragon	มังกร	mang-gon
giant	ยักษ์	yák

123. Zodiac Signs

Aries	ราศีเมษ	raa-sěe mâyt
Taurus	ราศีพฤษภ	raa-sěe phréut-sòp
Gemini	ราศีมิถุน	raa-sěe me-thǔn
Cancer	ราศีกรกฎ	raa-sěe gor-rá-gòt
Leo	ราศีสิงห์	raa-sěe-sǐng
Virgo	ราศีกันย์	raa-sěe gan
Libra	ราศีตุล	raa-sěe dtun
Scorpio	ราศีพฤศจิก	raa-sěe phréut-sà-jìk
Sagittarius	ราศีธันว์	raa-sěe than
Capricorn	ราศีมังกร	raa-sěe mang-gon
Aquarius	ราศีกุมภ์	raa-sěe gum
Pisces	ราศีมีน	raa-sěe meen
character	บุคลิก	bùk-khá-lík

character traits	ลักษณะบุคลิก	lák-sà-nà bùk-khá-lík
behavior	พฤติกรรม	phréut-dtì-gam
to tell fortunes	ทำนายชะตา	tham naai chá-dtaa
fortune-teller	หมอดู	mŏr doo
horoscope	ดวงชะตา	duang chá-dtaa

Arts

124. Theater

theater	โรงละคร	rohng lá-khon
opera	โอเปรา	oh-bprào
operetta	ละครเพลง	lá-khon phlayng
ballet	บัลเลต์	ban lây
theater poster	โปสเตอร์ละคร	bpòht-dtêr lá-khon
troupe (theatrical company)	คณะผู้แสดง	khá-ná phôo sà-daeng
tour	การออกแสดง	gaan òrk sà-daeng
to be on tour	ออกแสดง	òrk sà-daeng
to rehearse (vi, vt)	ซ้อม	sórm
rehearsal	การซ้อม	gaan sórm
repertoire	รายการละคร	raai gaan lá-khon
performance	การแสดง	gaan sà-daeng
theatrical show	การแสดง	gaan sà-daeng
	มหรสพ	má-hŏr-rá-sòp
play	ละคร	lá-khon
ticket	ตั๋ว	dtŭa
box office (ticket booth)	ช่องจำหน่ายตั๋ว	chôrng jam-nàai dtŭa
lobby, foyer	ล็อบบี้	lórp-bêe
coat check (cloakroom)	ที่รับฝากเสื้อโค้ท	thêe ráp fàak sêua khóht
coat check tag	ป้ายรับเสื้อ	bpâai ráp sêua
binoculars	กล้องสองสองตา	glôrng sòrng sŏrng dtaa
usher	พนักงานที่นำ	phá-nák ngaan thêe nam
	ไปยังที่นั่ง	bpai yang thêe nâng
orchestra seats	ที่นั่งชั้นล่าง	thêe nâng chán lâang
balcony	ที่นั่งชั้นสอง	thêe nâng chán sŏrng
dress circle	ที่นั่งชั้นบน	thêe nâng chán bon
box	ที่นั่งพิเศษ	thêe nâng phí-sàyt
row	แถว	thăe
seat	ที่นั่ง	thêe nâng
audience	ผู้ชม	phôo chom
spectator	ผู้เข้าชม	phôo khâo chom
to clap (vi, vt)	ปรบมือ	bpròp meu
applause	การปรบมือ	gaan bpròp meu
ovation	การปรบมือให้เกียรติ	gaan bpròp meu hâi gìat
stage	เวที	way-thee
curtain	ฉาก	chàak

scenery	ฉาก	chàak
backstage	หลังเวที	lăng way-thee
scene (e.g., the last ~)	ตอน	dtorn
act	องค์	ong
intermission	ช่วงหยุดพัก	chûang yùt phák

125. Cinema

actor	นักแสดงชาย	nák sà-daeng chaai
actress	นักแสดงหญิง	nák sà-daeng yĭng
movies (industry)	ภาพยนตร์	phâap-phá-yon
movie	หนัง	năng
episode	ตอน	dtorn
detective movie	หนังประโลมโลกสืบสวน	năng sèup sŭan
action movie	หนังแอ็คชั่น	năng áek-chân
adventure movie	หนังผจญภัย	năng phà-jon phai
sci-fi movie	หนังนิยาย วิทยาศาสตร์	năng ní-yaai wít-thá-yaa sàat
horror movie	หนังสยองขวัญ	năng sà-yŏrng khwăn
comedy movie	หนังตลก	năng dtà-lòk
melodrama	หนังประโลมโลก	năng bprà-lohm lôhk
drama	หนังดรามา	năng draa maa
fictional movie	หนังเรื่องแต่ง	năng rêuang dtàeng
documentary	หนังสารคดี	năng săa-rá-khá-dee
cartoon	การ์ตูน	gaa-dtoon
silent movies	หนังเงียบ	năng ngîap
role (part)	บทบาท	bòt bàat
leading role	บทบาทนำ	bòt bàat nam
to play (vi, vt)	แสดง	sà-daeng
movie star	ดาราภาพยนตร์	daa-raa phâap-phá-yon
well-known (adj)	เป็นที่รู้จักดี	bpen thêe róo jàk dee
famous (adj)	ชื่อดัง	chêu dang
popular (adj)	ที่นิยม	thêe ní-yom
script (screenplay)	บท	bòt
scriptwriter	คนเขียนบท	khon khĭan bòt
movie director	ผู้กำกับ ภาพยนตร์	phôo gam-gàp phâap-phá-yon
producer	ผู้อำนวยการสร้าง	phôo am-nuay gaan sâang
assistant	ผู้ช่วย	phôo chûay
cameraman	ช่างกล้อง	châang glôrng
stuntman	นักแสดงแทน	nák sà-daeng thaen
double (stand-in)	นักแสดงแทน	nák sà-daeng thaen

to shoot a movie	ถ่ายทำภาพยนตร์	thàai tham phâap-phá-yon
audition, screen test	การคัดนักแสดง	gaan khát nák sà-daeng
shooting	การถ่ายทำ	gaan thàai tham
movie crew	กลุ่มคนถ่าย ภาพยนต	glùm khon thàai phâa-pha-yon
movie set	สถานที่ ถ่ายทำภาพยนตร์	sà-thǎan thêe thàai tham phâap-phá-yon
camera	กล้อง	glôrng
movie theater	โรงภาพยนตร์	rohng phâap-phá-yon
screen (e.g., big ~)	หน้าจอ	nâa jor
to show a movie	ฉายภาพยนตร์	chǎai phâap-phá-yon
soundtrack	เสียงซาวด์แทร็ก	sǐang saao tráek
special effects	เอฟเฟ็กต์พิเศษ	àyf-fék phí-sàyt
subtitles	ซับ	sáp
credits	เครดิต	khray-dìt
translation	การแปล	gaan bplae

126. Painting

art	ศิลปะ	sǐn-lá-bpà
fine arts	วิจิตรศิลป์	wí-jìt sǐn
art gallery	หอศิลป์	hǒr sǐn
art exhibition	การจัดแสดง ศิลปะ	gaan jàt sà-daeng sǐn-lá-bpà
painting (art)	จิตรกรรม	jìt-dtrà-gam
graphic art	เลขนศิลป์	lâyk-ná-sǐn
abstract art	ศิลปะนามธรรม	sǐn-lá-bpà naam-má-tham
impressionism	ลัทธิประทับใจ	lát-thí bprà-tháp jai
picture (painting)	ภาพ	phâap
drawing	ภาพวาด	phâap-wâat
poster	โปสเตอร์	bpòht-dtêr
illustration (picture)	ภาพประกอบ	phâap bprà-gòrp
miniature	รูปปั้นขนาดยอ	rôop bpân khà-nàat yôr
copy (of painting, etc.)	สำเนา	sǎm-nao
reproduction	การทำซ้ำ	gaan tham sám
mosaic	โมเสก	moh-sàyk
stained glass window	หน้าต่างกระจกสี	nâa dtàang grà-jòk sěe
fresco	ภาพผนัง	phâap phà-nǎng
engraving	การแกะลาย	gaan gàe laai
bust (sculpture)	รูปปั้นครึ่งตัว	rôop bpân khrêung dtua
sculpture	รูปปั้นแกะสลัก	rôop bpân gàe sà-làk
statue	รูปปั้น	rôop bpân
plaster of Paris	ปูนปลาสเตอร์	bpoon bpláat-dtêr

plaster (as adj)	ปูนปลาสเตอร์	bpoon bpláat-dtêr
portrait	ภาพเหมือน	phâap měuan
self-portrait	ภาพเหมือนของ ตนเอง	phâap měuan khǒrng dton ayng
landscape painting	ภาพภูมิทัศน์	phâap phoom-mi -thát
still life	ภาพหุ่นนิ่ง	phâap hùn nîng
caricature	ภาพลอ	phâap-lór
sketch	ภาพสเก็ตช์	phâap sà-gèt
paint	สี	sěe
watercolor paint	สีน้ำ	sěe náam
oil (paint)	สีน้ำมัน	sěe náam man
pencil	ดินสอ	din-sǒr
India ink	หมึกสีดำ	mèuk sěe dam
charcoal	ถ่าน	thàan
to draw (vi, vt)	วาด	wâat
to paint (vi, vt)	ระบายสี	rá-baai sěe
to pose (vi)	จัดท่า	jàt thâa
artist's model (masc.)	แบบภาพวาด	bàep phâap-wâat
artist's model (fem.)	แบบภาพวาด	bàep phâap-wâat
artist (painter)	ช่างวาดรูป	châang wâat rôop
work of art	งานศิลปะ	ngaan sǐn-lá-bpà
masterpiece	งานชิ้นเอก	ngaan chín àyk
studio (artist's workroom)	สตูดิโอ	sà-dtoo dì oh
canvas (cloth)	ผ้าใบ	phâa bai
easel	ขาตั้งกระดาน วาดรูป	khǎa dtâng grà daan wâat rôop
palette	จานสี	jaan sěe
frame (picture ~, etc.)	กรอบ	gròrp
restoration	การฟื้นฟู	gaan féun foo
to restore (vt)	ฟื้นฟู	féun foo

127. Literature & Poetry

literature	วรรณคดี	wan-ná-khá-dee
author (writer)	ผู้แต่ง	phôo dtàeng
pseudonym	นามปากกา	naam bpàak gaa
book	หนังสือ	nǎng-sěu
volume	เล่ม	lêm
table of contents	สารบัญ	sǎa-rá-ban
page	หน้า	nâa
main character	ตัวละครหลัก	dtua lá-khon làk
autograph	ลายเซ็น	laai sen
short story	เรื่องสั้น	rêuang sân

story (novella)	เรื่องราว	rêuang raao
novel	นิยาย	ní-yaai
work (writing)	งานเขียน	ngaan khĭan
fable	นิทาน	ní-thaan
detective novel	นิยายสืบสวน	ní-yaai sèup sŭan
poem (verse)	กลอน	glorn
poetry	บทกลอน	bòt glorn
poem (epic, ballad)	บทกวี	bòt gà-wee
poet	นักกวี	nák gà-wee
fiction	เรื่องแต่ง	rêuang dtàeng
science fiction	นิยายวิทยาศาสตร์	ní-yaai wít-thá-yaa sàat
adventures	นิยายผจญภัย	ní-yaai phà-jon phai
educational literature	วรรณกรรม การศึกษา	wan-ná-gam gaan sèuk-săa
children's literature	วรรณกรรมสำหรับเด็ก	wan-ná-gam săm-ràp dèk

128. Circus

circus	ละครสัตว์	lá-khon sàt
traveling circus	ละครสัตว์เล่รอน	lá-khon sàt lây rôrn
program	รายการการแสดง	raai gaan gaan sà-daeng
performance	การแสดง	gaan sà-daeng
act (circus ~)	การแสดง	gaan sà-daeng
circus ring	เวทีละครสัตว์	way-thee lá-kon sàt
pantomime (act)	ละครใบ้	lá-khon bâi
clown	ตัวตลก	dtua dtà-lòk
acrobat	นักกายกรรม	nák gaai-yá-gam
acrobatics	กายกรรม	gaai-yá-gam
gymnast	นักกายกรรม	nák gaai-yá-gam
acrobatic gymnastics	กายกรรม	gaai-yá-gam
somersault	การตีลังกา	gaan dtee lang-gaa
athlete (strongman)	นักกีฬา	nák gee-laa
tamer (e.g., lion ~)	ผู้ฝึกสัตว์	phôo fèuk sàt
rider (circus horse ~)	นักขี่	nák khèe
assistant	ผู้ช่วย	phôo chûay
stunt	ผาดโผน	phàat phŏhn
magic trick	มายากล	maa-yaa gon
conjurer, magician	นักมายากล	nák maa-yaa gon
juggler	นักมายากล โยนของ	nák maa-yaa gon yohn khŏrng
to juggle (vi, vt)	โยนของ	yohn khŏrng
animal trainer	ผู้ฝึกสัตว์	phôo fèuk sàt

animal training	การฝึกสัตว์	gaan fèuk sàt
to train (animals)	ฝึก	fèuk

129. Music. Pop music

music	ดนตรี	don-dtree
musician	นักดนตรี	nák don-dtree
musical instrument	เครื่องดนตรี	khrêuang don-dtree
to play ...	เล่น	lên
guitar	กีตาร์	gee-dtâa
violin	ไวโอลิน	wai-oh-lin
cello	เชลโล	chayn-lôh
double bass	ดับเบิลเบส	dàp-bern bàyt
harp	พิณ	phin
piano	เปียโน	bpia noh
grand piano	แกรนด์เปียโน	graen bpia-noh
organ	ออร์แกน	or-gaen
wind instruments	เครื่องเป่า	khrêuang bpào
oboe	โอโบ	oh-boh
saxophone	แซ็กโซโฟน	sáek-soh-fohn
clarinet	แคลริเน็ต	khlae-rí-nét
flute	ฟลูต	flút
trumpet	ทรัมเป็ต	thram-bpèt
accordion	หีบเพลงชัก	hèep phlayng chák
drum	กลอง	glorng
duo	คู่	khôo
trio	วงทริโอ	wong thrí-oh
quartet	กลุ่มที่มีสี่คน	glùm thêe mee sèe khon
choir	คณะประสานเสียง	khá-ná bprà-sǎan sǐang
orchestra	วงดุริยางค์	wong dù-rí-yaang
pop music	เพลงป็อป	phlayng bpòp
rock music	เพลงร็อค	phlayng rók
rock group	วงร็อค	wong rórk
jazz	แจซ	jáet
idol	ไอดอล	ai-dorn
admirer, fan	แฟน	faen
concert	คอนเสิร์ต	khon-sèrt
symphony	ซิมโฟนี	sím-foh-nee
composition	การแต่งเพลง	gaan dtàeng phlayng
to compose (write)	แต่ง	dtàeng
singing (n)	การร้องเพลง	gaan róng playng
song	เพลง	phlayng

tune (melody)	เสียงเพลง	sǐang phlayng
rhythm	จังหวะ	jang wà
blues	บลูส	bloo
sheet music	โน้ตเพลง	nóht phlayng
baton	ไม้สั้นของ	máai sân khǒrng
	วาทยากร	wâa-tha-yaa gon
bow	คันชอ	khan sor
string	สาย	sǎai
case (e.g., guitar ~)	กลอง	glòrng

Rest. Entertainment. Travel

130. Trip. Travel

English	Thai	Transcription
tourism, travel	การท่องเที่ยว	gaan thôrng thîeow
tourist	นักท่องเที่ยว	nák thôrng thîeow
trip, voyage	การเดินทาง	gaan dern thaang
adventure	การผจญภัย	gaan phà-jon phai
trip, journey	การเดินทาง	gaan dern thaang
vacation	วันหยุดพักผ่อน	wan yùt phák phòrn
to be on vacation	หยุดพักผ่อน	yùt phák phòrn
rest	การพัก	gaan phák
train	รถไฟ	rót fai
by train	โดยรถไฟ	doi rót fai
airplane	เครื่องบิน	khrêuang bin
by airplane	โดยเครื่องบิน	doi khrêuang bin
by car	โดยรถยนต์	doi rót-yon
by ship	โดยเรือ	doi reua
luggage	สัมภาระ	săm-phaa-rá
suitcase	กระเป๋าเดินทาง	grà-bpăo dern-thaang
luggage cart	รถขนสัมภาระ	rót khŏn săm-phaa-rá
passport	หนังสือเดินทาง	năng-sěu dern-thaang
visa	วีซา	wee-sâa
ticket	ตั๋ว	dtŭa
air ticket	ตั๋วเครื่องบิน	dtŭa khrêuang bin
guidebook	หนังสือแนะนำ	năng-sěu náe nam
map (tourist ~)	แผนที่	phăen thêe
area (rural ~)	เขต	khàyt
place, site	สถานที่	sà-thăan thêe
exotica (n)	สิ่งแปลกใหม่	sìng bplàek mài
exotic (adj)	ต่างแดน	dtàang daen
amazing (adj)	น่าประหลาดใจ	nâa bprà-làat jai
group	กลุ่ม	glùm
excursion, sightseeing tour	การเดินทาง ท่องเที่ยว	gaan dern taang thôrng thîeow
guide (person)	มัคคุเทศก์	mák-khú-thâyt

131. Hotel

hotel	โรงแรม	rohng raem
motel	โรงแรม	rohng raem
three-star (~ hotel)	สามดาว	săam daao
five-star	ห้าดาว	hâa daao
to stay (in a hotel, etc.)	พัก	phák
room	ห้อง	hôrng
single room	ห้องเดี่ยว	hôrng dìeow
double room	ห้องคู่	hôrng khôo
to book a room	จองห้อง	jorng hôrng
half board	พักครึ่งวัน	phák khrêung wan
full board	พักเต็มวัน	phák dtem wan
with bath	มีห้องอาบน้ำ	mee hôrng àap náam
with shower	มีฝักบัว	mee fàk bua
satellite television	โทรทัศน์ดาวเทียม	thoh-rá-thát daao thiam
air-conditioner	เครื่องปรับอากาศ	khrêuang bpràp-aa-gàat
towel	ผ้าเช็ดตัว	phâa chét dtua
key	กุญแจ	gun-jae
administrator	นักบริหาร	nák bor-rí-hăan
chambermaid	แม่บ้าน	mâe bâan
porter, bellboy	พนักงาน, ขนกระเป๋า	phá-nák ngaan khŏn grà-bpăo
doorman	พนักงานเปิดประตู	phá-nák ngaan bpèrt bprà-dtoo
restaurant	ร้านอาหาร	ráan aa-hăan
pub, bar	บาร์	baa
breakfast	อาหารเช้า	aa-hăan cháo
dinner	อาหารเย็น	aa-hăan yen
buffet	บุฟเฟ่ต์	bùf-fây
lobby	ล็อบบี้	lórp-bêe
elevator	ลิฟต์	líf
DO NOT DISTURB	ห้ามรบกวน	hâam róp guan
NO SMOKING	ห้ามสูบบุหรี่	hâam sòop bù rèe

132. Books. Reading

book	หนังสือ	năng-sĕu
author	ผู้แต่ง	phôo dtàeng
writer	นักเขียน	nák khĭan
to write (~ a book)	เขียน	khĭan

reader	ผู้อ่าน	phôo àan
to read (vi, vt)	อ่าน	àan
reading (activity)	การอ่าน	gaan àan
silently (to oneself)	อย่างเงียบๆ	yàang ngîap ngîap
aloud (adv)	ออกเสียงดัง	òrk sĭang dang
to publish (vt)	ตีพิมพ์	dtee phim
publishing (process)	การตีพิมพ์	gaan dtee phim
publisher	ผู้พิมพ์	phôo phim
publishing house	สำนักพิมพ์	săm-nák phim
to come out (be released)	ออก	òrk
release (of a book)	การออก	gaan òrk
print run	จำนวน	jam-nuan
bookstore	ร้านหนังสือ	ráan năng-sĕu
library	ห้องสมุด	hông sà-mùt
story (novella)	เรื่องราว	rêuang raao
short story	เรื่องสั้น	rêuang sân
novel	นิยาย	ní-yaai
detective novel	นิยายสืบสวน	ní-yaai sèup sŭan
memoirs	บันทึกความท
รงจำ	ban-théuk khwaam
song jam
legend	ตำนาน	dtam naan
myth	นิทานปรัมปรา	ní-thaan bpram bpraa
poetry, poems	บทกวี	bòt gà-wee
autobiography	อัตชีวประวัติ	àt-chee-wá-bprà-wàt
selected works	งานที่ผ่าน
การคัดเลือก	ngaan thêe phàan
gaan khát lêuak
science fiction	นิยายวิทยาศาสตร์	ní-yaai wít-thá-yaa sàat
title	ชื่อเรื่อง	chêu rêuang
introduction	บทนำ	bòt nam
title page	หน้าแรก	nâa râek
chapter	บท	bòt
extract	ข้อความที่
คัดออกมา	khôr khwaam thêe
khát òk maa
episode	ตอน	dtorn
plot (storyline)	เค้าเรื่อง	kháo rêuang
contents	เนื้อหา	néua hăa
table of contents	สารบัญ	săa-rá-ban
main character	ตัวละครหลัก	dtua lá-khon làk
volume	เล่ม	lêm
cover	ปก	bpòk
binding	สัน	săn

bookmark	ที่คั่นหนังสือ	thêe khân năng-sěu
page	หน้า	nâa
to page through	เปิดผ่านๆ	bpèrt phàan phàan
margins	ระยะขอบ	rá-yá khòrp
annotation (marginal note, etc.)	ความเห็นประกอบ	khwaam hěn bprà-gòp
footnote	เชิงอรรถ	cherng àt-tha

text	บท	bòt
type, font	ตัวพิมพ์	dtua phim
misprint, typo	ความพิมพ์ผิด	khwaam phim phìt

translation	คำแปล	kham bplae
to translate (vt)	แปล	bplae
original (n)	ต้นฉบับ	dtôn chà-bàp

famous (adj)	โด่งดัง	dòhng dang
unknown (not famous)	ไม่เป็นที่รู้จัก	mâi bpen thêe róo jàk
interesting (adj)	น่าสนใจ	nâa sǒn jai
bestseller	ขายดี	khǎai dee

dictionary	พจนานุกรม	phót-jà-naa-nú-grom
textbook	หนังสือเรียน	năng-sěu rian
encyclopedia	สารานุกรม	sǎa-raa-nú-grom

133. Hunting. Fishing

hunting	การล่าสัตว์	gaan lâa sàt
to hunt (vi, vt)	ล่าสัตว์	lâa sàt
hunter	นักล่าสัตว์	nák lâa sàt

to shoot (vi)	ยิง	ying
rifle	ปืนไรเฟิล	bpeun rai-fern
bullet (shell)	กระสุนปืน	grà-sǔn bpeun
shot (lead balls)	กระสุน	grà-sǔn

steel trap	กับดักเหล็ก	gàp dàk lèk
snare (for birds, etc.)	กับดัก	gàp dàk
to fall into the steel trap	ติดกับดัก	dtìt gàp dàk
to lay a steel trap	วางกับดัก	waang gàp dàk

poacher	ผู้ลักลอบล่าสัตว์	phôo lák lôrp lâa sàt
game (in hunting)	สัตว์ที่ถูกล่า	sàt têe thòok lâa
hound dog	หมาล่าเนื้อ	mǎa lâa néua
safari	ซาฟารี	saa-faa-ree
mounted animal	สัตว์สตาฟ	sàt sà-dtàaf

fisherman, angler	คนประมง	khon bprà-mong
fishing (angling)	การจับปลา	gaan jàp bplaa
to fish (vi)	จับปลา	jàp bplaa

fishing rod	คันเบ็ด	khan bèt
fishing line	สายเบ็ด	săai bèt
hook	ตะขอ	dtà-khŏr
float, bobber	ทุ่น	thûn
bait	เหยื่อ	yèua
to cast a line	เหวี่ยงเบ็ด	wìang bèt
to bite (ab. fish)	งับเหยื่อ	ngáp yèua
catch (of fish)	ปลาจับ	bpla jàp
ice-hole	ช่องน้ำแข็ง	chôrng nám khăeng
fishing net	แหจับปลา	hăe jàp bplaa
boat	เรือ	reua
to net (to fish with a net)	จับปลาด้วยแห	jàp bplaa dûay hăe
to cast[throw] the net	เหวี่ยงแห	wìang hăe
to haul the net in	ลากอวน	lâak uan
to fall into the net	ติดแห	dtìt hăe
whaler (person)	นักล่าปลาวาฬ	nák lâa bplaa waan
whaleboat	เรือล่าปลาวาฬ	reua lâa bplaa waan
harpoon	ฉมวก	chà-mùak

134. Games. Billiards

billiards	บิลเลียด	bin-lîat
billiard room, hall	ห้องบิลเลียด	hôrng bin-lîat
ball (snooker, etc.)	ลูก	lôok
to pocket a ball	แทงลูกลงหลุม	thaeng lôok long lŭm
cue	ไม้คิว	máai khiw
pocket	หลุม	lŭm

135. Games. Playing cards

diamonds	ข้าวหลามตัด	khâao lăam dtàt
spades	โพดำ	phoh dam
hearts	โพแดง	phoh daeng
clubs	ดอกจิก	dòrk jìk
ace	เอส	àyt
king	คิง	king
queen	แหม่ม	màem
jack, knave	แจค	jáek
playing card	ไพ่	phâi
cards	ไพ่	phâi
trump	ไต๋	dtăi
deck of cards	สำรับไพ่	săm-ráp phâi

point	แต้ม	dtâem
to deal (vi, vt)	แจกไพ่	jàek phâi
to shuffle (cards)	สับไพ่	sàp phâi
lead, turn (n)	ที	thee
cardsharp	คนโกงไพ่	khon gohng phâi

136. Rest. Games. Miscellaneous

to stroll (vi, vt)	เดินเล่น	dern lên
stroll (leisurely walk)	การเดินเลน	gaan dern lên
car ride	การนั่งรถ	gaan nâng rót
adventure	การผจญภัย	gaan phà-jon phai
picnic	ปิคนิค	bpìk-ník
game (chess, etc.)	เกม	gaym
player	ผู้เล่น	phôo lên
game (one ~ of chess)	เกม	gaym
collector (e.g., philatelist)	นักสะสม	nák sà-sŏm
to collect (stamps, etc.)	สะสม	sà-sŏm
collection	การสะสม	gaan sà-sŏm
crossword puzzle	ปริศนาอักษรไขว้	bprìt-sà-nǎa àk-sŏn khwâi
racetrack (horse racing venue)	ลู่แข่ง	lôo khàeng
disco (discotheque)	ดิสโก้	dít-gôh
sauna	ซาวน่า	saao-nâa
lottery	สลากกินแบ่ง	sà-làak gin bàeng
camping trip	การเดินทาง ตั้งแคมป์	gaan dern thaang dtâng-khaem
camp	แคมป์	khaem
tent (for camping)	เต็นท์	dtáyn
compass	เข็มทิศ	khěm thít
camper	ผู้เดินทาง ตั้งแคมป์	phôo dern thaang dtâng-khaem
to watch (movie, etc.)	ดู	doo
viewer	ผู้ชมทีวี	phôo chom thee wee
TV show (TV program)	รายการทีวี	raai gaan thee wee

137. Photography

camera (photo)	กล้อง	glôrng
photo, picture	ภาพถ่าย	phâap thàai
photographer	ช่างถ่ายภาพ	châang thàai phâap
photo studio	ห้องถ่ายภาพ	hôrng thàai phâap

photo album	อัลบั้มภาพถ่าย	an-bâm phâap-thàai
camera lens	เลนส์กล้อง	len glôrng
telephoto lens	เลนส์ถ่ายไกล	len thàai glai
filter	ฟิลเตอร์	fin-dtêr
lens	เลนส์	len

optics (high-quality ~)	ออปติก	orp-dtìk
diaphragm (aperture)	รูรับแสง	roo ráp sǎeng
exposure time	เวลาในการ	way-laa nai gaan
(shutter speed)	ถ่ายภาพ	thàai phâap
viewfinder	เครื่องจับภาพ	khrêuang jàp phâap

digital camera	กล้องดิจิตอล	glôrng dì-jì-dton
tripod	ขาตั้งกล้อง	khǎa dtâng glông
flash	แฟลช	flâet

to photograph (vt)	ถ่ายภาพ	thàai phâap
to take pictures	ถ่ายภาพ	thàai phâap
to have one's picture taken	ได้รับการ ~	dâai ráp gaan
	ถ่ายภาพให้	thàai phâap hâi

focus	โฟกัส	foh-gát
to focus	โฟกัส	foh-gát
sharp, in focus (adj)	คมชัด	khom chát
sharpness	ความคมชัด	khwaam khom chát

| contrast | ความเปรียบต่าง | khwaam bprìap dtàang |
| contrast (as adj) | เปรียบต่าง | bprìap dtàang |

picture (photo)	ภาพ	phâap
negative (n)	ภาพเนกาทีฟ	phâap nay gaa thêef
film (a roll of ~)	ฟิล์ม	fim
frame (still)	เฟรม	fraym
to print (photos)	พิมพ์	phim

138. Beach. Swimming

beach	ชายหาด	chaai hàat
sand	ทราย	saai
deserted (beach)	ร้าง	ráang

suntan	ผิวคล้ำแดด	phǐw khlám dàet
to get a tan	ตากแดด	dtàak dàet
tan (adj)	มีผิวคล้ำแดด	mee phǐw khlám dàet
sunscreen	ครีมกันแดด	khreem gan dàet

bikini	บิกินี่	bì-gì-nee
bathing suit	ชุดว่ายน้ำ	chút wâai náam
swim trunks	กางเกงว่ายน้ำ	gaang-gayng wâai náam
swimming pool	สระว่ายน้ำ	sà wâai náam

to swim (vi)	ว่ายน้ำ	wâai náam
shower	ฝักบัว	fàk bua
to change (one's clothes)	เปลี่ยนชุด	bplìan chút
towel	ผ้าเช็ดตัว	phâa chét dtua
boat	เรือ	reua
motorboat	เรือยนต์	reua yon
water ski	สกีน้ำ	sà-gee nám
paddle boat	เรือถีบ	reua thèep
surfing	การโต้คลื่น	gaan dtôh khlêun
surfer	นักโต้คลื่น	nák dtôh khlêun
scuba set	อุปกรณ์ดำน้ำ	u-bpà-gon dam náam
flippers (swim fins)	ตีนกบ	dteen gòp
mask (diving ~)	หน้ากากดำน้ำ	nâa gàak dam náam
diver	นักประดาน้ำ	nák bprà-daa náam
to dive (vi)	ดำน้ำ	dam náam
underwater (adv)	ใต้น้ำ	dtâi nám
beach umbrella	ร่มชายหาด	rôm chaai hàat
sunbed (lounger)	เตียงอาบแดด	dtiang àap dàet
sunglasses	แว่นกันแดด	wâen gan dàet
air mattress	ที่นอนเป่าลม	thêe non bpào lom
to play (amuse oneself)	เล่น	lên
to go for a swim	ไปว่ายน้ำ	bpai wâai náam
beach ball	บอล	bon
to inflate (vt)	เติมลม	dterm lom
inflatable, air (adj)	แบบเติมลม	bàep dterm lom
wave	คลื่น	khlêun
buoy (line of ~s)	ทุ่นลอย	thûn loi
to drown (ab. person)	จมน้ำ	jom náam
to save, to rescue	ช่วยชีวิต	chûay chee-wít
life vest	เสื้อชูชีพ	sêua choo chêep
to observe, to watch	สังเกตการณ์	sǎng-gàyt gaan
lifeguard	ไลฟ์การ์ด	lai-gàat

TECHNICAL EQUIPMENT. TRANSPORTATION

Technical equipment

139. Computer

computer	คอมพิวเตอร์	khorm-phiw-dtêr
notebook, laptop	โน้ตบุ๊ค	nóht búk
to turn on	เปิด	bpèrt
to turn off	ปิด	bpìt
keyboard	แป้นพิมพ์	bpâen phim
key	ปุ่ม	bpùm
mouse	เมาส์	mao
mouse pad	แผ่นรองเมาส์	phàen rorng mao
button	ปุ่ม	bpùm
cursor	เคอร์เซอร์	khêr-sêr
monitor	จอมอนิเตอร์	jor mor-ní-dtêr
screen	หน้าจอ	nâa jor
hard disk	ฮาร์ดดิสก์	hâat-dìt
hard disk capacity	ความจุฮาร์ดดิสก์	kwaam jù hâat-dìt
memory	หน่วยความจำ	nùay khwaam jam
random access memory	หน่วยความจำ เขาถึงโดยสุ่ม	nùay khwaam jam khâo thěung doi sùm
file	ไฟล์	fai
folder	โฟลเดอร์	fohl-dêr
to open (vt)	เปิด	bpèrt
to close (vt)	ปิด	bpìt
to save (vt)	บันทึก	ban-théuk
to delete (vt)	ลบ	lóp
to copy (vt)	คัดลอก	khát lôrk
to sort (vt)	จัดเรียง	jàt riang
to transfer (copy)	ทำสำเนา	tham sǎm-nao
program	โปรแกรม	bproh-graem
software	ซอฟต์แวร์	sôf-wae
programmer	นักเขียนโปรแกรม	nák khǐan bproh-graem
to program (vt)	เขียนโปรแกรม	khǐan bproh-graem
hacker	แฮ็กเกอร์	háek-gêr

password	รหัสผ่าน	rá-hàt phàan
virus	ไวรัส	wai-rát
to find, to detect	ตรวจพบ	dtrùat phóp
byte	ไบท์	bai
megabyte	เมกะไบท์	may-gà-bai
data	ข้อมูล	khôr moon
database	ฐานขอมูล	thăan khôr moon
cable (USB, etc.)	สายเคเบิล	săai khay-bêrn
to disconnect (vt)	ตัดการเชื่อมต่อ	dtàt gaan chêuam dtòr
to connect (sth to sth)	เชื่อมต่อ	chêuam dtòr

140. Internet. E-mail

Internet	อินเทอร์เน็ต	in-thêr-nét
browser	เบราวเซอร์	brao-sêr
search engine	โปรแกรมคนหา	bproh-graem khón hăa
provider	ผู้ใหบริการ	phôo hâi bor-rí-gaan
webmaster	เว็บมาสเตอร์	wép-mâat-dtêr
website	เว็บไซต์	wép sai
webpage	เว็บเพจ	wép phâyt
address (e-mail ~)	ที่อยู่	thêe yòo
address book	สมุดที่อยู่	sà-mùt thêe yòo
mailbox	กล่องจดหมายอีเมลล์	glòrng jòt măai ee-mayn
mail	จดหมาย	jòt măai
full (adj)	เต็ม	dtem
message	ข้อความ	khôr khwaam
incoming messages	ขอความขาเข้า	khôr khwaam khăa khâo
outgoing messages	ขอความขาออก	khôr khwaam khăa òrk
sender	ผู้ส่ง	phôo sòng
to send (vt)	ส่ง	sòng
sending (of mail)	การส่ง	gaan sòng
receiver	ผู้รับ	phôo ráp
to receive (vt)	รับ	ráp
correspondence	การติดต่อกัน	gaan dtìt dtòr gan
	ทางจดหมาย	thaang jòt măai
to correspond (vi)	ติดต่อกันทา	dtìt dtòr gan thaang
	งจดหมาย	jòt măai
file	ไฟล์	fai
to download (vt)	ดาวน์โหลด	daao lòht

to create (vt)	สร้าง	sâang
to delete (vt)	ลบ	lóp
deleted (adj)	ถูกลบ	thòok lóp

connection (ADSL, etc.)	การเชื่อมต่อ	gaan chêuam dtòr
speed	ความเร็ว	khwaam reo
modem	โมเด็ม	moh-dem
access	การเข้าถึง	gaan khâo thěung
port (e.g., input ~)	พอรท	phôt

| connection (make a ~) | การเชื่อมต่อ | gaan chêuam dtòr |
| to connect to ... (vi) | เชื่อมต่อกับ... | chêuam dtòr gàp... |

| to select (vt) | เลือก | lêuak |
| to search (for ...) | ค้นหา | khón hăa |

Transportation

141. Airplane

airplane	เครื่องบิน	khrêuang bin
air ticket	ตั๋วเครื่องบิน	dtŭa khrêuang bin
airline	สายการบิน	săai gaan bin
airport	สนามบิน	sà-năam bin
supersonic (adj)	ความเร็วเหนือเสียง	khwaam reo nĕua-sĭang
captain	กัปตัน	gàp dtan
crew	ลูกเรือ	lôok reua
pilot	นักบิน	nák bin
flight attendant (fem.)	พนักงานต้อนรับ บนเครื่องบิน	phá-nák ngaan dtôrn ráp bon khrêuang bin
navigator	ต้นหน	dtôn hŏn
wings	ปีก	bpèek
tail	หาง	hăang
cockpit	ห้องนักบิน	hôrng nák bin
engine	เครื่องยนต์	khrêuang yon
undercarriage (landing gear)	โครงส่วนล่าง ของเครื่องบิน	khrorng sùan lâang khŏrng khrêuang bin
turbine	กังหัน	gang-hăn
propeller	ใบพัด	bai phát
black box	กล่องดำ	glòrng dam
yoke (control column)	คันบังคับ	khan bang-kháp
fuel	เชื้อเพลิง	chéua phlerng
safety card	คู่มือความ ปลอดภัย	khôo meu khwaam bplòt phai
oxygen mask	หน้ากากอ็อกซิเจน	nâa gàak ók sí jayn
uniform	เครื่องแบบ	khrêuang bàep
life vest	เสื้อชูชีพ	sêua choo chêep
parachute	ร่มชูชีพ	rôm choo chêep
takeoff	การบินขึ้น	gaan bin khêun
to take off (vi)	บินขึ้น	bin khêun
runway	ทางวิ่งเครื่องบิน	thaang wîng khrêuang bin
visibility	ทัศนวิสัย	thát sá ná wí-săi
flight (act of flying)	การบิน	gaan bin
altitude	ความสูง	khwaam sŏong
air pocket	หลุมอากาศ	lŭm aa-gàat
seat	ที่นั่ง	thêe nâng

headphones	หูฟัง	hŏo fang
folding tray (tray table)	ถาดพับเก็บได้	thàat pháp gèp dâai
airplane window	หน้าต่างเครื่องบิน	nâa dtàang khrêuang bin
aisle	ทางเดิน	thaang dern

142. Train

train	รถไฟ	rót fai
commuter train	รถไฟชานเมือง	rót fai chaan meuang
express train	รถไฟด่วน	rót fai dùan
diesel locomotive	รถจักรดีเซล	rót jàk dee-sayn
steam locomotive	รถจักรไอน้ำ	rót jàk ai náam

| passenger car | ตู้โดยสาร | dtôo doi săan |
| dining car | ตูเสบียง | dtôo sà-biang |

rails	รางรถไฟ	raang rót fai
railroad	ทางรถไฟ	thaang rót fai
railway tie	หมอนรองราง	mŏrn rorng raang

platform (railway ~)	ชานชลา	chaan-chá-laa
track (~ 1, 2, etc.)	ราง	raang
semaphore	ไฟสัญญาณรถไฟ	fai săn-yaan rót fai
station	สถานี	sà-thăa-nee

engineer (train driver)	คนขับรถไฟ	khon khàp rót fai
porter (of luggage)	พนักงาน,	phá-nák ngaan
	ยกกระเป๋า	yók grà-bpăo
car attendant	พูนักงานรถไฟ	phá-nák ngaan rót fai
passenger	ผู้โดยสาร	phôo doi săan
conductor	พนักงานตรวจตั๋ว	phá-nák ngaan dtrùat dtŭa
(ticket inspector)		

| corridor (in train) | ทางเดิน | thaang dern |
| emergency brake | เบรคฉุกเฉิน | bràyk chùk-chĕrn |

compartment	ตู้นอน	dtôo norn
berth	เตียง	dtiang
upper berth	เตียงบน	dtiang bon
lower berth	เตียงล่าง	dtiang lâang
bed linen, bedding	ชุดเครื่องนอน	chút khrêuang norn

ticket	ตั๋ว	dtŭa
schedule	ตารางเวลา	dtaa-raang way-laa
information display	ฉระดานแสดง	grà daan sà-daeng
	ขอมูล	khôr moon

to leave, to depart	ออกเดินทาง	òrk dern thaang
departure (of train)	การออกเดินทาง	gaan òrk dern thaang
to arrive (ab. train)	มาถึง	maa thĕung

arrival	การมาถึง	gaan maa thĕung
to arrive by train	มาถึงโดยรถไฟ	maa thĕung doi rót fai
to get on the train	ขึ้นรถไฟ	khêun rót fai
to get off the train	ลงจากรถไฟ	long jàak rót fai

| train wreck | รถไฟตกราง | rót fai dtòk raang |
| to derail (vi) | ตกราง | dtòk raang |

steam locomotive	หัวรถจักรไอน้ำ	hŭa rót jàk ai náam
stoker, fireman	คนควบคุมเตาไฟ	khon khûap khum dtao fai
firebox	เตาไฟ	dtao fai
coal	ถ่านหิน	thàan hĭn

143. Ship

| ship | เรือ | reua |
| vessel | เรือ | reua |

steamship	เรือจักรไอน้ำ	reua jàk ai náam
riverboat	เรือลองแมน้ำ	reua lông mâe náam
cruise ship	เรือเดินสมุทร	reua dern sà-mùt
cruiser	เรือลาดตระเวน	reua lâat dtrà-wayn

yacht	เรือยอชต์	reua yôt
tugboat	เรือลากจูง	reua lâak joong
barge	เรือบรรทุก	reua ban-thúk
ferry	เรือขามฟาก	reua khâam fâak

sailing ship	เรือใบ	reua bai
brigantine	เรือใบสอง	reua bai sŏrng
	เสากระโดง	săo grà-dohng

| ice breaker | เรือตัดน้ำแข็ง | reua dtàt náam khăeng |
| submarine | เรือดำน้ำ | reua dam náam |

boat (flat-bottomed ~)	เรือพาย	reua phaai
dinghy	เรือบดเล็ก	reua bòt lék
lifeboat	เรือชูชีพ	reua choo chêep
motorboat	เรือยนต์	reua yon

captain	กัปตัน	gàp dtan
seaman	นาวิน	naa-win
sailor	คนเรือ	khon reua
crew	กะลาสี	gà-laa-sĕe

boatswain	สรั่ง	sà-ràng
ship's boy	คนช่วยงาน	khon chûay ngaan
	ในเรือ	nai reua
cook	กุ๊ก	gúk
ship's doctor	แพทย์เรือ	phâet reua

deck	ดาดฟ้าเรือ	dàat-fáa reua
mast	เสากระโดงเรือ	săo grà-dohng reua
sail	ใบเรือ	bai reua
hold	ท้องเรือ	thórng-reua
bow (prow)	หัวเรือ	hŭa-reua
stern	ท้ายเรือ	tháai reua
oar	ไม้พาย	máai phaai
screw propeller	ใบจักร	bai jàk
cabin	ห้องพัก	hôrng phák
wardroom	ห้องอาหาร	hôrng aa-hăan
engine room	ห้องเครื่องยนต์	hôrng khrêuang yon
bridge	สะพานเดินเรือ	sà-phaan dern reua
radio room	ห้องวิทยุ	hôrng wít-thá-yú
wave (radio)	คลื่นความถี่	khlêun khwaam thèe
logbook	สมุดบันทึก	sà-mùt ban-théuk
spyglass	กล้องส่องทางไกล	glôrng sòrng thaang glai
bell	ระฆัง	rá-khang
flag	ธง	thorng
hawser (mooring ~)	เชือก	chêuak
knot (bowline, etc.)	ปม	bpom
deckrails	ราว	raao
gangway	ไม้พาดให้ขึ้นลงเรือ	mái phâat hâi khêun long reua
anchor	สมอ	sà-mŏr
to weigh anchor	ถอนสมอ	thŏrn sà-mŏr
to drop anchor	ทอดสมอ	thôrt sà-mŏr
anchor chain	โซ่สมอเรือ	sôh sà-mŏr reua
port (harbor)	ท่าเรือ	thâa reua
quay, wharf	ทา	thâa
to berth (moor)	จอดเทียบท่า	jòt thîap tâa
to cast off	ออกจากทา	òrk jàak tâa
trip, voyage	การเดินทาง	gaan dern thaang
cruise (sea trip)	การล่องเรือ	gaan lôrng reua
course (route)	เส้นทาง	sên thaang
route (itinerary)	เส้นทาง	sên thaang
fairway (safe water channel)	ร่องเรือเดิน	rông reua dern
shallows	โขด	khòht
to run aground	เกยตื้น	goie dtêun
storm	พายุ	phaa-yú
signal	สัญญาณ	săn-yaan
to sink (vi)	ลม	lôm

Man overboard!	คนตกเรือ!	kon dtòk reua
SOS (distress signal)	SOS	es-o-es
ring buoy	ห่วงยาง	hùang yaang

144. Airport

airport	สนามบิน	sà-nǎam bin
airplane	เครื่องบิน	khrêuang bin
airline	สายการบิน	sǎai gaan bin
air traffic controller	เจ้าหน้าที่ควบคุม	jâo nâa-thêe khûap khum
	จราจรทางอากาศ	jà-raa-jon thaang aa-gàat
departure	การออกเดินทาง	gaan òrk dern thaang
arrival	การมาถึง	gaan maa thěung
to arrive (by plane)	มาถึง	maa thěung
departure time	เวลาขาไป	way-laa khǎa bpai
arrival time	เวลามาถึง	way-laa maa thěung
to be delayed	ถูกเลื่อน	thòok lêuan
flight delay	เลื่อนเที่ยวบิน	lêuan thieow bin
information board	ฏระดานแสดง	grà daan sà-daeng
	ข้อมูล	khôr moon
information	ข้อมูล	khôr moon
to announce (vt)	ประกาศ	bprà-gàat
flight (e.g., next ~)	เที่ยวบิน	thîeow bin
customs	ศุลกากร	sǔn-lá-gaa-gon
customs officer	เจ้าหน้าที่	jâo nâa-thêe
	ศุลกากร	sǔn-lá-gaa-gon
customs declaration	แบบฟอร์มการเสีย	bàep form gaan sǐa
	ภาษีศุลกากร	phaa-sěe sǔn-lá-gaa-gon
to fill out (vt)	กรอก	gròrk
to fill out the declaration	กรอกแบบฟอร์ม	gròrk bàep form
	การเสียภาษี	gaan sǐa paa-sěe
passport control	จุดตรวจหนังสือ	jùt dtrùat nǎng-sěu
	เดินทาง	dern-thaang
luggage	สัมภาระ	sǎm-phaa-rá
hand luggage	กระเป๋าถือ	grà-bpǎo thěu
luggage cart	รถขนสัมภาระ	rót khǒn sǎm-phaa-rá
landing	การลงจอด	gaan long jòrt
landing strip	ลานบินลงจอด	laan bin long jòrt
to land (vi)	ลงจอด	long jòrt
airstair (passenger stair)	ทางขึ้นลง	thaang khêun long
	เครื่องบิน	khrêuang bin
check-in	การเช็คอิน	gaan chék in

check-in counter	เคาน์เตอร์เช็คอิน	khao-dtêr chék in
to check-in (vi)	เช็คอิน	chék in
boarding pass	บัตรที่นั่ง	bàt thêe nâng
departure gate	ซองเขา	chôrng khâo

transit	การต่อเที่ยวบิน	gaan tòr thîeow bin
to wait (vt)	รอ	ror
departure lounge	ห้องผู้โดยสาร	hôrng phôo doi săan
	ขาออก	khăa òk
to see off	ไปส่ง	bpai sòng
to say goodbye	บอกลา	bòrk laa

145. Bicycle. Motorcycle

bicycle	รถจักรยาน	rót jàk-grà-yaan
scooter	สกูตเตอร์	sà-góot-dtêr
motorcycle, bike	รถมอเตอร์ไซค์	rót mor-dtêr-sai

to go by bicycle	ขี่จักรยาน	khèe jàk-grà-yaan
handlebars	พวงมาลัยรถ	phuang maa-lai rót
pedal	แป้นเหยียบ	bpâen yìap
brakes	เบรก	bràyk
bicycle seat (saddle)	ที่นั่งจักรยาน	thêe nâng jàk-grà-yaan

pump	ปั้ม	bpám
luggage rack	ที่วางสัมภาระ	thêe waang săm-phaa-rá
front lamp	ไฟหน้า	fai nâa
helmet	หมวกนิรภัย	mùak ní-rá-phai

wheel	ล้อ	lór
fender	บังโคลน	bang khlon
rim	ขอบล้อ	khòp lór
spoke	กานล้อ	gâan lór

Cars

146. Types of cars

automobile, car	รถยนต์	rót yon
sports car	รถสปอร์ต	rót sà-bpòt
limousine	รถลีมูซีน	rót lee moo seen
off-road vehicle	รถเอสยูวี	rót àyt yoo wee
convertible (n)	รถยนต์เปิดประทุน	rót yon bpèrt bprà-thun
minibus	รถบัสเล็ก	rót bàt lék
ambulance	รถพยาบาล	rót phá-yaa-baan
snowplow	รถไถหิมะ	rót thǎi hì-má
truck	รถบรรทุก	rót ban-thúk
tanker truck	รถบรรทุกน้ำมัน	rót ban-thúk nám man
van (small truck)	รถตู้	rót dtôo
road tractor (trailer truck)	รถลาก	rót lâak
trailer	รถพ่วง	rót phûang
comfortable (adj)	สะดวก	sà-dùak
used (adj)	มือสอง	meu sǒrng

147. Cars. Bodywork

hood	กระโปรงรถ	grà bprohng rót
fender	บังโคลน	bang khlon
roof	หลังคา	lǎng khaa
windshield	กระจกหน้ารถ	grà-jòk nâa rót
rear-view mirror	กระจกมองหลัง	grà-jòk morng lǎng
windshield washer	ที่ฉีดน้ำลวง	thêe chèet nám
	กระจกหนารถ	láang grà-jòk nâa rót
windshield wipers	ที่ปัดล้างกระจก	thêe bpàt láang grà-jòk
	หน้ารถ	nâa rót
side window	กระจกข้าง	grà-jòk khâang
window lift (power window)	กระจกไฟฟ้า	grà-jòk fai-fáa
antenna	เสาอากาศ	sǎo aa-gàat
sunroof	หลังคารับแดด	lǎng khaa ráp dàet
bumper	กันชน	gan chon
trunk	ท้ายรถ	tháai rót

roof luggage rack	ชั้นวางสัมภาระ	chán waang săm-phaa-rá
door	ประตู	bprà-dtoo
door handle	ที่เปิดประตู	thêe bpèrt bprà-dtoo
door lock	ล็อคประตูรถ	lók bprà-dtoo rót

license plate	ป้ายทะเบียน	bpâai thá-bian
muffler	ท่อไอเสีย	thôr ai sĭa
gas tank	ถังน้ำมัน	thăng náam man
tailpipe	ท่อไอเสีย	thôr ai sĭa

gas, accelerator	เร่ง	râyng
pedal	แป้นเหยียบ	bpâen yìap
gas pedal	คันเร่ง	khan râyng

brake	เบรก	bràyk
brake pedal	แป้นเบรค	bpâen bràyk
to brake (use the brake)	เบรก	bràyk
parking brake	เบรกมือ	bràyk meu

clutch	คลัตช์	khlát
clutch pedal	แป้นคลัตช์	bpâen khlát
clutch disc	จวนคลัตช์	jaan khlát
shock absorber	โชคอัพ	chóhk-àp

wheel	ล้อ	lór
spare tire	ลอสำรอง	lór săm-rorng
tire	ยางรถ	yaang rót
hubcap	ลอแม็ก	lór-máek

driving wheels	ล้อพวงมาลัย	lór phuang maa-lai
front-wheel drive (as adj)	ขับเคลื่อนลูอหน้า	khàp khlêuan lór nâa
rear-wheel drive (as adj)	ขับเคลื่อนลูอหลัง	khàp khlêuan lór lăng
all-wheel drive (as adj)	ขับเคลื่อนสี่ลอ	khàp khlêuan sèe lór

| gearbox | กระปุกเกียร์ | grà-bpùk gia |
| automatic (adj) | อัตโนมัติ | àt-noh-mát |

| mechanical (adj) | กลไก | gon-gai |
| gear shift | คันเกียร์ | khan gia |

| headlight | ไฟหน้า | fai nâa |
| headlights | ไฟหน้า | fai nâa |

low beam	ไฟต่ำ	fai dtàm
high beam	ไฟสูง	fai sŏong
brake light	ไฟเบรก	fai bràyk

parking lights	ไฟจอดรถ	fai jòt rót
hazard lights	ไฟฉุกเฉิน	fai chùk-chĕrn
fog lights	ไฟตัดหมอก	fai dtàt mòk
turn signal	ไฟเลี้ยว	fai líeow
back-up light	ไฟรถถอย	fai rót thŏi

148. Cars. Passenger compartment

car inside (interior)	ภายในรถ	phaai nai rót
leather (as adj)	หนัง	năng
velour (as adj)	กำมะหยี่	gam-má-yèe
upholstery	เครื่องเบาะ	khrêuang bòr
instrument (gage)	อุปกรณ์	ù-bpà-gon
dashboard	แผงหน้าปัด	phăeng nâa bpàt
speedometer	มาตรวัดความเร็ว	mâat wát khwaam reo
needle (pointer)	เข็มชี้วัด	khĕm chée wát
odometer	มิเตอร์วัดระยะทาง	mí-dtêr wát rá-yá thaang
indicator (sensor)	มิเตอร์วัด	mí-dtêr wát
level	ระดับ	rá-dàp
warning light	ไฟเตือน	fai dteuan
steering wheel	พวงมาลัยรถ	phuang maa-lai rót
horn	แตร	dtrae
button	ปุ่ม	bpùm
switch	สวิตช์	sà-wít
seat	ที่นั่ง	thêe nâng
backrest	พนักพิง	phá-nák phing
headrest	ที่พิงศีรษะ	thêe phing sĕe-sà
seat belt	เข็มขัดนิรภัย	khĕm khàt ní-rá-phai
to fasten the belt	คาดเข็มขัดนิรภัย	khâat khĕm khàt ní-rá-phai
adjustment (of seats)	การปรับ	gaan bpràp
airbag	ถุงลมนิรภัย	thŭng lom ní-rá-phai
air-conditioner	เครื่องปรับอากาศ	khrêuang bpràp-aa-gàat
radio	วิทยุ	wít-thá-yú
CD player	เครื่องเล่น CD	khrêuang lên see-dee
to turn on	เปิด	bpèrt
antenna	เสาอากาศ	săo aa-gàat
glove box	ชองเก็บของ	chôrng gèp khŏrng
	ขางคนขับ	khâang khon khàp
ashtray	ที่เขี่ยบุหรี่	thêe khìa bù rèe

149. Cars. Engine

engine	เครื่องยนต์	khrêuang yon
motor	มอเตอร	mor-dtêr
diesel (as adj)	ดีเซล	dee-sayn
gasoline (as adj)	น้ำมันเบนซิน	nám man bayn-sin
engine volume	ขนาดเครื่องยนต์	khà-nàat khrêuang yon
power	กำลัง	gam-lang

horsepower	แรงม้า	raeng máa
piston	ก้านลูกสูบ	gâan lôok sòop
cylinder	กระบอกสูบ	grà-bòrk sòop
valve	วาลว	waao

injector	หัวฉีด	hǔa chèet
generator (alternator)	เครื่องกำเนิดไฟฟ้า	khrêuang gam-nèrt fai fáa
carburetor	คาร์บูเรเตอร์	khaa-boo-ray-dtêr
motor oil	น้ำมันเครื่อง	nám man khrêuang

radiator	หม้อน้ำ	môr náam
coolant	สารทำความเย็น	sǎan tham khwaam yen
cooling fan	พัดลมระบาย ความร้อน	phát lom rá-baai khwaam rón

battery (accumulator)	แบตเตอรี่	bàet-dter-rêe
starter	มอเตอรสตาร์ต	mor-dtêr sà-dtàat
ignition	การจุดระเบิด	gaan jùt rá-bèrt
spark plug	หัวเทียน	hǔa thian

terminal (of battery)	ขั้วแบตเตอรี่	khûa bàet-dter-rêe
positive terminal	ขั้วบวก	khûa bùak
negative terminal	ขั้วลบ	khûa lóp
fuse	ฟิวส์	fiw

air filter	เครื่องกรองอากาศ	khrêuang grorng aa-gàat
oil filter	ไส้กรองน้ำมัน	sâi grorng nám man
fuel filter	ไส้กรองน้ำมัน เชื้อเพลิง	sâi grorng nám man chéua phlerng

150. Cars. Crash. Repair

car crash	อุบัติเหตุรถชน	u-bàt hàyt rót chon
traffic accident	อุบัติเหตุจราจร	u-bàt hàyt jà-raa-jon
to crash (into the wall, etc.)	ชน	chon

to get smashed up	ชนโครม	chon khrohm
damage	ความเสียหาย	khwaam sǐa hǎai
intact (unscathed)	ไม่มีความเสียหาย	mâi mee khwaam sǐa hǎai

breakdown	การเสีย	gaan sǐa
to break down (vi)	ตาย	dtaai
towrope	เชือกลากรถยนต์	chêuak lâak rót yon

puncture	ยางรั่ว	yaang rûa
to be flat	ทำให้ยางแบน	tham hâi yaang baen
to pump up	เติมลมยาง	dterm lom yaang
pressure	แรงดัน	raeng dan
to check (to examine)	ตรวจสอบ	dtrùat sòrp
repair	การซ่อม	gaan sôrm

auto repair shop	ร้านซ่อมรถยนต์	ráan sôrm rót yon
spare part	อะไหล่	a lài
part	ชิ้นส่วน	chín sùan
bolt (with nut)	สลักเกลียว	sà-làk glieow
screw (fastener)	สกรู	sà-groo
nut	แหวนสกรู	wăen sà-groo
washer	แหวนเล็ก	wăen lék
bearing (e.g., ball ~)	แบริง	bae-ring
tube	ท่อ	thôr
gasket (head ~)	ปะเก็น	bpà gen
cable, wire	สายไฟ	săai fai
jack	แม่แรง	mâe raeng
wrench	ปูระแจ	bprà-jae
hammer	ค้อน	khórn
pump	ปั๊ม	bpám
screwdriver	ไขควง	khăi khuang
fire extinguisher	ถังดับเพลิง	thăng dàp phlerng
warning triangle	ป้ายเตือน	bpâai dteuan
to stall (vi)	มีเครื่องดับ	mee khrêuang dàp
stall (n)	การดับ	gaan dàp
to be broken	เสีย	sĭa
to overheat (vi)	ร้อนเกิน	rórn gern
to be clogged up	อุดตัน	ùt dtan
to freeze up (pipes, etc.)	เยือกแข็ง	yêuak khăeng
to burst (vi, ab. tube)	แตก	dtàek
pressure	แรงดัน	raeng dan
level	ระดับ	rá-dàp
slack (~ belt)	อ่อน	òrn
dent	รอยบุบ	roi bùp
knocking noise (engine)	เสียงเครื่องยนต์ดับ	sĭang khrêuang yon dàp
crack	รอยแตก	roi dtàek
scratch	รอยขูด	roi khòot

151. Cars. Road

road	ถนน	thà-nŏn
highway	ทางหลวง	thaang lŭang
freeway	ทางด่วน	thaang dùan
direction (way)	ทิศทาง	thít thaang
distance	ระยะทาง	rá-yá thaang
bridge	สะพาน	sà-phaan
parking lot	ลานจอดรถ	laan jòrt rót

square	จัตุรัส	jàt-dtù-ràt
interchange	ทางแยกต่างระดับ	thaang yâek dtàang rá-dàp
tunnel	อุโมงค์	u-mohng
gas station	ปั๊มน้ำมัน	bpám náam man
parking lot	ลานจอดรถ	laan jòrt rót
gas pump (fuel dispenser)	ที่เติมน้ำมัน	thêe dterm náam man
auto repair shop	รานซ่อมรถยนต์	ráan sôrm rót yon
to get gas (to fill up)	เติมน้ำมัน	dterm náam man
fuel	น้ำมันเชื้อเพลิง	nám man chéua phlerng
jerrycan	ถังน้ำมัน	thăng náam man
asphalt	ถนนลาดยาง	thà-nŏn lâat yaang
road markings	เครื่องหมายจราจร บนพื้นทาง	khrêuang măai jà-raa-jon bon phéun thaang
curb	ขอบถนน	khòrp thà-nŏn
guardrail	รั้วกั้น	rúa gân
ditch	คู	khoo
roadside (shoulder)	ข้างถนน	khâang thà-nŏn
lamppost	เสาไฟ	săo fai
to drive (a car)	ขับ	khàp
to turn (e.g., ~ left)	เลี้ยว	líeow
to make a U-turn	กลับรถ	glàp rót
reverse (~ gear)	ถอยรถ	thŏri rót
to honk (vi)	บีบแตร	bèep dtrae
honk (sound)	เสียงบีบแตร	sĭang bèep dtrae
to get stuck (in the mud, etc.)	ติด	dtìt
to spin the wheels	หมุนล้อ	mŭn lór
to cut, to turn off (vt)	ปิด	bpìt
speed	ความเร็ว	khwaam reo
to exceed the speed limit	ขับเร็วเกิน	khàp reo gern
to give a ticket	ให้ใบสั่ง	hâi bai sàng
traffic lights	ไฟสัญญาณจราจร	fai săn-yaan jà-raa-jon
driver's license	ใบขับขี่	bai khàp khèe
grade crossing	ทางข้ามรถไฟ	thaang khâam rót fai
intersection	สี่แยก	sèe yâek
crosswalk	ทางม้าลาย	thaang máa laai
bend, curve	ทางโค้ง	thaang khóhng
pedestrian zone	ถนนคนเดิน	thà-nŏn khon dern

PEOPLE. LIFE EVENTS

Life events

152. Holidays. Event

celebration, holiday	วันหยุดเฉลิมฉลอง	wan yùt chà-lĕrm chà-lŏng
national day	วันชาติ	wan châat
public holiday	วันหยุดนักขัตฤกษ์	wan yùt nák-kàt-rêrk
to commemorate (vt)	เฉลิมฉลอง	chà-lĕrm chà-lŏrng

event (happening)	เหตุการณ์	hàyt gaan
event (organized activity)	งานอีเวนต์	ngaan ee wayn
banquet (party)	งานเลี้ยง	ngaan líang
reception (formal party)	งานเลี้ยง	ngaan líang
feast	งานฉลอง	ngaan chà-lŏrng

anniversary	วันครบรอบ	wan khróp rôrp
jubilee	วันครบรอบปี	wan khróp rôrp bpee
to celebrate (vt)	ฉลอง	chà-lŏrng

New Year	ปีใหม่	bpee mài
Happy New Year!	สวัสดีปีใหม่!	sà-wàt-dee bpee mài
Santa Claus	ซานตาคลอส	saan-dtaa-khlôrt

Christmas	คริสต์มาส	khrít-mâat
Merry Christmas!	สุขสันต์วันคริสต์มาส	sùk-săn wan khrít-mâat
Christmas tree	ต้นคริสต์มาส	dtôn khrít-mâat
fireworks (fireworks show)	ดอกไม้ไฟ	dòrk máai fai

wedding	งานแต่งงาน	ngaan dtàeng ngaan
groom	เจ้าบ่าว	jâo bàao
bride	เจ้าสาว	jâo săao

| to invite (vt) | เชิญ | chern |
| invitation card | บัตรเชิญ | bàt chern |

guest	แขก	khàek
to visit	ไปเยี่ยม	bpai yîam
(~ your parents, etc.)		
to meet the guests	ตอนรับแขก	dton ráp khàek

gift, present	ของขวัญ	khŏrng khwăn
to give (sth as present)	ให้	hâi
to receive gifts	รับของขวัญ	ráp khŏrng khwăn

bouquet (of flowers)	ช่อดอกไม้	chôr dòrk máai
congratulations	คำแสดง	kham sà-daeng
	ความยินดี	khwaam yin-dee
to congratulate (vt)	แสดงความยินดี	sà-daeng khwaam yin dee

greeting card	บัตรอวยพร	bàt uay phon
to send a postcard	ส่งโปสการ์ด	sòng bpòht-gàat
to get a postcard	รับโปสการ์ด	ráp bpòht-gàat

toast	ดื่มอวยพร	dèum uay phon
to offer (a drink, etc.)	เลี้ยงเครื่องดื่ม	líang khrêuang dèum
champagne	แชมเปญ	chaem-bpayn

to enjoy oneself	มีความสุข	mee khwaam sùk
merriment (gaiety)	ความรื่นเริง	khwaam rêun-rerng
joy (emotion)	ความสุขสันต์	khwaam sùk-sǎn

| dance | การเต้น | gaan dtên |
| to dance (vi, vt) | เต้น | dtên |

| waltz | วอลทซ์ | wɔ:lts |
| tango | แทงโก้ | thaeng-gôh |

153. Funerals. Burial

cemetery	สุสาน	sù-sǎan
grave, tomb	หลุมศพ	lǔm sòp
cross	ไม้กางเขน	máai gaang khǎyn
gravestone	ป้ายหลุมศพ	bpâai lǔm sòp
fence	รั้ว	rúa
chapel	โรงสวด	rohng sùat

death	ความตาย	khwaam dtaai
to die (vi)	ตาย	dtaai
the deceased	ผู้เสียชีวิต	phôo sǐa chee-wít
mourning	การไว้อาลัย	gaan wái aa-lai

to bury (vt)	ฝังศพ	fǎng sòp
funeral home	บริษัทรับ	bor-rí-sàt ráp
	จัดงานศพ	jàt ngaan sòp
funeral	งานศพ	ngaan sòp

wreath	พวงหรีด	phuang rèet
casket, coffin	โลงศพ	lohng sòp
hearse	รถขนศพ	rót khǒn sòp
shroud	ผ้าห่อศพ	phâa hòr sòp

funeral procession	พิธีศพ	phí-tee sòp
funerary urn	โกศ	gòht
crematory	เมรุ	mayn

obituary	ข่าวมรณกรรม	khàao mor-rá-ná-gam
to cry (weep)	ร้องไห้	rórng hâi
to sob (vi)	สะอื้น	sà-êun

154. War. Soldiers

platoon	หมวด	mùat
company	กองร้อย	gorng rói
regiment	กรม	grom
army	กองทัพ	gorng tháp
division	กองพล	gorng phon-la

| section, squad | หมู่ | mòo |
| host (army) | กองทัพ | gorng tháp |

| soldier | ทหาร | thá-hǎan |
| officer | นายทหาร | naai thá-hǎan |

private	พลทหาร	phon-thá-hǎan
sergeant	สิบเอก	sìp àyk
lieutenant	ร้อยโท	rói thoh
captain	ร้อยเอก	rói àyk
major	พลตรี	phon-dtree
colonel	พันเอก	phan àyk
general	นายพล	naai phon

sailor	กะลาสี	gà-laa-sěe
captain	กัปตัน	gàp dtan
boatswain	สรั่งเรือ	sà-ràng reua

artilleryman	ทหารปืนใหญ่	thá-hǎan bpeun yài
paratrooper	พลร่ม	phon-rôm
pilot	นักบิน	nák bin
navigator	ต้นหน	dtôn hǒn
mechanic	ช่างเครื่อง	châang khrêuang

pioneer (sapper)	ทหารช่าง	thá-hǎan châang
parachutist	ทหารราบอากาศ	thá-hǎan râap aa-gàat
reconnaissance scout	ทหารพราน	thá-hǎan phraan
sniper	พลซุ่มยิง	phon sûm ying

patrol (group)	หน่วยลาดตระเวน	nùay lâat dtrà-wayn
to patrol (vt)	ลาดตระเวน	lâat dtrà-wayn
sentry, guard	ทหารยาม	tá-hǎan yaam

warrior	นักรบ	nák róp
patriot	ผู้รักชาติ	phôo rák châat
hero	วีรบุรุษ	wee-rá-bù-rùt
heroine	วีรสตรี	wee rá-sot dtree
traitor	ผู้ทรยศ	phôo thor-rá-yót

to betray (vt)	ทรยศ	thor-rá-yót
deserter	ทหารหนีทัพ	thá-hǎan něe tháp
to desert (vi)	หนีทัพ	něe tháp

mercenary	ทหารรับจ้าง	thá-hǎan ráp jâang
recruit	เกณฑ์ทหาร	gayn thá-hǎan
volunteer	อาสาสมัคร	aa-sǎa sà-màk

dead (n)	คนถูกฆ่า	khon thòok khâa
wounded (n)	ผู้ได้รับบาดเจ็บ	phôo dâai ráp bàat jèp
prisoner of war	เชลยศึก	chá-loie sèuk

155. War. Military actions. Part 1

war	สงคราม	sǒng-khraam
to be at war	ทำสงคราม	tham sǒng-khraam
civil war	สงคราม กลางเมือง	sǒng-khraam glaang-meuang

treacherously (adv)	ตลบตะแลง	dtà-lòp-dtà-laeng
declaration of war	การประกาศ สงคราม	gaan bprà-gàat sǒng-khraam
to declare (~ war)	ประกาศสงคราม	bprà-gàat sǒng-khraam
aggression	การรุกราน	gaan rúk-raan
to attack (invade)	บุกรุก	bùk rúk

to invade (vt)	บุกรุก	bùk rúk
invader	ผู้บุกรุก	phôo bùk rúk
conqueror	ผู้ยึดครอง	phôo yéut khrorng

defense	การป้องกัน	gaan bpôrng gan
to defend (a country, etc.)	ปกป้อง	bpòk bpôrng
to defend (against ...)	ป้องกัน	bpôrng gan

enemy	ศัตรู	sàt-dtroo
foe, adversary	ข้าศึก	khâa sèuk
enemy (as adj)	ศัตรู	sàt-dtroo

| strategy | ยุทธศาสตร์ | yút-thá-sàat |
| tactics | ยุทธวิธี | yút-thá-wí-thee |

order	คำสั่ง	kham sàng
command (order)	คำบัญชาการ	kham ban-chaa gaan
to order (vt)	สั่ง	sàng
mission	ภารกิจ	phaa-rá-gìt
secret (adj)	อย่างลับ	yàang láp

battle, combat	การรบ	gaan róp
attack	การจู่โจม	gaan jòo johm
charge (assault)	การเข้าจู่โจม	gaan khâo jòo johm

to storm (vt)	บุกจู่โจม	bùk jòo johm
siege (to be under ~)	การโอบล้อมโจมตี	gaan òhp lóm johm dtee
offensive (n)	การโจมตี	gaan johm dtee
to go on the offensive	โจมตี	johm dtee
retreat	การถอย	gaan thŏi
to retreat (vi)	ถอย	thŏi
encirclement	การปิดล้อม	gaan bpìt lórm
to encircle (vt)	ปิดล้อม	bpìt lórm
bombing (by aircraft)	การทิ้งระเบิด	gaan thíng rá-bèrt
to drop a bomb	ทิ้งระเบิด	thíng rá-bèrt
to bomb (vt)	ทิ้งระเบิด	thíng rá-bèrt
explosion	การระเบิด	gaan rá-bèrt
shot	การยิง	gaan ying
to fire (~ a shot)	ยิง	ying
firing (burst of ~)	การยิง	gaan ying
to aim (to point a weapon)	เล็ง	leng
to point (a gun)	ชี้	chée
to hit (the target)	ถูกเป้าหมาย	thòok bpâo măai
to sink (~ a ship)	จม	jom
hole (in a ship)	รู	roo
to founder, to sink (vi)	จม	jom
front (war ~)	แนวหน้า	naew nâa
evacuation	การอพยพ	gaan òp-phá-yóp
to evacuate (vt)	อพยพ	òp-phá-yóp
trench	สนามเพลาะ	sà-năam phlór
barbwire	ลวดหนาม	lûat năam
barrier (anti tank ~)	สิ่งกีดขวาง	sìng gèet-khwăang
watchtower	หอสังเกตการณ์	hŏr săng-gàyt gaan
military hospital	โรงพยาบาล	rohng phá-yaa-baan
	ทหาร	thá-hăan
to wound (vt)	ทำให้บาดเจ็บ	tham hâi bàat jèp
wound	แผล	phlăe
wounded (n)	ผู้ได้รับบาดเจ็บ	phôo dâai ráp bàat jèp
to be wounded	ได้รับบาดเจ็บ	dâai ráp bàat jèp
serious (wound)	รายแรง	ráai raeng

156. Weapons

weapons	อาวุธ	aa-wút
firearms	อาวุธปืน	aa-wút bpeun

cold weapons (knives, etc.)	อาวุธเย็น	aa-wút yen
chemical weapons	อาวุธเคมี	aa-wút khay-mee
nuclear (adj)	นิวเคลียร์	niw-khlia
nuclear weapons	อาวุธนิวเคลียร์	aa-wút niw-khlia
bomb	ลูกระเบิด	lôok rá-bèrt
atomic bomb	ลูกระเบิดปรมาณู	lôok rá-bèrt bpà-rá-maa-noo
pistol (gun)	ปืนพก	bpeun phók
rifle	ปืนไรเฟิล	bpeun rai-fern
submachine gun	ปืนกลมือ	bpeun gon meu
machine gun	ปืนกล	bpeun gon
muzzle	ปากประบอกปืน	bpàak bprà bòrk bpeun
barrel	ลำกลอง	lam glôrng
caliber	ขนาดลำกล้อง	khà-nàat lam glôrng
trigger	ไกปืน	gai bpeun
sight (aiming device)	ศูนย์เล็ง	sǒon leng
magazine	แม็กกาซีน	máek-gaa-seen
butt (shoulder stock)	พานท้ายปืน	phaan tháai bpeun
hand grenade	ระเบิดมือ	rá-bèrt meu
explosive	วัตถุระเบิด	wát-thù rá-bèrt
bullet	ลูกกระสุน	lôok grà-sǔn
cartridge	ตลับกระสุน	dtà-làp grà-sǔn
charge	กระสุน	grà-sǔn
ammunition	อาวุธยุทธภัณฑ์	aa-wút yút-thá-phan
bomber (aircraft)	เครื่องบินทิ้งระเบิด	khrêuang bin thíng rá-bèrt
fighter	เครื่องบินขับไล่	khrêuang bin khàp lâi
helicopter	เฮลิคอปเตอร์	hay-lí-khôrp-dtêr
anti-aircraft gun	ปืนต่อสู้อากาศยาน	bpeun dtòr sôo aa-gàat-sà-yaan
tank	รถถัง	rót thǎng
tank gun	ปืนรถถัง	bpeun rót thǎng
artillery	ปืนใหญ่	bpeun yài
gun (cannon, howitzer)	ปืน	bpeun
to lay (a gun)	เล็งเป้าปืน	leng bpâo bpeun
shell (projectile)	กระสุน	grà-sǔn
mortar bomb	กระสุนปืนครก	grà-sǔn bpeun khrók
mortar	ปืนครก	bpeun khrók
splinter (shell fragment)	สะเก็ดระเบิด	sà-gèt rá-bèrt
submarine	เรือดำน้ำ	reua dam náam
torpedo	ตอร์ปิโต	dtor-bpì-doh

missile	ขีปนาวุธ	khĕe-bpà-naa-wút
to load (gun)	ใส่กระสุน	sài grà-sŭn
to shoot (vi)	ยิง	ying
to point at (the cannon)	เล็ง	leng
bayonet	ดาบปลายปืน	dàap bplaai bpeun

rapier	เรเปียร์	ray-bpia
saber (e.g., cavalry ~)	ดาบโค้ง	dàap khóhng
spear (weapon)	หอก	hòrk
bow	ธนู	thá-noo
arrow	ลูกธนู	lôok-thá-noo
musket	ปืนคาบศิลา	bpeun khâap sì-laa
crossbow	หน้าไม้	nâa máai

157. Ancient people

primitive (prehistoric)	แบบดั้งเดิม	bàep dâng derm
prehistoric (adj)	ยุคก่อนประวัติศาสตร์	yúk gòn bprà-wàt sàat
ancient (~ civilization)	โบราณ	boh-raan

Stone Age	ยุคหิน	yúk hĭn
Bronze Age	ยุคสำริด	yúk săm-rít
Ice Age	ยุคน้ำแข็ง	yúk nám khăeng

tribe	เผ่า	phào
cannibal	ผู้ที่กินเนื้อคน	phôo thêe gin néua khon
hunter	นักล่าสัตว์	nák lâa sàt
to hunt (vi, vt)	ล่าสัตว์	lâa sàt
mammoth	ช้างแมมมอธ	cháang-maem-môt

cave	ถ้ำ	thâm
fire	ไฟ	fai
campfire	กองไฟ	gorng fai
cave painting	ภาพวาดในถ้ำ	phâap-wâat nai thâm

tool (e.g., stone ax)	เครื่องมือ	khrêuang meu
spear	หอก	hòrk
stone ax	ขวานหิน	khwăan hĭn
to be at war	ทำสงคราม	tham sŏng-khraam
to domesticate (vt)	เชื่อง	chêuang

idol	เทวรูป	theu-rôop
to worship (vt)	บูชา	boo-chaa
superstition	ความเชื่องมงาย	khwaam chêua ngom-ngaai
rite	พิธีกรรม	phí-thee gam

evolution	วิวัฒนาการ	wí-wát-thá-naa-gaan
development	การพัฒนา	gaan phát-thá-naa
disappearance (extinction)	การสูญพันธุ์	gaan sŏon phan

to adapt oneself	ปรับตัว	bpràp dtua
archeology	โบราณคดี	boh-raan khá-dee
archeologist	นักโบราณคดี	nák boh-raan-ná-khá-dee
archeological (adj)	ทางโบราณคดี	thaang boh-raan khá-dee
excavation site	แหล่งขุดค้น	làeng khùt khón
excavations	การขุดคน	gaan khùt khón
find (object)	สิ่งที่คูนพบ	sìng thêe khón phóp
fragment	เศษชิ้นสวน	sàyt chín sùan

158. Middle Ages

people (ethnic group)	ชาติพันธุ์	châat-dtì-phan
peoples	ชุติพันธุ์	châat-dtì-phan
tribe	เผา	phào
tribes	เผา	phào
barbarians	อนารยชน	à-naa-rá-yá-chon
Gauls	ชาวโกล	chaao gloh
Goths	ชาวกอธ	chaao gòt
Slavs	ชาวสลาฟ	chaao sà-làaf
Vikings	ชาวไวกิ้ง	chaao wai-gîng
Romans	ชาวโรมัน	chaao roh-man
Roman (adj)	โรมัน	roh-man
Byzantines	ชาวไบแซนไทน์	chaao bai-saen-tpai
Byzantium	ไบแซนเทียม	bai-saen-thiam
Byzantine (adj)	ไบแซนไทน์	bai-saen-thai
emperor	จักรพรรดิ	jàk-grà-phát
leader, chief (tribal ~)	ผู้นำ	phôo nam
powerful (~ king)	ทรงพลัง	song phá-lang
king	มูหากษัตริย์	má-hǎa gà-sàt
ruler (sovereign)	ผู้ปกครอง	phôo bpòk khrorng
knight	อัศวิน	àt-sà-win
feudal lord	เจาครองนคร	jâo khrorng ná-khon
feudal (adj)	ระบบศักดินา	rá-bòp sàk-gà-dì naa
vassal	เจ้าของที่ดิน	jâo khǒrng thêe din
duke	ดยุค	dà-yúk
earl	เอิร์ล	ern
baron	บารอน	baa-rorn
bishop	พระบิชอป	phrá bì-chôp
armor	เกราะ	gròr
shield	โล	lôh
sword	ดาบ	dàap
visor	กะบังหน้าของหมวก	gà-bang nâa khǒrng mùak

chainmail	เสื้อเกราะถัก	sêua gròr thàk
Crusade	สงครามครูเสด	sŏng-khraam khroo-sàyt
crusader	ผู้ทำสงคราม ศาสนา	phôo tham sŏng-kraam sàat-sà-năa

territory	อาณาเขต	aa-naa khàyt
to attack (invade)	โจมตี	johm dtee
to conquer (vt)	ยึดครอง	yéut khrorng
to occupy (invade)	บุกยึด	bùk yéut

siege (to be under ~)	การโอบล้อมโจมตี	gaan òhp lóm johm dtee
besieged (adj)	ถูกล้อมกรอบ	thòok lóm gròp
to besiege (vt)	ล้อมโจมตี	lóm johm dtee

inquisition	การไต่สวน	gaan dtài sŭan
inquisitor	ผู้ไต่สวน	phôo dtài sŭan
torture	การทูรมาน	gaan thor-rá-maan
cruel (adj)	โหดร้าย	hòht ráai
heretic	ผู้นอกรีต	phôo nôrk rêet
heresy	ความนอกรีต	khwaam nôrk rêet

seafaring	การเดินเรือทะเล	gaan dern reua thá-lay
pirate	โจรสลัด	john sà-làt
piracy	การปล้นสะดม ในนานน้ำทะเล	gaan bplôn-sà-dom nai nâan náam thá-lay
boarding (attack)	การบุกขึ้นเรือ	gaan bùk khêun reua
loot, booty	ของที่ปล้น สะดมมา	khŏrng têe bplôn-sà-dom maa
treasures	สมบัติ	sŏm-bàt

discovery	การค้นพบ	gaan khón phóp
to discover (new land, etc.)	คนพบ	khón phóp
expedition	การสำรวจ	gaan săm-rùat

musketeer	ทหารถือ ปืนคาบศิลา	thá-hăan thĕu bpeun khâap sì-laa
cardinal	พระคาร์ดินัล	phrá khaa-dì-nan
heraldry	มุทราศาสตร์	mút-raa sàat
heraldic (adj)	ทางมุทราศาสตร์	thaang mút-raa sàat

159. Leader. Chief. Authorities

king	ราชา	raa-chaa
queen	ราชินี	raa-chí-nee
royal (adj)	เกี่ยวกับราชวงศ์	gìeow gàp râat-cha-wong
kingdom	ราชอาณาจักร	râat aa-naa jàk

prince	เจ้าชาย	jâo chaai
princess	เจาหญิง	jâo yĭng
president	ประธานาธิบดี	bprà-thaa-naa-thí-bor-dee

vice-president	รองประธา นาธิบดี	rorng bprà-thaa-naa-thí-bor-dee
senator	สมาชิกวุฒิสภา	sà-maa-chík wút-thí sà-phaa
monarch	กษัตริย์	gà-sàt
ruler (sovereign)	ผู้ปกครอง	phôo bpòk khrorng
dictator	เผด็จการ	phà-dèt gaan
tyrant	ทูรราช	thor-rá-râat
magnate	ผู้มีอิทธิ พลสูง	phôo mee ìt-thí phon sŏong
director	ผู้อำนวยการ	phôo am-nuay gaan
chief	หัวหน้า	hŭa-nâa
manager (director)	ผู้จัดการ	phôo jàt gaan
boss	หัวหน้า	hŭa-nâa
owner	เจาของ	jâo khŏrng
leader	ผู้นำ	phôo nam
head (~ of delegation)	หัวหน้า	hŭa-nâa
authorities	เจาหน้าที่	jâo nâa-thêe
superiors	ผู้บังคับบัญชา	phôo bang-kháp ban-chaa
governor	ผู้ว่าการ	phôo wâa gaan
consul	กงสุล	gong-sŭn
diplomat	นักการทูต	nák gaan thôot
mayor	นายกเทศ มนตรี	naa-yók thâyt-sà-mon-dtree
sheriff	นายอำเภอ	naai am-pher
emperor	จักรพรรดิ	jàk-grà-phát
tsar, czar	ซาร์	saa
pharaoh	ฟาโรห์	faa-roh
khan	ขาน	khàan

160. Breaking the law. Criminals. Part 1

bandit	โจร	john
crime	อาชญากรรม	àat-yaa-gam
criminal (person)	อาชญากร	àat-yaa-gon
thief	ขโมย	khà-moi
to steal (vi, vt)	ขโมย	khà-moi
stealing (larceny)	การลักขโมย	gaan lák khà-moi
theft	การลักทรัพย์	gaan lák sáp
to kidnap (vt)	ลักพาตัว	lák phaa dtua
kidnapping	การลักพาตัว	gaan lák phaa dtua
kidnapper	ผู้ลักพาตัว	phôo lák phaa dtua
ransom	คาไถ	khâa thài

to demand ransom	เรียกเงินค่าไถ่	rîak ngern khâa thài
to rob (vt)	ปล้น	bplôn
robbery	การปล้น	gaan bplôn
robber	ขโมยขโจร	khà-moi khà-john
to extort (vt)	รีดไถ	rêet thăi
extortionist	ผู้รีดไถ	phôo rêet thăi
extortion	การรีดไถ	gaan rêet thăi
to murder, to kill	ฆ่า	khâa
murder	ฆาตกรรม	khâat-dtà-gaam
murderer	ฆาตกร	khâat-dtà-gon
gunshot	การยิงปืน	gaan ying bpeun
to fire (~ a shot)	ยิง	ying
to shoot to death	ยิงให้ตาย	ying hâi dtaai
to shoot (vi)	ยิง	ying
shooting	การยิง	gaan ying
incident (fight, etc.)	เหตุการณ์	hàyt gaan
fight, brawl	การต่อสู้	gaan dtòr sôo
Help!	ขอช่วย	khŏr chûay
victim	เหยื่อ	yèua
to damage (vt)	ทำความเสียหาย	tham khwaam sĭa hăai
damage	ความเสียหาย	khwaam sĭa hăai
dead body, corpse	ศพ	sòp
grave (~ crime)	รายแรง	ráai raeng
to attack (vt)	จู่โจม	jòo johm
to beat (to hit)	ตี	dtee
to beat up	ซ้อม	sórm
to take (rob of sth)	ปล้น	bplôn
to stab to death	แทงให้ตาย	thaeng hâi dtaai
to maim (vt)	ทำให้บาดเจ็บสาหัส	tham hâi bàat jèp săa hàt
to wound (vt)	บาด	bàat
blackmail	การกรรโชก	gaan-gan-chôhk
to blackmail (vt)	กรรโชก	gan-chôhk
blackmailer	ผู้ขูกรรโชก	phôo khòo gan-chôhk
protection racket	การคุมครอง ผิดกฎหมาย	gaan khum khrorng phìt gòt măai
racketeer	ผู้ที่หาเงิน จากกิจกรรมที่ ผิดกฎหมาย	phôo thêe hăa ngern jàak gìt-jà-gam thêe phìt gòt măai
gangster	เหล่าร้าย	lào ráai
mafia, Mob	มาเฟีย	maa-fia
pickpocket	ขโมยล้วงกระเป๋า	khà-moi lúang grà-bpăo
burglar	ขโมยย่องเบา	khà-moi yôong bao
smuggling	การลักลอบ	gaan lák-lôrp

smuggler	ผู้ลักลอบ	phôo lák lôrp
forgery	การปลอมแปลง	gaan bplorm bplaeng
to forge (counterfeit)	ปลอมแปลง	bplorm bplaeng
fake (forged)	ปลอม	bplorm

161. Breaking the law. Criminals. Part 2

rape	การข่มขืน	gaan khòm khěun
to rape (vt)	ข่มขืน	khòm khěun
rapist	โจรขุมขืน	john khòm khěun
maniac	คนบ้า	khon bâa

prostitute (fem.)	โสเภณี	sǒh-phay-nee
prostitution	การค้าประเวณี	gaan kháa bprà-way-nee
pimp	แมงดา	maeng-daa

| drug addict | ผู้ติดยาเสพติด | phôo dtìt yaa-sàyp-dtìt |
| drug dealer | พอค้ายาเสพติด | phôr kháa yaa-sàyp-dtìt |

to blow up (bomb)	ระเบิด	rá-bèrt
explosion	การระเบิด	gaan rá-bèrt
to set fire	เผา	phǎo
arsonist	ผู้ลอบวางเพลิง	phôo lôp waang phlerng

terrorism	การก่อการร้าย	gaan gòr gaan ráai
terrorist	ผู้ก่อการร้าย	phôo gòr gaan ráai
hostage	ตัวประกัน	dtua bprà-gan

to swindle (deceive)	ล่อลวง	lôr luang
swindle, deception	การลอลวง	gaan lôr luang
swindler	นักตมตุ๋น	nák dtôm dtǔn

to bribe (vt)	ติดสินบน	dtìt sǐn-bon
bribery	การติดสินบน	gaan dtìt sǐn-bon
bribe	สินบน	sǐn bon

poison	ยาพิษ	yaa phít
to poison (vt)	วางยาพิษ	waang-yaa phít
to poison oneself	กินยาตาย	gin yaa dtaai

| suicide (act) | การฆ่าตัวตาย | gaan khâa dtua dtaai |
| suicide (person) | ผู้ฆ่าตัวตาย | phôo khâa dtua dtaai |

to threaten (vt)	ขู่	khòo
threat	คำขู่	kham khòo
to make an attempt	พยายามฆ่า	phá-yaa-yaam khâa
attempt (attack)	การพยายามฆ่า	gaan phá-yaa-yaam khâa

| to steal (a car) | จี้ | jêe |
| to hijack (a plane) | จี้ | jêe |

| revenge | การแก้แค้น | gaan gâe kháen |
| to avenge (get revenge) | แกแค้น | gâe kháen |

to torture (vt)	ทรมาณ	thon-maan
torture	การทรมาน	gaan thor-rá-maan
to torment (vt)	ทำทารุณ	tam taa-run

pirate	โจรสลัด	john sà-làt
hooligan	นักเลง	nák-layng
armed (adj)	มีอาวุธ	mee aa-wút
violence	ความรุนแรง	khwaam run raeng
illegal (unlawful)	ผิดกฎหมาย	phìt gòt mǎai

| spying (espionage) | จารกรรม | jaa-rá-gam |
| to spy (vi) | ลวงความลับ | lúang khwaam láp |

162. Police. Law. Part 1

| justice | ยุติธรรม | yút-dtì-tham |
| court (see you in ~) | ศาล | sǎan |

judge	ผู้พิพากษา	phôo phí-phâak-sǎa
jurors	ลูกขุน	lôok khǔn
jury trial	การไต่สวนคดี	gaan dtài sǔan khá-dee
	แบบมีลูกขุน	bàep mee lôok khǔn
to judge, to try (vt)	พิพากษา	phí-phâak-sǎa

lawyer, attorney	ทนายความ	thá-naai khwaam
defendant	จำเลย	jam loie
dock	คอกจำเลย	khôrk jam loie

| charge | ข้อกล่าวหา | khôr glàao hǎa |
| accused | ถูกกล่าวหา | thòok glàao hǎa |

| sentence | การลงโทษ | gaan long thôht |
| to sentence (vt) | พิพากษา | phí-phâak-sǎa |

guilty (culprit)	ผู้กระทำ	phôo grà-tham
	ความผิด	khwaam phìt
to punish (vt)	ลงโทษ	long thôht
punishment	การลงโทษ	gaan long thôht

fine (penalty)	ปรับ	bpràp
life imprisonment	การจำคุก	gaan jam khúk
	ตลอดชีวิต	dtà-lòt chee-wít
death penalty	โทษประหาร	thôht-bprà-hǎan
electric chair	เก้าอี้ไฟฟ้า	gâo-êe fai-fáa
gallows	ตะแลงแกง	dtà-laeng-gaeng
to execute (vt)	ประหาร	bprà-hǎan
execution	การประหาร	gaan bprà-hǎan

prison, jail	คุก	khúk
cell	ห้องขัง	hôrng khǎng
escort (convoy)	ผู้ควบคุมตัว	phôo khûap khum dtua
prison guard	ผู้คุม	phôo khum
prisoner	นักโทษ	nák thôht
handcuffs	กุญแจมือ	gun-jae meu
to handcuff (vt)	ใส่กุญแจมือ	sài gun-jae meu
prison break	การแหกคุก	gaan hàek khúk
to break out (vi)	แหก	hàek
to disappear (vi)	หายตัวไป	hǎai dtua bpai
to release (from prison)	ถูกปล่อยตัว	thòok bplòi dtua
amnesty	การนิรโทษกรรม	gaan ní-rá-thôht gam
police	ตำรวจ	dtam-rùat
police officer	เจ้าหน้าที่ตำรวจ	jâo nâa-thêe dtam-rùat
police station	สถานีตำรวจ	sà-thǎa-nee dtam-rùat
billy club	กระบองตำรวจ	grà-bong dtam-rùat
bullhorn	โทรโข่ง	toh-ra -khòhng
patrol car	รถลาดตระเวน	rót lâat dtrà-wayn
siren	หวอ	wǒr
to turn on the siren	เปิดหวอ	bpèrt wǒr
siren call	เสียงหวอ	sǐang wǒr
crime scene	ที่เกิดเหตุ	thêe gèrt hàyt
witness	พยาน	phá-yaan
freedom	อิสระ	ìt-sà-rà
accomplice	ผู้ร่วมกระทำผิด	phôo rûam grà-tham phìt
to flee (vi)	หนี	něe
trace (to leave a ~)	ร่องรอย	rông roi

163. Police. Law. Part 2

search (investigation)	การสืบสวน	gaan sèup sǔan
to look for ...	หาตัว	hǎa dtua
suspicion	ความสงสัย	khwaam sǒng-sǎi
suspicious (e.g., ~ vehicle)	น่าสงสัย	nâa sǒng-sǎi
to stop (cause to halt)	เรียกให้หยุด	rîak hâi yùt
to detain (keep in custody)	กักตัว	gàk dtua
case (lawsuit)	คดี	khá-dee
investigation	การสืบสวน	gaan sèup sǔan
detective	นักสืบ	nák sèup
investigator	นักสอบสวน	nák sòrp sǔan
hypothesis	สันนิษฐาน	sǎn-nít-thǎan
motive	เหตุจูงใจ	hàyt joong jai
interrogation	การสอบปากคำ	gaan sòb bpàak kham

to interrogate (vt)	สอบสวน	sòrp sŭan
to question	ไถ่ถาม	thài thăam
(~ neighbors, etc.)		
check (identity ~)	การตรวจสอบ	gaan dtrùat sòp
round-up (raid)	การรวบตัว	gaan rûap dtua
search (~ warrant)	การตรวจคน	gaan dtrùat khón
chase (pursuit)	การไล่ล่า	gaan lâi lâa
to pursue, to chase	ไล่ล่า	lâi lâa
to track (a criminal)	สืบ	sèup
arrest	การจับกุม	gaan jàp gum
to arrest (sb)	จับกุม	jàp gum
to catch (thief, etc.)	จับ	jàp
capture	การจับ	gaan jàp
document	เอกสาร	àyk săan
proof (evidence)	หลักฐาน	làk thăan
to prove (vt)	พิสูจน์	phí-sòot
footprint	รอยเท้า	roi tháo
fingerprints	รอยนิ้วมือ	roi níw meu
piece of evidence	หลักฐาน	làk thăan
alibi	ข้อแก้ตัว	khôr gâe dtua
innocent (not guilty)	พ้นผิด	phón phìt
injustice	ความอยุติธรรม	khwaam a-yút-dtì-tam
unjust, unfair (adj)	ไม่เป็นธรรม	mâi bpen-tham
criminal (adj)	อาชญากร	àat-yaa-gon
to confiscate (vt)	ยึด	yéut
drug (illegal substance)	ยาเสพติด	yaa sàyp dtìt
weapon, gun	อาวุธ	aa-wút
to disarm (vt)	ปลดอาวุธ	bplòt aa-wút
to order (command)	ออกคำสั่ง	òrk kham sàng
to disappear (vi)	หายตัวไป	hăai dtua bpai
law	กฎหมาย	gòt măai
legal, lawful (adj)	ตามกฎหมาย	dtaam gòt măai
illegal, illicit (adj)	ผิดกฎหมาย	phìt gòt măai
responsibility (blame)	ความรับผิดชอบ	khwaam ráp phìt chôp
responsible (adj)	รับผิดชอบ	ráp phìt chôp

NATURE

The Earth. Part 1

164. Outer space

space	อวกาศ	a-wá-gàat
space (as adj)	ทางอวกาศ	thang a-wá-gàat
outer space	อวกาศ	a-wá-gàat
world	โลก	lôhk
universe	จักรวาล	jàk-grà-waan
galaxy	ดาราจักร	daa-raa jàk
star	ดาว	daao
constellation	กลุ่มดาว	glùm daao
planet	ดาวเคราะห์	daao khrór
satellite	ดาวเทียม	daao thiam
meteorite	ดาวตก	daao dtòk
comet	ดาวหาง	daao hǎang
asteroid	ดาวเคราะห์น้อย	daao khrór nói
orbit	วงโคจร	wong khoh-jon
to revolve (~ around the Earth)	เวียน	wian
atmosphere	บรรยากาศ	ban-yaa-gàat
the Sun	ดวงอาทิตย์	duang aa-thít
solar system	ระบบสุริยะ	rá-bòp sù-rí-yá
solar eclipse	สุริยุปราคา	sù-rí-yú-bpà-raa-kaa
the Earth	โลก	lôhk
the Moon	ดวงจันทร์	duang jan
Mars	ดาวอังคาร	daao ang-khaan
Venus	ดาวศุกร	daao sùk
Jupiter	ดาวพฤหัส	daao phá-réu-hàt
Saturn	ดาวเสาร	daao sǎo
Mercury	ดาวพุธ	daao phút
Uranus	ดาวยูเรนัส	daao-yoo-ray-nát
Neptune	ดาวเนปจูน	daao-nâyp-joon
Pluto	ดาวพลูโต	daao phloo-dtoh
Milky Way	ทางช้างเผือก	thaang cháang phèuak

Great Bear (Ursa Major)	กลุ่มดาวหมีใหญ่	glùm daao mĕe yài
North Star	ดาวเหนือ	daao nĕua
Martian	ชาวดาวอังคาร	chaao daao ang-khaan
extraterrestrial (n)	มนุษย์ต่างดาว	má-nút dtàang daao
alien	มนุษย์ต่างดาว	má-nút dtàang daao
flying saucer	จานบิน	jaan bin
spaceship	ยานอวกาศ	yaan a-wá-gàat
space station	สถานีอวกาศ	sà-thăa-nee a-wá-gàat
blast-off	การปล่อยจรวด	gaan bplòi jà-rùat
engine	เครื่องยนต์	khrêuang yon
nozzle	ท่อไอพ่น	thôr ai phôn
fuel	เชื้อเพลิง	chéua phlerng
cockpit, flight deck	ที่นั่งคนขับ	thêe nâng khon khàp
antenna	เสาอากาศ	săo aa-gàat
porthole	ช่อง	chôrng
solar panel	อุปกรณ์พลังงานแสงอาทิตย์	ù-bpà-gon phá-lang ngaan săeng aa-thít
spacesuit	ชุดอวกาศ	chút a-wá-gàat
weightlessness	สภาพไร้น้ำหนัก	sà-phâap rái nám nàk
oxygen	อ็อกซิเจน	ók sí jayn
docking (in space)	การเทียบท่า	gaan thîap thâa
to dock (vi, vt)	เทียบท่า	thîap thâa
observatory	หอดูดาว	hŏr doo daao
telescope	กล้องโทรทรรศน์	glôrng thoh-rá-thát
to observe (vt)	เฝ้าสังเกต	fâo săng-gàyt
to explore (vt)	สำรวจ	săm-rùat

165. The Earth

the Earth	โลก	lôhk
the globe (the Earth)	ลูกโลก	lôok lôhk
planet	ดาวเคราะห์	daao khrór
atmosphere	บรรยากาศ	ban-yaa-gàat
geography	ภูมิศาสตร์	phoo-mí-sàat
nature	ธรรมชาติ	tham-má-châat
globe (table ~)	ลูกโลก	lôok lôhk
map	แผนที่	phăen thêe
atlas	หนังสือแผนที่โลก	năng-sĕu phăen thêe lôhk
Europe	ยุโรป	yú-ròhp
Asia	เอเชีย	ay-chia

| Africa | แอฟริกา | àef-rí-gaa |
| Australia | ออสเตรเลีย | òrt-dtray-lia |

America	อเมริกา	a-may-rí-gaa
North America	อเมริกาเหนือ	a-may-rí-gaa nĕua
South America	อเมริกาใต้	a-may-rí-gaa dtâi

| Antarctica | แอนตาร์กติกา | aen-dtàak-dtì-gaa |
| the Arctic | อาร์กติค | àak-dtìk |

166. Cardinal directions

north	เหนือ	nĕua
to the north	ทิศเหนือ	thít nĕua
in the north	ที่ภาคเหนือ	thêe phâak nĕua
northern (adj)	ทางเหนือ	thaang nĕua

south	ใต้	dtâi
to the south	ทิศใต้	thít dtâi
in the south	ที่ภาคใต้	thêe phâak dtâi
southern (adj)	ทางใต้	thaang dtâi

west	ตะวันตก	dtà-wan dtòk
to the west	ทิศตะวันตก	thít dtà-wan dtòk
in the west	ที่ภาคตะวันตก	thêe phâak dtà-wan dtòk
western (adj)	ทางตะวันตก	thaang dtà-wan dtòk

east	ตะวันออก	dtà-wan òrk
to the east	ทิศตะวันออก	thít dtà-wan òrk
in the east	ที่ภาคตะวันออก	thêe phâak dtà-wan òrk
eastern (adj)	ทางตะวันออก	thaang dtà-wan òrk

167. Sea. Ocean

sea	ทะเล	thá-lay
ocean	มุหาสมุทร	má-hăa sà-mùt
gulf (bay)	อ่าว	àao
straits	ช่องแคบ	chôrng khâep

| land (solid ground) | พื้นดิน | phéun din |
| continent (mainland) | ทวีป | thá-wêep |

island	เกาะ	gòr
peninsula	คาบสมุทร	khâap sà-mùt
archipelago	หมู่เกาะ	mòo gòr

| bay, cove | อ่าว | àao |
| harbor | ท่าเรือ | thâa reua |

lagoon	ลากูน	laa-goon
cape	แหลม	lǎem
atoll	อะทอลล์	à-thorn
reef	แนวปะการัง	naew bpà-gaa-rang
coral	ปะการัง	bpà gaa-rang
coral reef	แนวปะการัง	naew bpà-gaa-rang
deep (adj)	ลึก	léuk
depth (deep water)	ความลึก	khwaam léuk
abyss	หุบเหวลึก	hùp wǎy léuk
trench (e.g., Mariana ~)	ร่องลึกก้นสมุทร	rông léuk gôn sà-mùt
current (Ocean ~)	กระแสน้ำ	grà-sǎe náam
to surround (bathe)	ล้อมรอบ	lórm rôrp
shore	ชายฝั่ง	chaai fàng
coast	ชายฝั่ง	chaai fàng
flow (flood tide)	น้ำขึ้น	náam khêun
ebb (ebb tide)	น้ำลง	náam long
shoal	หาดตื้น	hàat dtêun
bottom (~ of the sea)	ก้นทะเล	gôn thá-lay
wave	คลื่น	khlêun
crest (~ of a wave)	ม้วนคลื่น	múan khlêun
spume (sea foam)	ฟองคลื่น	forng khlêun
storm (sea storm)	พายุ	phaa-yú
hurricane	พายุเฮอร์ริเคน	phaa-yú her-rí-khayn
tsunami	คลื่นยักษ์	khlêun yák
calm (dead ~)	ภาวะไร้ลมพัด	phaa-wá rái lom phát
quiet, calm (adj)	สงบ	sà-ngòp
pole	ขั้วโลก	khûa lôhk
polar (adj)	ขั้วโลก	khûa lôhk
latitude	เส้นรุ้ง	sên rúng
longitude	เสนแวง	sên waeng
parallel	เส้นขนาน	sên khà-nǎan
equator	เส้นศูนย์สูตร	sên sǒon sòot
sky	ท้องฟ้า	thórng fáa
horizon	ขอบฟ้า	khòrp fáa
air	อากาศ	aa-gàat
lighthouse	ประภาคาร	bprà-phaa-khaan
to dive (vi)	ดำ	dam
to sink (ab. boat)	จม	jom
treasures	สมบัติ	sǒm-bàt

168. Mountains

mountain	ภูเขา	phoo khǎo
mountain range	ทิวเขา	thiw khǎo
mountain ridge	สันเขา	sǎn khǎo
summit, top	ยอดเขา	yôrt khǎo
peak	ยอด	yôrt
foot (~ of the mountain)	ตีนเขา	dteun khǎo
slope (mountainside)	ไหลเขา	lài khǎo
volcano	ภูเขาไฟ	phoo khǎo fai
active volcano	ภูเขาไฟ มีพลัง	phoo khǎo fai mee phá-lang
dormant volcano	ภูเขาไฟ ที่ดับแล้ว	phoo khǎo fai thêe dàp láew
eruption	ภูเขาไฟระเบิด	phoo khǎo fai rá-bèrt
crater	ปล่องภูเขาไฟ	bplòng phoo khǎo fai
magma	หินหนืด	hǐn nèut
lava	ลาวา	laa-waa
molten (~ lava)	หลอมเหลว	lǒrm lěo
canyon	หุบเขาลึก	hùp khǎo léuk
gorge	ช่องเขา	chôrng khǎo
crevice	รอยแตกภูเขา	roi dtàek phoo khǎo
abyss (chasm)	หุบเหวลึก	hùp wǎy léuk
pass, col	ทางผ่าน	thaang phàan
plateau	ที่ราบสูง	thêe râap sǒong
cliff	หน้าผา	nâa phǎa
hill	เนินเขา	nern khǎo
glacier	ธารน้ำแข็ง	thaan náam khǎeng
waterfall	น้ำตก	nám dtòk
geyser	น้ำพุร้อน	nám phú rórn
lake	ทะเลสาบ	thá-lay sàap
plain	ที่ราบ	thêe râap
landscape	ภูมิทัศน์	phoom thát
echo	เสียงสะท้อน	sǐang sà-thón
alpinist	นักปีนเขา	nák bpeen khǎo
rock climber	นักไต่เขา	nák dtài khǎo
to conquer (in climbing)	ไต่เขาถึงยอด	dtài khǎo thěung yôt
climb (an easy ~)	การปีนเขา	gaan bpeen khǎo

169. Rivers

river	แม่น้ำ	mâe náam
spring (natural source)	แหล่งน้ำแร่	làeng náam râe

riverbed (river channel)	เส้นทางแม่น้ำ	sên thaang mâe náam
basin (river valley)	ลุ่มน้ำ	lûm náam
to flow into ...	ไหลไปสู่...	lǎi bpai sòo...

| tributary | สาขา | sǎa-khǎa |
| bank (of river) | ฝั่งแม่น้ำ | fàng mâe náam |

current (stream)	กระแสน้ำ	grà-sǎe náam
downstream (adv)	ตามกระแสน้ำ	dtaam grà-sǎe náam
upstream (adv)	ทวนน้ำ	thuan náam

inundation	น้ำท่วม	nám thûam
flooding	น้ำท่วม	nám thûam
to overflow (vi)	เอ่อล้น	èr lón
to flood (vt)	ท่วม	thûam

| shallow (shoal) | บริเวณน้ำตื้น | bor-rí-wayn nám dtêun |
| rapids | กระแสน้ำเชี่ยว | grà-sǎe nám-chîeow |

dam	เขื่อน	khèuan
canal	คลอง	khlorng
reservoir (artificial lake)	ที่เก็บกักน้ำ	thêe gèp gàk náam
sluice, lock	ประตูระบายน้ำ	bprà-dtoo rá-baai náam

water body (pond, etc.)	พื้นน้ำ	phéun náam
swamp (marshland)	บึง	beung
bog, marsh	ห้วย	hûay
whirlpool	น้ำวน	nám won

stream (brook)	ลำธาร	lam thaan
drinking (ab. water)	น้ำดื่มได้	nám dèum dâai
fresh (~ water)	น้ำจืด	nám jèut

| ice | น้ำแข็ง | nám khǎeng |
| to freeze over (ab. river, etc.) | แช่แข็ง | châe khǎeng |

170. Forest

| forest, wood | ป่าไม้ | bpàa máai |
| forest (as adj) | ป่า | bpàa |

thick forest	ป่าทึบ	bpàa théup
grove	ป่าละเมาะ	bpàa lá-mór
forest clearing	ทุ่งโล่ง	thûng lôhng

thicket	ป่าละเมาะ	bpàa lá-mór
scrubland	ป่าละเมาะ	bpàa lá-mór
footpath (troddenpath)	ทางเดิน	thaang dern
gully	ร่องธาร	rông thaan

tree	ต้นไม้	dtôn máai
leaf	ใบไม้	bai máai
leaves (foliage)	ใบไม้	bai máai
fall of leaves	ใบไม้ร่วง	bai máai rûang
to fall (ab. leaves)	ร่วง	rûang
top (of the tree)	ยอด	yôrt
branch	กิ่ง	gìng
bough	กานไม้	gâan mái
bud (on shrub, tree)	ยอดอ่อน	yôrt òrn
needle (of pine tree)	เข็ม	khěm
pine cone	ลูกสน	lôok sŏn
tree hollow	โพรงไม้	phrohng máai
nest	รัง	rang
burrow (animal hole)	โพรง	phrohng
trunk	ลำต้น	lam dtôn
root	ราก	râak
bark	เปลือกไม้	bplèuak máai
moss	มอส	môt
to uproot (remove trees or tree stumps)	ถอนราก	thŏrn râak
to chop down	โค่น	khôhn
to deforest (vt)	ตัดไม้ทำลายป่า	dtàt mái tham laai bpàa
tree stump	ตอไม้	dtor máai
campfire	กองไฟ	gorng fai
forest fire	ไฟป่า	fai bpàa
to extinguish (vt)	ดับไฟ	dàp fai
forest ranger	เจ้าหน้าที่ดูแลป่า	jâo nâa-thêe doo lae bpàa
protection	การปกป้อง	gaan bpòk bpôrng
to protect (~ nature)	ปกป้อง	bpòk bpôrng
poacher	นักลอบล่าสัตว์	nák lôrp lâa sàt
steel trap	กับดักเหล็ก	gàp dàk lèk
to gather, to pick (vt)	เก็บ	gèp
to lose one's way	หลงทาง	lŏng thaang

171. Natural resources

natural resources	ทรัพยากร ธรรมชาติ	sáp-pá-yaa-gon tham-má-châat
minerals	แร่	râe
deposits	ตะกอน	dtà-gorn
field (e.g., oilfield)	บ่อ	bòr
to mine (extract)	ขุดแร่	khùt râe

mining (extraction)	การขุดแร่	gaan khùt râe
ore	แร่	râe
mine (e.g., for coal)	เหมืองแร่	měuang râe
shaft (mine ~)	ช่องเหมือง	chôrng měuang
miner	คนงานเหมือง	khon ngaan měuang
gas (natural ~)	แก๊ส	gáet
gas pipeline	ท่อแก๊ส	thôr gáet
oil (petroleum)	น้ำมัน	nám man
oil pipeline	ท่อน้ำมัน	thôr náam man
oil well	บ่อน้ำมัน	bòr náam man
derrick (tower)	ปั้นจั่นขนาดใหญ่	bpân jàn khà-nàat yài
tanker	เรือบรรทุกน้ำมัน	reua ban-thúk nám man
sand	ทราย	saai
limestone	หินปูน	hǐn bpoon
gravel	กรวด	grùat
peat	พีต	phêet
clay	ดินเหนียว	din nǐeow
coal	ถ่านหิน	thàan hǐn
iron (ore)	เหล็ก	lèk
gold	ทอง	thorng
silver	เงิน	ngern
nickel	นิเกิล	ní-gêrn
copper	ทองแดง	thorng daeng
zinc	สังกะสี	sǎng-gà-sěe
manganese	แมงกานีส	maeng-gaa-nêet
mercury	ปรอท	bpa -ròrt
lead	ตะกั่ว	dtà-gùa
mineral	แร่	râe
crystal	ผลึก	phà-lèuk
marble	หินอ่อน	hǐn òrn
uranium	ยูเรเนียม	yoo-ray-niam

The Earth. Part 2

172. Weather

weather	สภาพอากาศ	sà-phâap aa-gàat
weather forecast	พยากรณ์ สภาพอากาศ	phá-yaa-gon sà-phâap aa-gàat
temperature	อุณหภูมิ	un-hà-phoom
thermometer	ปรอทวัดอุณหภูมิ	bpà-ròrt wát un-hà-phoom
barometer	เครื่องวัดความดัน บรรยากาศ	khrêuang wát khwaam dan ban-yaa-gàat
humid (adj)	ชื้น	chéun
humidity	ความชื้น	khwaam chéun
heat (extreme ~)	ความร้อน	khwaam rórn
hot (torrid)	ร้อน	rórn
it's hot	มันร้อน	man rórn
it's warm	มันอุ่น	man ùn
warm (moderately hot)	อุ่น	ùn
it's cold	อากาศเย็น	aa-gàat yen
cold (adj)	เย็น	yen
sun	ดวงอาทิตย์	duang aa-thít
to shine (vi)	สองแสง	sòrng săeng
sunny (day)	มีแสงแดด	mee săeng dàet
to come up (vi)	ขึ้น	khêun
to set (vi)	ตก	dtòk
cloud	เมฆ	mâyk
cloudy (adj)	มีเมฆมาก	mee mâyk mâak
rain cloud	เมฆฝน	mâyk fŏn
somber (gloomy)	มืดครึ้ม	mêut khréum
rain	ฝน	fŏn
it's raining	ฝนตก	fŏn dtòk
rainy (~ day, weather)	ฝนตก	fŏn dtòk
to drizzle (vi)	ฝนปรอย	fòn bproi
pouring rain	ฝนตกหนัก	fŏn dtòk nàk
downpour	ฝนห่าใหญ่	fŏn hàa yài
heavy (e.g., ~ rain)	หนัก	nàk
puddle	หลุมน้ำ	lòm nám
to get wet (in rain)	เปียก	bpìak

fog (mist)	หมอก	mòrk
foggy	หมอกจัด	mòrk jàt
snow	หิมะ	hì-má
it's snowing	หิมะตก	hì-má dtòk

173. Severe weather. Natural disasters

thunderstorm	พายุฟ้าคะนอง	phaa-yú fáa khá-nong
lightning (~ strike)	ฟ้าผา	fáa phàa
to flash (vi)	แลบ	lâep
thunder	ฟ้าคะนอง	fáa khá-norng
to thunder (vi)	มีฟ้าคะนอง	mee fáa khá-norng
it's thundering	มีฟ้าร้อง	mee fáa rórng
hail	ลูกเห็บ	lôok hèp
it's hailing	มีลูกเห็บตก	mee lôok hèp dtòk
to flood (vt)	ท่วม	thûam
flood, inundation	น้ำท่วม	nám thûam
earthquake	แผ่นดินไหว	phàen din wăi
tremor, shoke	ไหว	wăi
epicenter	จุดเหนือศูนย์	jùt nĕua sŏon
	แผ่นดินไหว	phàen din wăi
eruption	ภูเขาไฟระเบิด	phoo khăo fai rá-bèrt
lava	ลาวา	laa-waa
twister	พายุหมุน	phaa-yú mŭn
tornado	พายุทอร์เนโด	phaa-yú thor-nay-doh
typhoon	พายุไต้ฝุ่น	phaa-yú dtâi fùn
hurricane	พายุเฮอร์ริเคน	phaa-yú her-rí-khayn
storm	พายุ	phaa-yú
tsunami	คลื่นสึนามิ	khlêun sèu-naa-mí
cyclone	พายุไซโคลน	phaa-yú sai-khlohn
bad weather	อากาศไม่ดี	aa-gàat mâi dee
fire (accident)	ไฟไหม	fai mâi
disaster	ความหายนะ	khwaam hăa-yá-ná
meteorite	อุกกาบาต	ùk-gaa-bàat
avalanche	หิมะถล่ม	hì-má thà-lòm
snowslide	หิมะถลม	hì-má thà-lòm
blizzard	พายุหิมะ	phaa-yú hì-má
snowstorm	พายุหิมะ	phaa-yú hì-má

Fauna

174. Mammals. Predators

predator	สัตว์กินเนื้อ	sàt gin néua
tiger	เสือ	sěua
lion	สิงโต	sǐng dtoh
wolf	หมาป่า	mǎa bpàa
fox	หมาจิ้งจอก	mǎa jîng-jòk
jaguar	เสือจากัวร์	sěua jaa-gua
leopard	เสือดาว	sěua daao
cheetah	เสือชีตาห์	sěua chee-dtaa
black panther	เสือดำ	sěua dam
puma	สิงโตภูเขา	sǐng-dtoh phoo khǎo
snow leopard	เสือดาวหิมะ	sěua daao hì-má
lynx	แมวป่า	maew bpàa
coyote	โคโยตี้	khoh-yoh-dtêe
jackal	หมาจิ้งจอกทอง	mǎa jîng-jòk thorng
hyena	ไฮยีนา	hai-yee-naa

175. Wild animals

animal	สัตว์	sàt
beast (animal)	สัตว์	sàt
squirrel	กระรอก	grà rôk
hedgehog	เม่น	mâyn
hare	กระต่ายป่า	grà-dtàai bpàa
rabbit	กระต่าย	grà-dtàai
badger	แบดเจอร์	baet-jer
raccoon	แร็คคูน	ráek khoon
hamster	หนูแฮมสเตอร์	nǒo haem-sà-dtêr
marmot	มาร์มอต	maa-môt
mole	ตุ่น	dtùn
mouse	หนู	nǒo
rat	หนู	nǒo
bat	ค้างคาว	kháang khaao
ermine	เออร์มิน	er-min
sable	เซเบิล	say bern

marten	มาร์เทิน	maa thern
weasel	เพียงพอน	phiang phon
	สีน้ำตาล	sĕe nám dtaan
mink	เพียงพอน	phiang phorn
beaver	บีเวอร์	bee-wer
otter	นาก	nâak
horse	ม้า	máa
moose	กวางมูส	gwaang môot
deer	กวาง	gwaang
camel	อูฐ	òot
bison	วัวป่า	wua bpàa
wisent	วัวป่าออรอช	wua bpàa or rôt
buffalo	ควาย	khwaai
zebra	ม้าลาย	máa laai
antelope	แอนทีโลป	aen-thi-lòp
roe deer	กวางโรเดียร์	gwaang roh-dia
fallow deer	กวางแฟลโลว์	gwaang flae-loh
chamois	เลียงผา	liang-phăa
wild boar	หมูป่า	mŏo bpàa
whale	วาฬ	waan
seal	แมวน้ำ	maew náam
walrus	ช้างน้ำ	cháang náam
fur seal	แมวน้ำมีขน	maew náam mee khŏn
dolphin	โลมา	loh-maa
bear	หมี	mĕe
polar bear	หมีขั้วโลก	mĕe khûa lôhk
panda	หมีแพนดา	mĕe phaen-dâa
monkey	ลิง	ling
chimpanzee	ลิงชิมแปนซี	ling chim-bpaen-see
orangutan	ลิงอุรังอุตัง	ling u-rang-u-dtang
gorilla	ลิงกอริลลา	ling gor-rin-lâa
macaque	ลิงแม็กแคก	ling mâk-khâk
gibbon	ชะนี	chá-nee
elephant	ช้าง	cháang
rhinoceros	แรด	râet
giraffe	ยีราฟ	yee-râaf
hippopotamus	ฮิปโปโปเตมัส	híp-bpoh-bpoh-dtay-mát
kangaroo	จิงโจ้	jing-jôh
koala (bear)	หมีโคอาล่า	mĕe khoh aa lâa
mongoose	พังพอน	phang phon
chinchilla	คินคิลลา	khin-khin laa
skunk	สกังก์	sà-gang
porcupine	เมน	mâyn

176. Domestic animals

cat	แมวตัวเมีย	maew dtua mia
tomcat	แมวตัวผู้	maew dtua phôo
dog	สุนัข	sù-nák
horse	ม้า	máa
stallion (male horse)	ม้าตัวผู้	máa dtua phôo
mare	มาตัวเมีย	máa dtua mia
cow	วัว	wua
bull	กระทิง	grà-thing
ox	วัว	wua
sheep (ewe)	แกะตัวเมีย	gàe dtua mia
ram	แกะตัวผู้	gàe dtua phôo
goat	แพะตัวเมีย	pháe dtua mia
billy goat, he-goat	แพะตัวผู้	pháe dtua phôo
donkey	ลา	laa
mule	ลอ	lôr
pig, hog	หมู	mŏo
piglet	ลูกหมู	lôok mŏo
rabbit	กระต่าย	grà-dtàai
hen (chicken)	ไก่ตัวเมีย	gài dtua mia
rooster	ไก่ตัวผู้	gài dtua phôo
duck	เป็ดตัวเมีย	bpèt dtua mia
drake	เป็ดตัวผู้	bpèt dtua phôo
goose	ห่าน	hàan
tom turkey, gobbler	ไก่งวงตัวผู้	gài nguang dtua phôo
turkey (hen)	ไกงวงตัวเมีย	gài nguang dtua mia
domestic animals	สัตว์เลี้ยง	sàt líang
tame (e.g., ~ hamster)	เลี้ยง	líang
to tame (vt)	เชื่อง	chêuang
to breed (vt)	ขยายพันธุ์	khà-yăai phan
farm	ฟาร์ม	faam
poultry	สัตว์ปีก	sàt bpèek
cattle	วัวควาย	wua khwaai
herd (cattle)	ฝูง	fŏong
stable	คอกม้า	khôrk máa
pigpen	คอกหมู	khôrk mŏo
cowshed	คอกวัว	khôrk wua
rabbit hutch	คอกกระต่าย	khôrk grà-dtàai
hen house	เลาไก่	láo gài

177. Dogs. Dog breeds

dog	สุนัข	sù-nák
sheepdog	สุนัขเลี้ยงแกะ	sù-nák líang gàe
German shepherd	เยอรมันเชฟเฟิร์ด	yer-rá-man chayf-fêrt
poodle	พูเดิ้ล	phoo dêrn
dachshund	ดัชชุน	dàt chun
bulldog	บูลด็อก	boon dòrk
boxer	บ๊อกเซอร์	bòk-sêr
mastiff	มัสตีฟ	mát-dtèef
Rottweiler	ร็อตไวเลอร์	rót-wai-ler
Doberman	โดเบอร์แมน	doh-ber-maen
basset	บาสเซ็ต	bàat-sét
bobtail	บ็อบเทล	bòp-thayn
Dalmatian	ดัลเมเชียน	dan-may-chian
cocker spaniel	ค็อกเกอรสเปเนียล	khórk-gêr sà-bpay-nian
Newfoundland	นิวฟาวน์ดฮาวน์ดแลนด์	niw-faao-dà-haao-dà-lăen
Saint Bernard	เซนตเบอรนารด	sayn ber nâat
husky	ฮัสกี้	hát-gêe
Chow Chow	เชาเชา	chao chao
spitz	สปิตซ	sà-bpìt
pug	ปัก	bpák

178. Sounds made by animals

barking (n)	เสี่ยงเห่า	sìang hào
to bark (vi)	เห่า	hào
to meow (vi)	รองเหมียว	rórng mǐeow
to purr (vi)	ทำเสี่ยงคราง	tham sìang khraang
to moo (vi)	ร้องมอๆ	rórng mor mor
to bellow (bull)	สงเสี่ยงคำราม	sòng sǐang kham-raam
to growl (vi)	โฮก	hôhk
howl (n)	เสียงหอน	sǐang hǒn
to howl (vi)	หอน	hǒrn
to whine (vi)	ครางหงิงๆ	khraang ngǐng ngǐng
to bleat (sheep)	ร้องแบะๆ	rórng bàe bàe
to oink, to grunt (pig)	ร้องอูดๆ	rórng ùut ùut
to squeal (vi)	ร้องเสียงแหลม	rórng sǐang lǎem
to croak (vi)	รองอบๆ	rórng ôp ôp
to buzz (insect)	หึ่ง	hèung
to chirp (crickets, grasshopper)	ทำเสียงจ๊อกแจ๊ก	tham sǐang jòrk jáek

179. Birds

bird	นก	nók
pigeon	นกพิราบ	nók phí-râap
sparrow	นกกระจิบ	nók grà-jìp
tit (great tit)	นกติ๊ด	nók dtít
magpie	นกสาลิกา	nók sǎa-lí gaa
raven	นกอีกา	nók ee-gaa
crow	นกกา	nók gaa
jackdaw	นกจำพวกกา	nók jam phûak gaa
rook	นกการูค	nók gaa róok
duck	เป็ด	bpèt
goose	ห่าน	hàan
pheasant	ไก่ฟ้า	gài fáa
eagle	นกอินทรี	nók in-see
hawk	นกเหยี่ยว	nók yìeow
falcon	นกเหยี่ยว	nók yìeow
vulture	นกแร้ง	nók ráeng
condor (Andean ~)	นกแร้งขนาดใหญ่	nók ráeng kà-nàat yài
swan	นกหงส์	nók hǒng
crane	นกกระเรียน	nók grà rian
stork	นกกระสา	nók grà-sǎa
parrot	นกแก้ว	nók gâew
hummingbird	นกฮัมมิ่งเบิร์ด	nók ham-mîng-bèrt
peacock	นกยูง	nók yoong
ostrich	นกกระจอกเทศ	nók grà-jòrk-thâyt
heron	นกยาง	nók yaang
flamingo	นกฟลามิงโก	nók flaa-ming-goh
pelican	นกกระทุง	nók-grà-thung
nightingale	นกไนติงเกล	nók-nai-dting-gayn
swallow	นกนางแอ่น	nók naang-àen
thrush	นกเดินดง	nók dern dong
song thrush	นกเดินดง รองเพลง	nók dern dong rórng phlayng
blackbird	นกเดินดงสีดำ	nók-dern-dong sěe dam
swift	นกแอ่น	nók àen
lark	นกลาร์ค	nók lâak
quail	นกคุ่ม	nók khûm
woodpecker	นกหัวขวาน	nók hǔa khwǎan
cuckoo	นกดุเหวา	nók dù hǎy wâa
owl	นกฮูก	nók hôok

eagle owl	นกเค้าใหญ่	nók kháo yài
wood grouse	ไก่ป่า	gài bpàa
black grouse	ไก่ดำ	gài dam
partridge	นกกระทา	nók-grà-thaa

starling	นกกิ้งโครง	nók-gîng-khrohng
canary	นกขมิ้น	nók khà-mîn
hazel grouse	ไก่น้ำตาล	gài nám dtaan
chaffinch	นกจาบ	nók-jàap
bullfinch	นกบูลฟินช์	nók boon-fin

seagull	นกนางนวล	nók naang-nuan
albatross	นกอัลบาทรอส	nók an-baa-thrôt
penguin	นกเพนกวิน	nók phayn-gwin

180. Birds. Singing and sounds

to sing (vi)	ร้องเพลง	rórng phlayng
to call (animal, bird)	ร้อง	rórng
to crow (rooster)	ร้องขัน	rórng khǎn
cock-a-doodle-doo	เสียงขัน	sǐang khǎn

to cluck (hen)	ร้องกุ๊กๆ	rórng gúk gúk
to caw (crow call)	ร้องเสียงกาๆ	rórng sǐang gaa gaa
to quack (duck call)	ร้องกาบๆ	rórng gâap gâap
to cheep (vi)	ร้องเสียงจิ๊บ ๆ	rórng sǐang jíp jíp
to chirp, to twitter	ร้องจอกแจก	rórng jòk jáek

181. Fish. Marine animals

bream	ปลาบรีม	bplaa bpreem
carp	ปลาคาร์ป	bplaa khâap
perch	ปลาเพิร์ช	bplaa phêrt
catfish	ปลาดุก	bplaa-dùk
pike	ปลาไพค์	bplaa phai

| salmon | ปลาแซลมอน | bplaa saen-morn |
| sturgeon | ปลาสเตอร์เจียน | bpláa sà-dtêr jian |

herring	ปลาเฮอร์ริง	bplaa her-ring
Atlantic salmon	ปลาแซลมอน แอตแลนติก	bplaa saen-mon àet-laen-dtìk
mackerel	ปลาซาบะ	bplaa saa-bà
flatfish	ปลาลิ้นหมา	bplaa lín-mǎa

zander, pike perch	ปลาไพค์เพิร์ช	bplaa phái phert
cod	ปลาค็อด	bplaa khót
tuna	ปลาทูนา	bplaa thoo-nâa

trout	ปลาเทราท์	bplaa thrau
eel	ปลาไหล	bplaa lăi
electric ray	ปลากระเบนไฟฟ้า	bplaa grà-bayn-fai-fáa
moray eel	ปลาไหลมอเรย์	bplaa lăi mor-ray
piranha	ปลาปิรันยา	bplaa bpì-ran-yâa
shark	ปลาฉลาม	bplaa chà-lăam
dolphin	โลมา	loh-maa
whale	วาฬ	waan
crab	ปู	bpoo
jellyfish	แมงกะพรุน	maeng gà-phrun
octopus	ปลาหมึก	bplaa mèuk
starfish	ปลาดาว	bplaa daao
sea urchin	หอยเม่น	hŏi mâyn
seahorse	ม้าน้ำ	máa nám
oyster	หอยนางรม	hŏi naang rom
shrimp	กุ้ง	gûng
lobster	กุ้งมังกร	gûng mang-gon
spiny lobster	กุ้งมังกร	gûng mang-gon

182. Amphibians. Reptiles

snake	งู	ngoo
venomous (snake)	พิษ	phít
viper	งูแมวเซา	ngoo maew sao
cobra	งูเห่า	ngoo hào
python	งูเหลือม	ngoo lĕuam
boa	งูโบอา	ngoo boh-aa
grass snake	งูเล็กที่ไม่เป็นอันตราย	ngoo lék thêe mâi bpen an-dtà-raai
rattle snake	งูหางกระดิ่ง	ngoo hăang grà-dìng
anaconda	งูอนาคอนดา	ngoo a -naa-khon-daa
lizard	กิ้งก่า	gîng-gàa
iguana	อีกัวน่า	ee gua naa
monitor lizard	กิ้งกามอนิเตอร์	gîng-gàa mor-ní-dtêr
salamander	ซาลาแมนเดอร์	saa-laa-maen-dêr
chameleon	กิ้งก่าคามิเลียน	gîng-gàa khaa-mí-lian
scorpion	แมงป่อง	maeng bpòrng
turtle	เต่า	dtào
frog	กบ	gòp
toad	คางคก	khaang-kók
crocodile	จระเข้	jor-rá-khây

183. Insects

insect, bug	แมลง	má-laeng
butterfly	ผีเสื้อ	phěe sêua
ant	มด	mót
fly	แมลงวัน	má-laeng wan
mosquito	ยุง	yung
beetle	แมลงปีกแข็ง	má-laeng bpèek khǎeng
wasp	ต่อ	dtòr
bee	ผึ้ง	phêung
bumblebee	ผึ้งบัมเบิลบี	phêung bam-bern bee
gadfly (botfly)	เหลือบ	lèuap
spider	แมงมุม	maeng mum
spiderweb	ใยแมงมุม	yai maeng mum
dragonfly	แมลงปอ	má-laeng bpor
grasshopper	ตั๊กแตน	dták-gà-dtaen
moth (night butterfly)	ผีเสื้อกลางคืน	phěe sêua glaang kheun
cockroach	แมลงสาบ	má-laeng sàap
tick	เห็บ	hèp
flea	หมัด	màt
midge	ริ้น	rín
locust	ตั๊กแตน	dták-gà-dtaen
snail	หอยทาก	hǒi thâak
cricket	จิ้งหรีด	jîng-rèet
lightning bug	หิ่งห้อย	hìng-hôi
ladybug	แมลงเต่าทอง	má-laeng dtào thorng
cockchafer	แมงอีนูน	maeng ee noon
leech	ปูลิง	bpling
caterpillar	บุ้ง	bûng
earthworm	ไส้เดือน	sâi deuan
larva	ตัวอ่อน	dtua òrn

184. Animals. Body parts

beak	จงอยปาก	ja-ngoi bpàak
wings	ปีก	bpèek
foot (of bird)	เท้า	tháo
feathers (plumage)	ขนนก	khǒn nók
feather	ขนนก	khǒn nók
crest	ขนหัว	khǒn hǔa
gills	เหงือก	ngèuak
spawn	ไข่ปลา	khài-bplaa

larva	ตัวอ่อน	dtua òrn
fin	ครีบ	khrêep
scales (of fish, reptile)	เกล็ด	glèt
fang (canine)	เขี้ยว	khîeow
paw (e.g., cat's ~)	เท้า	tháo
muzzle (snout)	จมูกและปาก	jà-mòok láe bpàak
maw (mouth)	ปาก	bpàak
tail	หาง	hăang
whiskers	หนวด	nùat
hoof	กีบ	gèep
horn	เขา	khăo
carapace	กระดอง	grà dorng
shell (of mollusk)	เปลือก	bplèuak
eggshell	เปลือกไข่	bplèuak khài
animal's hair (pelage)	ขน	khŏn
pelt (hide)	หนัง	năng

185. Animals. Habitats

habitat	ที่อยู่อาศัย	thêe yòo aa-săi
migration	การอพยพ	gaan òp-phá-yóp
mountain	ภูเขา	phoo khăo
reef	แนวปะการัง	naew bpà-gaa-rang
cliff	หน้าผา	nâa phăa
forest	ป่า	bpàa
jungle	ป่าดิบชื้น	bpàa dìp chéun
savanna	สะวันนา	sà wan naa
tundra	ทันดรา	than-draa
steppe	ทุ่งหญ้าสเตปป์	thûng yâa sà-dtàyp
desert	ทะเลทราย	thá-lay saai
oasis	โอเอซิส	oh-ay-sít
sea	ทะเล	thá-lay
lake	ทะเลสาบ	thá-lay sàap
ocean	มหาสมุทร	má-hăa sà-mùt
swamp (marshland)	บึง	beung
freshwater (adj)	น้ำจืด	nám jèut
pond	บ่อน้ำ	bòr náam
river	แม่น้ำ	mâe náam
den (bear's ~)	ถ้ำสัตว์	thâm sàt
nest	รัง	rang

tree hollow	โพรงไม้	phrohng máai
burrow (animal hole)	โพรง	phrohng
anthill	รังมด	rang mót

Flora

186. Trees

tree	ต้นไม้	dtôn máai
deciduous (adj)	ผลัดใบ	phlàt bai
coniferous (adj)	สน	săn
evergreen (adj)	ซึ่งเขียวชอุ่ม	sêung khǎeow chá-ùm
	ตลอดปี	dtà-lòrt bpee
apple tree	ต้นแอปเปิ้ล	dtôn àep-bpêrn
pear tree	ต้นแพร	dtôn phae
sweet cherry tree	ต้นเชอร์รี่ป่า	dtôn cher-rêe bpàa
sour cherry tree	ต้นเชอร์รี่	dtôn cher-rêe
plum tree	ต้นพลัม	dtôn phlam
birch	ต้นเบิร์ช	dtôn bèrt
oak	ต้นโอ๊ค	dtôn óhk
linden tree	ต้นไม้ดอกเหลือง	dtôn máai dòrk lûuang
aspen	ต้นแอสเพน	dtôn ae sà-phayn
maple	ต้นเมเปิ้ล	dtôn may bpêrn
spruce	ต้นเฟอร์	dtôn fer
pine	ต้นเกี๊ยะ	dtôn gía
larch	ต้นลารช	dtôn lâat
fir tree	ต้นเฟอร์	dtôn fer
cedar	ต้นซีดาร	dtôn-see-daa
poplar	ต้นปอปลาร์	dtôn bpor-bplaa
rowan	ต้นโรแวน	dtôn-roh-waen
willow	ต้นวิลโลว์	dtôn win-loh
alder	ต้นอัลเดอร์	dtôn an-dêr
beech	ต้นบีช	dtôn bèet
elm	ต้นเอลม	dtôn elm
ash (tree)	ต้นแอช	dtôn aesh
chestnut	ต้นเกาลัด	dtôn gao lát
magnolia	ต้นแมกโนเลีย	dtôn mâek-noh-lia
palm tree	ต้นปาลม	dtôn bpaam
cypress	ต้นไซเปรส	dtôn-sai-bpràyt
mangrove	ต้นโกงกาง	dtôn gohng gaang
baobab	ต้นเบาบับ	dtôn bao-bàp
eucalyptus	ต้นยูคาลิปตัส	dtôn yoo-khaa-líp-dtàt
sequoia	ต้นสนซีควัยยา	dtôn săn see kua yaa

187. Shrubs

bush	พุ่มไม้	phúm máai
shrub	ต้นไม้พุ่ม	dtôn máai phúm
grapevine	ต้นองุ่น	dtôn a-ngùn
vineyard	ไร่องุ่น	râi a-ngùn
raspberry bush	พุ่มราสเบอร์รี่	phúm râat-ber-rêe
blackcurrant bush	พุ่มแบล็คเคอร์แรนท์	phúm blàek-khêr-raen
redcurrant bush	พุ่มเรดเคอร์แรนท์	phúm râyt-khêr-raen
gooseberry bush	พุ่มกูสเบอรรี่	phúm gòot-ber-rêe
acacia	ต้นอาเคเชีย	dtôn aa-khay-chia
barberry	ต้นบาร์เบอร์รี่	dtôn baa-ber-rêe
jasmine	มะลิ	má-lí
juniper	ต้นจูนิเปอร์	dtôn joo-ní-bper
rosebush	พุ่มกุหลาบ	phúm gù làap
dog rose	พุ่มด็อกโรส	phúm dòrk-rôht

188. Mushrooms

mushroom	เห็ด	hèt
edible mushroom	เห็ดกินได้	hèt gin dâai
poisonous mushroom	เห็ดมีพิษ	hèt mee pít
cap (of mushroom)	ดอกเห็ด	dòrk hèt
stipe (of mushroom)	ตันเห็ด	dtôn hèt
cep (Boletus edulis)	เห็ดพอร์ชินี	hèt phor chí nee
orange-cap boletus	เห็ดพอร์ชินีดอกเหลือง	hèt phor chí nee dòrk lûuang
birch bolete	เห็ดตับเต่าที่ขึ้นบนตันเบิร์ช	hèt dtàp dtào thêe khêun bon dtôn-bèrt
chanterelle	เห็ดก่อเหลือง	hèt gòr lûuang
russula	เห็ดตะไค	hèt dtà khai
morel	เห็ดมอเรล	hèt mor rayn
fly agaric	เห็ดพิษหมวกแดง	hèt phít mùak daeng
death cap	เห็ดระโงกหิน	hèt rá ngôhk hĕn

189. Fruits. Berries

fruit	ผลไม้	phăn-lá-máai
fruits	ผลไม้	phăn-lá-máai
apple	แอปเปิ้ล	àep-bpêrn
pear	ลูกแพร	lôok phae

plum	พลัม	phlam
strawberry (garden ~)	สตรอว์เบอร์รี่	sà-dtror-ber-rêe
sour cherry	เชอร์รี่	cher-rêe
sweet cherry	เชอร์รี่ป่า	cher-rêe bpàa
grape	องุ่น	a-ngùn
raspberry	ราสเบอร์รี่	râat-ber-rêe
blackcurrant	แบล็คเคอรแรนท์	blàek khêr-raen
redcurrant	เรดเคอรแรนท	râyt-khêr-raen
gooseberry	กูสเบอร์รี่	gòot-ber-rêe
cranberry	แครนเบอร์รี่	khraen-ber-rêe
orange	ส้ม	sôm
mandarin	สมแมนดาริน	sôm maen daa rin
pineapple	สับปะรด	sàp-bpà-rót
banana	กล้วย	glúay
date	อินทผลัม	in-thá-phâ-lam
lemon	เลมอน	lay-mon
apricot	แอปริคอท	ae-bprì-khôrt
peach	ลูกทอ	lôok thór
kiwi	กีวี	gee wee
grapefruit	สมโอ	sôm oh
berry	เบอร์รี่	ber-rêe
berries	เบอร์รี่	ber-rêe
cowberry	คาวเบอร์รี่	khaao-ber-rêe
wild strawberry	สตรอวเบอร์รี่ป่า	sá-dtrorw ber-rêe bpàa
bilberry	บิลเบอร์รี่	bil-ber-rêe

190. Flowers. Plants

flower	ดอกไม้	dòrk máai
bouquet (of flowers)	ชอดอกไม้	chôr dòrk máai
rose (flower)	ดอกกุหลาบ	dòrk gù làap
tulip	ดอกทิวลิป	dòrk thiw-líp
carnation	ดอกคาร์เนชั่น	dòrk khaa-nay-chân
gladiolus	ดอกแกลดิโอลัส	dòrk gaen-dì-oh-lát
cornflower	ดอกคอร์นฟลาวเวอร์	dòrk khon-flaao-wer
harebell	ดอกระฆัง	dòrk rá-khang
dandelion	ดอกแดนดิไลออน	dòrk daen-dì-lai-on
camomile	ดอกคาโมมายล์	dòrk khaa-moh maai
aloe	ว่านหางจระเข้	wâan-hǐ ang-jor-rá-khây
cactus	ตะบองเพชร	dtà-bong-phét
rubber plant, ficus	ตนเลียบ	dtôn lîap
lily	ดอกลิลลี่	dòrk lí-lêe

geranium	ดอกเจอราเนียม	dòrk jer-raa-niam
hyacinth	ดอกไฮอะซินท์	dòrk hai-a-sin
mimosa	ดอกไมยราบ	dòrk mai râap
narcissus	ดอกนาร์ซิสซัส	dòrk naa-sít-sát
nasturtium	ดอกแนสเตอรชัม	dòrk nâet-dtêr-cham
orchid	ดอกกล้วยไม้	dòrk glúay máai
peony	ดอกโบตั๋น	dòrk boh-dtǐ n
violet	ดอกไวโอเล็ต	dòrk wai-oh-lét
pansy	ดอกแพนซี	dòrk phaen-see
forget-me-not	ดอกฟอร์เก็ตมีน็อต	dòrk for-gèt-mee-nót
daisy	ดอกเดซี	dòrk day see
poppy	ดอกป๊อปปี้	dòrk bpóp-bpêe
hemp	กัญชา	gan chaa
mint	สะระแหน่	sà-rá-nàe
lily of the valley	ดอกลิลลี่แห่งหุบเขา	dòrk lí-lá-lêe hàeng hùp khǐ o
snowdrop	ดอกหยาดหิมะ	dòrk yàat hì-má
nettle	ตำแย	dtam-yae
sorrel	ซอรเรล	sor-rayn
water lily	บัว	bua
fern	เฟิร์น	fern
lichen	ไลเคน	lai-khayn
conservatory (greenhouse)	เรือนกระจก	reuan grà-jòk
lawn	สนามหญ้า	sà-nǐ am yâa
flowerbed	สนามดอกไม้	sà-nǐ am-dòrk-máai
plant	พืช	phêut
grass	หญ้า	yâa
blade of grass	ใบหญ้า	bai yâa
leaf	ใบไม้	bai máai
petal	กลีบดอก	glèep dòrk
stem	ลำต้น	lam dtôn
tuber	หัวใต้ดิน	hǒa dtâi din
young plant (shoot)	ต้นอ่อน	dtôn òrn
thorn	หนาม	nǐ am
to blossom (vi)	บาน	baan
to fade, to wither	เหี่ยว	hìeow
smell (odor)	กลิ่น	glìn
to cut (flowers)	ตัด	dtàt
to pick (a flower)	เด็ด	dèt

191. Cereals, grains

grain	เมล็ด	má-lét
cereal crops	ธัญพืช	than-yá-phêut
ear (of barley, etc.)	รวงขาว	ruang khâao
wheat	ข้าวสาลี	khâao sĭ a-lee
rye	ข้าวไรย์	khâao rai
oats	ข้าวโอต	khâao óht
millet	ข้าวฟ่าง	khâao fâang
barley	ขาวบาร์เลย์	khâao baa-lây
corn	ข้าวโพด	khâao-phôht
rice	ขาว	khâao
buckwheat	บัควีท	bàk-wêet
pea plant	ถั่วลันเตา	thùa-lan-dtao
kidney bean	ถั่วรูปไต	thùa rôop dtai
soy	ถั่วเหลือง	thùa lŭuang
lentil	ถั่วเลนทิล	thùa layn thin
beans (pulse crops)	ถั่ว	thùa

REGIONAL GEOGRAPHY

Countries. Nationalities

192. Politics. Government. Part 1

politics	การเมือง	gaan meuang
political (adj)	ทางการเมือง	thang gaan meuang
politician	นักการเมือง	nák gaan meuang
state (country)	รัฐ	rát
citizen	พลเมือง	phon-lá-meuang
citizenship	สัญชาติ	săn-châat
national emblem	ตราประจำชาติ	dtraa bprà-jam châat
national anthem	เพลงชาติ	phlayng châat
government	รัฐบาล	rát-thà-baan
head of state	ผู้นำประเทศ	phôo nam bprà-thâyt
parliament	รัฐสภา	rát-thà-sà-phaa
party	พรรคการเมือง	phák gaan meuang
capitalism	ทุนนิยม	thun ní-yom
capitalist (adj)	แบบทุนนิยม	bàep thun ní-yom
socialism	สังคมนิยม	săng-khom ní-yom
socialist (adj)	แบบสังคมนิยม	bàep săng-khom ní-yom
communism	ลัทธิคอมมิวนิสต์	lát-thí khom-miw-nít
communist (adj)	แบบคอมมิวนิสต์	bàep khom-miw-nít
communist (n)	คนคอมมิวนิสต์	khon khom-miw-nít
democracy	ประชาธิปไตย	bprà-chaa-thíp-bpà-dtai
democrat	ผู้นิยมประชาธิปไตย	phôo ní-yom bprà-chaa-típ-bpà-dtai
democratic (adj)	แบบประชาธิปไตย	bàep bprà-chaa-thíp-bpà-dtai
Democratic party	พรรคประชาธิปัตย์	phák bprà-chaa-tí-bpàt
liberal (n)	ผู้เอียงเสรีนิยม	phôo iang săy-ree ní-yom
liberal (adj)	แบบเสรีนิยม	bàep săy-ree ní-yom
conservative (n)	ผู้เอียงอนุรักษ์นิยม	phôo iang a-nú rák ní-yom
conservative (adj)	แบบอนุรักษ์นิยม	bàep a-nú rák ní-yom
republic (n)	สาธารณรัฐ	săa-thaa-rá-ná rát

| republican (n) | รีพับลิกัน | ree pháp lí gan |
| Republican party | พรรครีพับลิกัน | phák ree-pháp-lí-gan |

elections	การเลือกตั้ง	gaan lêuak dtâng
to elect (vt)	เลือก	lêuak
elector, voter	ผู้ออกเสียง	phôo òrk sĭang
	ลงคะแนน	long khá-naen
election campaign	การรณรงค์	gaan ron-ná-rorng
	หาเสียง	hăa sĭang

voting (n)	การออกเสียง	gaan òrk sĭang
	ลงคะแนน	long khá-naen
to vote (vi)	ลงคะแนน	long khá-naen
suffrage, right to vote	สิทธิใน	sìt-thí nai
	การเลือกตั้ง	gaan lêuak dtâng

candidate	ผู้สมัคร	phôo sà-màk
to be a candidate	ลงสมัคร	long sà-màk
campaign	การรณรงค์	gaan ron-ná-rorng

| opposition (as adj) | ฝ่ายค้าน | fàai kháan |
| opposition (n) | ฝ่ายคาน | fàai kháan |

visit	การเยือน	gaan yeuan
official visit	การเยือนอย่างเป็น	gaan yeuan yàang bpen
	ทางการ	thaang gaan
international (adj)	แบบสากล	bàep săa-gon

| negotiations | การเจรจา | gaan jayn-rá-jaa |
| to negotiate (vi) | เจรจา | jayn-rá-jaa |

193. Politics. Government. Part 2

society	สังคม	săng-khom
constitution	รัฐธรรมนูญ	rát-thà-tham-má-noon
power (political control)	อำนาจ	am-nâat
corruption	การทุจริต	gaan thút-jà-rìt
	คอรัปชั่น	khor-ráp-chân

| law (justice) | กฎหมาย | gòt măai |
| legal (legitimate) | ทางกฎหมาย | thaang gòt măai |

| justice (fairness) | ความยุติธรรม | khwaam yút-dtì-tham |
| just (fair) | เป็นธรรม | bpen tham |

committee	คณะกรรมการ	khá-ná gam-má-gaan
bill (draft law)	ราง	râang
budget	งบประมาณ	ngóp bprà-maan
policy	นโยบาย	ná-yoh-baai
reform	ปฏิรูป	bpà-dtì rôop

radical (adj)	รุนแรง	run raeng
power (strength, force)	กำลัง	gam-lang
powerful (adj)	ทรงพลัง	song phá-lang
supporter	ผู้สนับสนุน	phôo sà-nàp-sà-nǔn
influence	อิทธิพล	ìt-thí pon

regime (e.g., military ~)	ระบอบการปกครอง	rá-bòrp gaan bpòk khrorng
conflict	ความขัดแย้ง	khwaam khàt yáeng
conspiracy (plot)	การคุบคิด	gaan khóp khít
provocation	การยั่วยุ	gaan yûa yú

to overthrow (regime, etc.)	ล้มล้วง	lóm láang
overthrow (of government)	การลม	gaan lóm
revolution	ปฏิวัติ	bpà-dtì-wát

coup d'état	รัฐประหาร	rát-thà-bprà-hǎan
military coup	การยึดอำนาจ	gaan yéut am-nâat
	ด้วยกำลังทหาร	dûay gam-lang thá-hǎan

crisis	วิกฤติ	wí-grìt
economic recession	ภาวะเศรษฐกิจ	phaa-wá sàyt-thà-gìt
	ถดถอย	thòt thǒi
demonstrator (protester)	ผู้ประท้วง	phôo bprà-thúang
demonstration	การประท้วง	gaan bprà-thúang
martial law	กฎอัยการศึก	gòt ai-yá-gaan sèuk
military base	ฐานทัพ	thǎan tháp

| stability | ความมั่นคง | khwaam mân-khong |
| stable (adj) | มั่นคง | mân khong |

| exploitation | การขูดรีด | gaan khòot rêet |
| to exploit (workers) | ขูดรีด | khòot rêet |

racism	คตินิยม	khá-dtì ní-yom
	เชื้อชาติ	chéua châat
racist	ผู้เหยียดผิว	phôo yìat phǐw
fascism	ลัทธิฟาสซิสต์	lát-thí fâat-sít
fascist	ผู้นิยมลัทธิฟาสซิสต์	phôo ní-yom lát-thí fâat-sít

194. Countries. Miscellaneous

foreigner	คนต่างชาติ	khon dtàang châat
foreign (adj)	ต่างชาติ	dtàang châat
abroad	ต่างประเทศ	dtàang bprà-thâyt
(in a foreign country)		

emigrant	ผู้อพยพ	phôo òp-phá-yóp
emigration	การอพยพ	gaan òp-phá-yóp
to emigrate (vi)	อพยพ	òp-phá-yóp
the West	ตะวันตก	dtà-wan dtòk

the East	ตะวันออก	dtà-wan òrk
the Far East	ตะวันออกไกล	dtà-wan òrk glai
civilization	อารยธรรม	aa-rá-yá-tham
humanity (mankind)	มนุษยชาติ	má-nút-sà-yá-châat
the world (earth)	โลก	lôhk
peace	ความสงบสุข	khwaam sà-ngòp-sùk
worldwide (adj)	ทั่วโลก	thûa lôhk
homeland	บ้านเกิด	bâan gèrt
people (population)	ประชาชน	bprà-chaa chon
population	ประชากร	bprà-chaa gon
people (a lot of ~)	ประชาชน	bprà-chaa chon
nation (people)	ชาติ	châat
generation	รุ่น	rûn
territory (area)	อาณาเขต	aa-naa khàyt
region	ภูมิภาค	phoo-mí-phâak
state (part of a country)	รัฐ	rát
tradition	ธรรมเนียม	tham-niam
custom (tradition)	ประเพณี	bprà-phay-nee
ecology	นิเวศวิทยา	ní-wâyt wít-thá-yaa
Indian (Native American)	อินเดียนแดง	in-dian daeng
Gypsy (masc.)	คนยิปซี	khon yíp-see
Gypsy (fem.)	คนยิปซี	khon yíp-see
Gypsy (adj)	ยิปซี	yíp see
empire	จักรวรรดิ	jàk-grà-wàt
colony	อาณานิคม	aa-naa ní-khom
slavery	การใช้แรงงาน	gaan chái raeng ngaan
	ทาส	thâat
invasion	การบุกรุก	gaan bùk rúk
famine	ความอดอยาก	khwaam òt yàak

195. Major religious groups. Confessions

religion	ศาสนา	sàat-sà-năa
religious (adj)	ศาสนา	sàat-sà-năa
faith, belief	ศรัทธา	sàt-thaa
to believe (in God)	นับถือ	náp thĕu
believer	ผู้ศรัทธา	phôo sàt-thaa
atheism	อเทวนิยม	a-thay-wá ní-yom
atheist	ผู้เชื่อว่า	phôo chêua wâa
	ไม่มีพระเจ้า	mâi mee phrá jâo
Christianity	ศาสนาคริสต์	sàat-sà-năa khrít
Christian (n)	ผู้นับถือ	phôo náp thĕu
	ศาสนาคริสต์	sàat-sà-năa khrít

Christian (adj)	ศาสนาคริสต์	sàat-sà-nǎa khrít
Catholicism	ศาสนาคาธอลิก	sàat-sà-nǎa khaa-thor-lík
Catholic (n)	ผู้นับถือ	phôo náp thěu
	ศาสนาคาธอลิก	sàat-sà-nǎa khaa-thor-lík
Catholic (adj)	คาธอลิก	khaa-thor-lík

Protestantism	ศาสนา	sàat-sà-nǎa
	โปรแตสแตนท์	bproh-dtàet-dtaen
Protestant Church	โบสถ์นิกาย	bòht ní-gaai
	โปรแตสแตนท์	bproh-dtàet-dtaen
Protestant (n)	ผู้นับถือศาสนา	phôo náp thěu sàat-sà-nǎa
	โปรแตสแตนท์	bproh-dtàet-dtaen

Orthodoxy	ศาสนาออร์ทอดอกซ์	sàat-sà-nǎa or-thor-dòrk
Orthodox Church	โบสถ์ศาสนา	bòht sàat-sà-nǎa
	ออร์ทอดอกซ์	or-thor-dòrk
Orthodox (n)	ผู้นับถือ	phôo náp thěu
	ศาสนาออร์ทอดอกซ์	sàat-sà-nǎa or-thor-dòrk

Presbyterianism	นิกายเพรสไบ	ní-gaai phrayt-bai-
	ที่เรียน	thee-rian
Presbyterian Church	โบสถ์นิกาย	bòht ní-gaai
	เพรสไบที่เรียน	phrayt-bai-thee-rian
Presbyterian (n)	ผู้นับถือนิกาย	phôo náp thěu ní-gaai
	เพรสไบที่เรียน	phrayt bai thee rian

Lutheranism	นิกายลูเทอแรน	ní-gaai loo-thay-a-rǎen
Lutheran (n)	ผู้นับถือนิกาย	phôo náp thěu ní-gaai
	ลูเทอแรน	loo-thay-a-rǎen

Baptist Church	นิกายแบ๊บติสท์	ní-gaai báep-dtìt
Baptist (n)	ผู้นับถือนิกาย	phôo náp thěu ní-gaai
	แบบติสท	báep-dtìt

Anglican Church	โบสถ์นิกาย	bòht ní-gaai
	แองกลิกัน	ae-ngók-lí-gan
Anglican (n)	ผู้นับถือนิกาย	phôo náp thěu ní-gaai
	แองกลิกัน	ae ngók lí gan

Mormonism	นิกายมอร์มอน	ní-gaai mor-mon
Mormon (n)	ผู้นับถือนิกาย	phôo náp thěu ní-gaai
	มอรมอน	mor-mon

| Judaism | ศาสนายิว | sàat-sà-nǎa yiw |
| Jew (n) | คนยิว | khon yiw |

Buddhism	ศาสนาพุธ	sàat-sà-nǎa phút
Buddhist (n)	ผู้นับถือ	phôo náp thěu
	ศาสนาพุธ	sàat-sà-nǎa phút
Hinduism	ศาสนาฮินดู	sàat-sà-nǎa hin-doo
Hindu (n)	ผู้นับถือ	phôo náp thěu
	ศาสนาฮินดู	sàat-sà-nǎa hin-doo

Islam	ศาสนาอิสลาม	sàat-sà-nǎa ìt-sà-laam
Muslim (n)	ผู้นับถือ	phôo náp thěu
	ศาสนาอิสลาม	sàat-sà-nǎa ìt-sà-laam
Muslim (adj)	มุสลิม	mút-sà-lim
Shiah Islam	ศาสนา	sàat-sà-nǎa
	อิสลามนิกายชีอะฮ์	ìt-sà-laam ní-gaai shi-à
Shiite (n)	ผู้นับถือนิกาย	phôo náp thěu ní-gaai
	ชีอะฮ์	shi-à
Sunni Islam	ศาสนาอิสลามนิ	sàat-sà-nǎa ìt-sà-laam ní-
	กายซุนนี	gaai sun-nee
Sunnite (n)	ผู้นับถือนิกาย	phôo náp thěu ní-gaai
	ซุนนี	sun-nee

196. Religions. Priests

priest	นักบวช	nák bùat
the Pope	พระสันตะปาปา	phrá sǎn-dtà-bpaa-bpaa
monk, friar	พระ	phrá
nun	แม่ชี	mâe chee
pastor	ศาสนาจารย์	sàat-sà-nǎa-jaan
abbot	เจ้าอาวาส	jâo aa-wâat
vicar (parish priest)	เจ้าอาวาส	jâo aa-wâat
bishop	มุขนายก	múk naa-yók
cardinal	พระคาร์ดินัล	phrá khaa-dì-nan
preacher	นักเทศน์	nák thâyt
preaching	การเทศนา	gaan thâyt-sà-nǎa
parishioners	ลูกวัด	lôok wát
believer	ผู้ศรัทธา	phôo sàt-thaa
atheist	ผู้เชื่อว่า	phôo chêua wâa
	ไม่มีพระเจ้า	mâi mee phrá jâo

197. Faith. Christianity. Islam

Adam	อาดัม	aa-dam
Eve	เอวา	ay-waa
God	พระเจ้า	phrá jâo
the Lord	พระเจ้า	phrá jâo
the Almighty	พระผู้เป็นเจ้า	phrá phôo bpen jâo
sin	บาป	bàap
to sin (vi)	ทำบาป	tham bàap
sinner (masc.)	คนบาป	khon bàap

sinner (fem.)	คนบาป	khon bàap
hell	นรก	ná-rók
paradise	สวรรค์	sà-wǎn
Jesus	พระเยซู	phrá yay-soo
Jesus Christ	พระเยซูคริสต์	phrá yay-soo khrít
the Holy Spirit	พระจิต	phrá jìt
the Savior	พระผู้ไถ่	phrá phôo thài
the Virgin Mary	พระนางมารีย์	phrá naang maa ree
	พรหมจารี	phrom-má-jaa-ree
the Devil	มาร	maan
devil's (adj)	ของมาร	khǒrng maan
Satan	ซาตาน	saa-dtaan
satanic (adj)	ซาตาน	saa-dtaan
angel	เทวทูต	thay-wá-thôot
guardian angel	เทวดาผู้	thay-wá-daa phôo
	คุมครอง	khúm khrorng
angelic (adj)	ของเทวดา	khǒrng thay-wá-daa
apostle	สาวก	sǎa-wók
archangel	หัวหน้าทูตสวรรค์	hǔa nâa thôot sà-wǎn
the Antichrist	ศัตรูของพระคริสต์	sàt-dtroo khǒrng phrá khrít
Church	โบสถ์	bòht
Bible	คัมภีร์ไบเบิ้ล	kham-phee bai-bêrn
biblical (adj)	ไบเบิ้ล	bai-bêrn
Old Testament	พันธสัญญาเดิม	phan-thá-sǎn-yaa derm
New Testament	พันธสัญญาใหม่	phan-thá-sǎn-yaa mài
Gospel	พระวรสาร	phrá won sǎan
Holy Scripture	พระคัมภีร์ไบเบิล	phrá kham-phee bai-bern
Heaven	สวรรค	sà-wǎn
Commandment	บัญญัติ	ban-yàt
prophet	ผู้เผยพระวจนะ	phôo phǒie phrá wá-jà-ná
prophecy	คำพยากรณ์	kham phá-yaa-gon
Allah	อัลลอฮ์	an-lor
Mohammed	พระมูฮัมหมัด	phrá moo ham màt
the Koran	อัลกุรอาน	an gù-rá-aan
mosque	สุเหรา	sù-rào
mullah	มุลละ	mun lá
prayer	บทสวดมนต์	bòt sùat mon
to pray (vi, vt)	สวด	sùat
pilgrimage	การจาริกแสวงบุญ	gaan jaa-rík sà-wǎeng bun
pilgrim	ผู้แสวงบุญ	phôo sà-wǎeng bun
Mecca	มักกะฮ	mák-gà
church	โบสถ์	bòht

temple	วิหาร	wí-hǎan
cathedral	มหาวิหาร	má-hǎa wí-hǎan
Gothic (adj)	แบบโกธิก	bàep goh-thík
synagogue	โบสถ์ของ	bòht khǒrng
	ศาสนายิว	sàat-sà-nǎa yiw
mosque	สุเหร่า	sù-rào
chapel	ห้องสวดมนต์	hôrng sùat mon
abbey	วัด	wát
convent	สำนักแม่ชี	sǎm-nák mâe chee
monastery	อาราม	aa raam
bell (church ~s)	ระฆัง	rá-khang
bell tower	หอระฆัง	hǒr rá-khang
to ring (ab. bells)	ตีระฆัง	dtee rá-khang
cross	ไม้กางเขน	mái gaang khǎyn
cupola (roof)	หลังคาทรงโดม	lǎng kaa song dohm
icon	รูปเคารพ	rôop kpao-róp
soul	วิญญาณ	win-yaan
fate (destiny)	ชะตากรรม	chá-dtaa gam
evil (n)	ความชั่วร้าย	khwaam chûa ráai
good (n)	ความดี	khwaam dee
vampire	ผีดูดเลือด	phěe dòot lêuat
witch (evil ~)	แม่มด	mâe mót
demon	ปีศาจ	bpee-sàat
spirit	ผี	phěe
redemption (giving us ~)	การไถ่ถอน	gaan thài thǒrn
to redeem (vt)	ไถ่ถอน	thài thǒrn
church service, mass	พิธีมิสซา	phí-tee mít-saa
to say mass	ประกอบพิธี	bprà-gòp phí-thee
	ศีลมหาสนิท	sěen má-hǎa sà-nìt
confession	การสารภาพ	gaan sǎa-rá-phâap
to confess (vi)	สารภาพ	sǎa-rá-phâap
saint (n)	นักบุญ	nák bun
sacred (holy)	ศักดิ์สิทธิ์	sàk-gà-dì sìt
holy water	น้ำมนต์	nám mon
ritual (n)	พิธีกรรม	phí-thee gam
ritual (adj)	แบบพิธีกรรม	bpaep phí-thee gam
sacrifice	การบูชายัญ	gaan boo-chaa yan
superstition	ความเชื่อ	khwaam chêua
	งมงาย	ngom-ngaai
superstitious (adj)	เชื่องมงาย	chêua ngom-ngaai
afterlife	ชีวิตหลัง	chee-wít lǎng
	ความตาย	khwaam dtaai
eternal life	ชีวิตอันเป็นนิรันดร์	chee-wít an bpen ní-ran

MISCELLANEOUS

198. Various useful words

background (green ~)	ฉากหลัง	chàak lăng
balance (of situation)	สมดุล	sà-má-dun
barrier (obstacle)	สิ่งกีดขวาง	sìng gèet-khwăang
base (basis)	ฐาน,	thăan
beginning	จุดเริ่มต้น	jùt rêrm-dtôn
category	หมวดหมู่	mùat mòo
cause (reason)	สาเหตุ	săa-hàyt
choice	ตัวเลือก	dtua lêuak
coincidence	ความบังเอิญ	khwaam bang-ern
comfortable (~ chair)	สะดวกสบาย	sà-dùak sà-baai
comparison	การเปรียบเทียบ	gaan bprìap thîap
compensation	การชดเชย	gaan chót-choie
degree (extent, amount)	ระดับ	rá-dàp
development	การพัฒนา	gaan phát-thá-naa
difference	ความแตกต่าง	khwaam dtàek dtàang
effect (e.g., of drugs)	ผลกระทบ	phŏn grà-thóp
effort (exertion)	ความพยายาม	khwaam phá-yaa-yaam
element	องค์ประกอบ	ong bprà-gòrp
end (finish)	จบ	jòp
example (illustration)	ตัวอย่าง	dtua yàang
fact	ข้อเท็จจริง	khôr thét jing
frequent (adj)	ถี่	thèe
growth (development)	การเติบโต	gaan dtèrp dtoh
help	ความช่วยเหลือ	khwaam chûay lĕua
ideal	อุดมคติ	u-dom khá-dtì
kind (sort, type)	ประเภท	bprà-phâyt
labyrinth	เขาวงกต	khăo-wong-gòt
mistake, error	ขอผิดพลาด	khôr phìt phlâat
moment	ช่วงเวลา	chûang way-laa
object (thing)	สิ่งของ	sìng khŏrng
obstacle	อุปสรรค	u-bpà-sàk
original (original copy)	ต้นฉบับ	dtôn chà-bàp
part (~ of sth)	สวน	sùan
particle, small part	อนุภาค	a-nú phâak
pause (break)	การหยุดพัก	gaan yùt phák

position	ตำแหน่ง	dtam-nàeng
principle	หลักการ	làk gaan
problem	ปัญหา	bpan-hǎa

process	กระบวนการ	grà-buan gaan
progress	ความก้าวหน้า	khwaam gâao nâa
property (quality)	คุณสมบัติ	khun-ná-sǒm-bàt
reaction	ปฏิกิริยา	bpà-dtì gì-rí-yaa
risk	ความเสี่ยง	khwaam sìang

secret	ความลับ	khwaam láp
series	ลำดับ	lam-dàp
shape (outer form)	รูปร่าง	rôop râang
situation	สถานการณ์	sà-thǎan gaan
solution	ทางแก	thaang gâe

standard (adj)	เป็นมาตรฐาน	bpen mâat-dtrà-thǎan
standard (level of quality)	มาตรฐาน	mâat-dtrà-thǎan
stop (pause)	การหยุด	gaan yùt
style	สไตล์	sà-dtai

system	ระบบ	rá-bòp
table (chart)	ตาราง	dtaa-raang
tempo, rate	จังหวะ	jang wà
term (word, expression)	คำ	kham

thing (object, item)	สิ่ง	sìng
truth (e.g., moment of ~)	ความจริง	khwaam jing
turn (please wait your ~)	ตา	dtaa
type (sort, kind)	ประเภท	bprà-phâyt
urgent (adj)	เร่งด่วน	râyng dùan

urgently (adv)	อย่างเร่งด่วน	yàang râyng dùan
utility (usefulness)	ความมีประโยชน์	khwaam mee bprà-yòht
variant (alternative)	ขอ	khôr
way (means, method)	วิธีทาง	wí-thěe thaang
zone	โซน	sohn